Additional Praise for *The Woman Babylon and the Marks of Empire*

"Dr. Shanell Smith offers a fascinating, sophisticated, and complex imaginative reader-engaged interpretation of the multilayered characterization of the woman/city Babylon as whore. She reads Revelation in a state of ambivalence and with 'ambi-veil-ence.' Dr. Smith both builds upon and reads differently from other Revelation scholars including African American interpreters, interrupting the conversation with her postcolonial womanist perspective. As an African American female scholar who embodies the tension of hybridity, Dr. Smith's entrance into the tension of the 'masculinist minority report' about the woman/city Babylon demonstrates that reading Revelation can be a complex and liberating experience for black women."

Mitzi J. Smith
Ashland Theological Seminary

"In this book, Shanell Smith articulates a postcolonial womanist approach to address one of Revelation's most troubling images—the Great Whore. In so doing, she adds an important dimension to our approaches to the text. Her writing modulates between personal insight and careful navigation of scholarly debate. This will be a book to return to multiple times!"

Lynn R. Huber
Elon University

The Woman Babylon and the Marks of Empire

The Woman Babylon and the Marks of Empire

Reading Revelation with a Postcolonial Womanist
Hermeneutics of Ambi*veil*ence

Shanell T. Smith

Fortress Press
Minneapolis

THE WOMAN BABYLON AND THE MARKS OF EMPIRE

Reading Revelation with a Postcolonial Womanist Hermeneutics of Ambi*veil*ence

Cover design: Alisha Lofgren

Library of Congress Cataloging-in-Publication Data

Print ISBN: 978-1-4514-7015-4

eBook ISBN: 978-1-4514-7243-1

The paper used in this publication meets the minimum requirements of American National Standard for Information Sciences — Permanence of Paper for Printed Library Materials, ANSI Z329.48-1984.

Manufactured in the U.S.A.

This book was produced using PressBooks.com, and PDF rendering was done by PrinceXML.

Contents

Acknowledgements

And then I breathed . . . *deeply*. This book, which is a revision of my dissertation, represents more than just a line on my CV, more than a debut of my scholarship; it represents the culmination of all the years in which "life happened," and I used my education as a distraction. I have distanced myself from the grief and pain that I felt from the deaths of my maternal grandparents, James and Barbara "Babs" Harris (I miss you both so much!), the near-death of my beloved sister, and much more. It was too much to bear, yet instead of "throwing in the towel" (thank you, Mom, for the intervention), I turned all of my energies to my work, completing my doctorate and obtaining a professorship in record time. Do not envy me; I am not bragging. The publication of this book makes me nervous, because it signals to me that it is time for release. It is time to face the pain of those tragic and life-altering events, and I am afraid. Throughout the years, colleagues have inquired, "How did you do it?" My response has always been, "There, but by the grace of God, go I." And this is how I shall move forward. I am thankful that I have a constant support system, and that I do not have to go it alone. I thank all of you in advance. Nevertheless, the publication of this book is also a time for celebration, so I now turn to the task at hand. While there are many that I could thank, there are a few that I need to mention by name.

I thank my best friend, the only one who has the amazing ability to cut through my stress and anxiety with words of comfort and reassurance, clearing a space for me to "just be," granting me an opportunity to smile, to be grateful, and to remember that "it's not that serious." To my husband, Clinton, I shake my head in awe of your grace, your strength, your patience, and your support of what I love to do. I thank God for your companionship, your faith in God, and your "ride-or-die" approach to your concern for me and our children. I love you.

To my princes, Clinton II, Peyton, and Justin: Mommy loves you! First, I thank you for the attention you need, because without you, I am certain that this book would have taken a lot longer to write. Since graduate school, you have made me one fiercely organized strategist for getting things done most expeditiously. I am grateful for the unconditional love that you give, and the laughs you provide—especially the ones I have when you do not know I am watching. To my mother, Sharon, "We did it!" Mommy, you are the smartest, most compassionate, and most faithful woman I know. You are *my* angel. To my dad, George, "Hi Dad!" I love you. I have never told you this, but you allow me to focus more on my work because I know that you are taking care of my mom. Thank you for your encouragement, your wit, and your love of God. To my *"sistas,"* Shakira and Leslie, what can I say, *"She did that!"* I can always count on you two to bring me back to earth, to remind me of what is most important, and to put a smile on my face. To my mother-in-law, Carole, I thank you for being who you are—a loving, caring, and supportive prayer-warrior. To my BJW family, there is no one like you, and I am blessed simply to be in the number.

I am so very grateful to have had the best dissertation committee that I could have had. To Stephen D. Moore (chair), Melanie Johnson-DeBaufre, and Althea Spencer Miller, I am so very appreciative of your scholarly insight, your attention to detail, and more importantly, I am thankful for your unceasing encouragement and respect. To my advisor, Stephen: You are a quiet soul with a beautiful spirit and a brilliant mind. You inspire me to be a great writer, teacher, and mentor. Thank you for being my friend.

The rest of my supportive network runs wide and deep. To my church family, Roseville Presbyterian Church (USA) in Newark, New Jersey, throughout all my years, I knew "somebody prayed for me." To my FTE family (now the Forum for Theological Exploration), I struggle to find the words to express my gratitude. If it were not for a presentation by our mother-mentor, Dr. Sharon Watson Fluker, I would not have known that obtaining a Ph.D. was an option. To James S. Logan, Jonathan L. Walton, and Nyasha Junior, you have no idea how great of an impact you had on me. Thank you so much. To my co-laboring sister-colleagues (you know who you are), your solidarity, level of intellectual sophistication, and love are unmatched. To my Drew University family—Acorn Academy, administrative assistants, library staff, the sweet ladies in the cafeteria, the maintenance women and men—I see you. I thank you for engaging me in conversation, for your smiles when I greeted you, and for all of the work you did to make my way easy. To my colleagues at Hartford Seminary, I am grateful to work with people with such passion; we have more groundbreaking interfaith work to do together. And to my ladies—the women who have finally stopped using the "f-word" with me, that is, *faculty*, I thank you for welcoming me, and I am glad that I have you in my life.

As I bring these acknowledgments to a close, I can hear my sister sweetly singing, "I will lift up my eyes to the hills from which cometh my help. My help cometh from the Lord" (Ps. 121). My help: O God, without you none of this would have been possible. I thank you for the unmerited grace and mercy you bestow upon me each day.

Throughout my entire life, you have truly showed up and showed out! You are a way maker, a protector and provider, and a healer. It is my heart's desire that the thoughts you have placed in my mind, what I attempted to put from pen to paper, will be a source of encouragement and enlightenment. Let it be acceptable to you, O Lord, my Rock and My Redeemer.

Introduction

"It loves me. It loves me not." This is the mantra I sometimes find myself reciting when I encounter the Bible, or people informed by its claims. Which phrase I utter depends on whether the text or its interpretations uplift, offend, or oppress me. Despite the subordinating rhetoric and violent imagery pervading the biblical text, or the negative experiences I encounter that result from an individual's or group's warped use of it, I cannot refrain from returning to its pages again and again—with a devout sentiment, no less. Some would say that it is a form of insanity—my continual engagement with the biblical texts, while expecting different results each time. However, my expectation is based not on the notion that the abrasive and ruthless passages of the Bible would magically be rewritten before our next encounter, but rather on the prospect of new tools and ways of reading that can help to deal with these types of texts so that they do not cause further harm.

Womanist biblical scholar Renita J. Weems notes the paradoxical relationship between the Bible and African American women that I have just described.[1] She highlights the fact that, despite the Bible's

---

1. *Womanist* is a term used by some women of color to reflect the unified aspects of their identity and experience in terms of race, sex, and class (to say the least). Certainly, the term *womanist* involves so much more—such as the power of naming oneself and the resistance to that which

1

use as a tool of oppression, it remains very influential in African American religious life.[2] As such, she rightly asserts that African American women must learn to read the Bible with caution and resistance, being careful not to internalize those things that offend them or threaten their dignity.[3] But what happens when the text reflects back to you aspects of your identity with which you either have not come to terms or refuse to embrace? How do you confront a text that forces you to recognize and admit certain realities—such as your privilege and participation in the capitalist structures of the United States—without limiting your ability to protest your simultaneous victimization within the same context? How do you deal with a text that frustrates your ability to efface inequalities, not only between yourself and others of your own racial/ethnic background and minority status, but also between yourself and your white (female) counterparts? How can you read the Bible "with caution and resistance" when what you read implicates you in the very things that may "offend" or "threaten the dignity" of others? These are the questions that emerge as I encounter the woman Babylon in the book of Revelation. A careful and comprehensive examination of this text reads like a mirror that reflects an image of myself that almost evokes the articulation of a new mantra: "I love me. I love me not." Well, almost.

"She is no ordinary woman." This was my thought after a careful engagement with her text. Many would suggest, and rightly so, that Babylon in Revelation is a metaphor. However, *she* is also a

---

attempts to undermine one's dignity—but one will have to turn to chapter 1 for such an in-depth discussion.

2. Renita J. Weems, "Reading *Her Way* through the Struggle: African American Women and the Bible," in *Stony the Road We Trod: African American Biblical Interpretation*, ed. Cain Hope Felder (Minneapolis: Fortress Press, 1991), 57.

3. Ibid., 63.

female literary character in a narrative, and therefore some form of imaginative readerly engagement is warranted. Thus, you should know that my book is more than a theoretical comparison of interpretations of Revelation. It is scholarship, yet also heavily infused with emotion, which, at times, is quite raw. You have been warned.

Although I have attempted to be the author's implied reader—the hypothetical hearer to which John's work is addressed—I cannot help but also read John's text resistantly. As a woman, and as an African American, his depiction of the woman Babylon incites many emotions within me, ranging from sadness and rage to joy and relief. Because I see so much of myself in her, she has become real to me. Therefore, whereas John intends to destroy the woman Babylon in order to depict the overtaking of the Roman Empire by God's empire, my appropriation of this female figure will empower and elevate her—an aim that runs counter to his. The words that John uses to paint a negative portrait of the woman Babylon are the very ones that I use to highlight her beautiful complexity. Some may say this is an effort to save myself. Perhaps it is, but I will address that later. For now, let me explain why the woman Babylon is no ordinary woman.

In the book of Revelation, the woman Babylon symbolizes imperial authority on the one hand, represented by her royal garb (17:4) and unspoken words (18:7),[4] and abject servitude on the other hand, represented by the term *pornē* applied to her via the inscription on her forehead, "Babylon the great, mother of whores and of earth's abominations" (17:5 NRSV), which, as will be argued below, suggests a punitive tattoo. This mark of ownership, and a more accurate understanding of the label *pornē*, suggest that the woman Babylon is not just a prostitute, as will also be argued below, but is also a

---

4. "As she glorified herself and lived luxuriously, so give her a like measure of torment and grief. Since in her heart she says, 'I rule as a queen/empress [*basilissa*]; I am no widow, and I will never see grief . . . '" (18:7), translation modified.

slave.[5] Representing both subjection (a slave woman) and prestige (an empress/imperial city), the woman Babylon is positioned on both sides of the colonial divide. Employing a postcolonial womanist critique,[6] I will argue that the woman Babylon is an object of ambivalent identification, which incites tension within this African American woman (and, potentially, other African American women as well) because she reflects ever so sharply and bitingly my continual conflicting reality of being simultaneously a victim of, and participant in, empire.[7] This is a truth for which I was not emotionally prepared.

My social location as a privileged African American woman urges me to adopt a particular stance in what is known as the "Great Whore" debate of Revelation 17. It refers to the scholarly discussion of the understanding of the woman Babylon as either a "whore" or a "city" and the implications of such classification. For the purposes of this book, I focus specifically on the work of Tina Pippin and Elisabeth Schüssler Fiorenza, as their work most clearly explicates both sides of the debate. Pippin employs a gender-critical approach to Revelation to critique the use and implications of gendered metaphors, which she asserts are not accidental, but reflect an inescapable androcentric, even misogynistic, perspective. She criticizes how feminist commentaries move beyond the troubling aspects of the annihilation of the woman Babylon (17:16); that is, most commonly by emphasizing that the woman refers to a city.

5. Jennifer A. Glancy and Stephen D. Moore argue that the widespread perception of the term *pornē* in the latter half of the first century c.e. suggests that it should be understood as "'brothel slave,' although scholars have tended to treat her as a *hetaera* [courtesan]" ("How Typical a Roman Prostitute Is Revelation's 'Great Whore'?" *Journal of Biblical Literature* 130 [2011]: 551–52, 557).

6. The term *postcolonial* with regard to biblical analysis refers to the critical study of empire, its effects on the parties involved, and any form of resistance to it. This explanation is a gross oversimplification; however, a more thorough discussion of this term is found in chapter one.

7. I seek to offer an African American woman's interpretation of the woman Babylon; however, it must be stated that I do not and cannot speak for all African American women.

Pippin points out that these interpretations are problematic because they obscure the "relationship between the fantastic world of the *Apocalypse* and reality."[8] Although "metaphoric violence against women is not the same as real violence," metaphor can still be dangerous and "harmful to real women because it shapes perceptions of reality and of gender relations for men and for women."[9] Thus, as Pippin notes, in Revelation the traditional hierarchical views of male over female—the object of the common feminist critique of hegemonic Christianity—remain untouched and undisturbed, such that both the women of the text and women of today remain subordinated and excluded from the realm of power.[10]

Schüssler Fiorenza agrees that this gender-critical reading is "crucially important to uncover and demystify the gender code of Revelation"; however, she asserts that it is also "in danger of re-valorizing the symbolic sex-gender system of the text while seeking to deconstruct it."[11] For Schüssler Fiorenza, this reification of the text's rhetoric lessens, if not destroys, the possibility for women to reread the text, resist its interlocking structures of domination, or produce liberating messages from the text.[12] She posits, therefore, that

8. Tina Pippin, "The Heroine and the Whore: The Apocalypse of John in Feminist Perspective," in *From Every People and Nation: The Book of Revelation in Intercultural Perspective*, ed. David Rhoads (Minneapolis: Fortress Press, 2005), 143.

9. J. Cheryl Exum, *Plotted, Shot, and Painted: Cultural Representations of Biblical Women* (Sheffield, UK: Sheffield Academic, 1996), 120n55.

10. Pippin, "The Heroine and the Whore," 143–44.

11. Schüssler Fiorenza, *The Power of the Word: Scripture and the Rhetoric of Empire* (Minneapolis: Fortress Press, 2007), 147. Schüssler Fiorenza's assertion is part of a long-standing debate between her and Pippin. Schüssler Fiorenza has long argued against "essentializing" individual images in Revelation, and instead suggests that they be viewed and analyzed "in relation to other images and within the 'strategic' positions [i.e. rhetoric] of the composition" (*The Book of Revelation: Justice and Judgment* [Philadelphia: Fortress Press, 1985], 188).

12. *Kyriarchy* is the term Schüssler Fiorenza coined to express the interlocking and overlapping systems of oppression that extend beyond the binary gender dualism of men versus women. It "seeks to express the intersecting structures of dominations and to replace the commonly used term, *patriarchy*, which is often understood in terms of binary gender dualism. As an analytic category . . . [it] does not restrict itself to gender analysis but seeks to comprehend the complex multiplicative interstructuring of gender, race, class, age, national, and colonial dominations

a feminist rhetorical-political analysis enables one to read John's use of rhetoric and gendered imagery not simply in gender terms, but in political terms as well.[13] Interpreting the text within this framework can help one to "discover a critique of empire in the conventionally coded feminine language for a city, which uses gender for constructing power," and, therefore, to negate any interpretations that suggest that "the vision of Babylon 'the Great' tells us anything about Revelation's understanding of actual women."[14]

The underlying question of the "Great Whore" debate is not whether metaphors matter and affect real women; each of these scholars would say that they do. Rather, the issue is *how to respond and read* for real women in one's analysis, both historically and theologically, and through which metaphors—woman or city. It is because of the work of these scholars, to whom I am indebted, that I have a foundation on which to build.

My reading of the woman Babylon provides an intervention in the "Great Whore" debate as it not only deconstructs the either/or dichotomy, but also, and more importantly, is the first to bring the categories of race, ethnicity, and class to bear on it. My sociocultural context impels me to be sensitive to such categories and, therefore, leads me to hold the two elements, woman and city, in tension, rather than deciding on one rather than the other. A postcolonial womanist interpretation of the woman Babylon highlights the simultaneous duality of her characterization—her depiction as both a brothel slavewoman *and* as an empress/imperial city.

In addition, my reading of the woman Babylon seeks to expand and complicate African American interpretations of Revelation, all of which ultimately and generally regard the text as essentially

and their imbrication with each other" (Schüssler Fiorenza, *The Power of the Word*, 14, emphasis original).

13. Ibid., 131–32.

14. Ibid., 136, 135, respectively.

liberating. Both Brian K. Blount and Clarice J. Martin, for example, posit John as a marginalized author who provides a critique—both social and religious—of the Roman Empire.[15] Blount, analyzing the entire book of Revelation through the lens of the African American experience, sees correlations between the situation of John's implicit reading community and that of the African American slaves and of the Black Church today. His main thesis is that the text of Revelation is a story of struggle and suffering, as well as active resistance, in the context of oppression—a story all too familiar to African American churches.

Martin focuses on the phrase *kai sōmatōn, kai psychas anthrōpōn* (usually translated as "slaves and human lives" or "slaves and human souls") in the cargo list of Rev. 18:13 and how it serves as a mirror into African American history.[16] As a womanist, she privileges black women's experience in her analysis and discerns how the text highlights and reflects the "historical experiences of subjectivity" of black women.[17] Her analysis reflects on the situation of African American slavery in order to highlight new ways to understand the rhetorical and ideological functions of the verse in its original context. Similar to Blount, Martin places John (and his community) and womanist thinkers in solidarity; they both "refract struggle, . . . untrammeled resistance and fearless resolve in pursuit of the liberated life."[18]

15. See Blount, *Can I Get a Witness: Reading Revelation through African American Culture* (Louisville: Westminster John Knox, 2005), and Martin, "Polishing the Unclouded Mirror: A Womanist Reading of *Revelation* 18:13," in *From Every People and Nation: The Book of Revelation in Intercultural Perspective*, ed. David Rhoads (Minneapolis: Fortress Press, 2005), 82–109.
16. Although *kai sōmatōn, kai psychas anthrōpōn* is literally translated as "bodies and souls of people," Martin rightly asserts that the words *sōmatōn* and *psychas anthrōpōn* "function as synonyms for 'slave'" ("Polishing the Unclouded Mirror," 89).
17. Ibid., 105.
18. Ibid., 106.

As an African American whose ancestors were victims of the American slave system—my great-great-grandmother was a former slave (Indiana Grant, 1851–1956)—I appreciate and applaud the works of these scholars that express the resistance to, and subversion of, imperial powers by colonized peoples. John as a voice of and for the oppressed is noteworthy. Nevertheless, another perspective is warranted, especially when the magnifying glass of postcolonial and womanist inquiry is positioned over the writings of John.

I move beyond the general African American notion that John is on the side of the marginalized people. Although his reinscription of imperial ideologies does not imply that he cannot be a minority, the way in which he depicts, discards, and destroys the *woman* Babylon causes me to question any meaningful form of resistance to empire in this text at all. For me as an African American woman, resistance to empire is null and void if it does not include the liberation of women. Martin makes a similar argument in an article on the *Haustafeln* (household codes), in which she calls the Black Church to practice consistent hermeneutics.[19] She powerfully asserts that "the African American interpretative tradition [is] marked by a forceful critique and rejection of a literalist interpretation of the slave regulations in the *Haustafeln*, but [is] not marked by an equally passionate critique and rejection of a literalist interpretation regarding the subordination of women to men in the *Haustafeln*."[20] This is problematic. Therefore, she insists that "African American believing communities need to assume a new and more profoundly integrative praxis that moves women 'from the margins'. . .'to the center.'"[21] This is what I intend to do with the woman Babylon of Revelation. By focusing the

19. Clarice J. Martin, "The *Haustafeln* (Household Codes) in African American Biblical Interpretation: 'Free Slaves' and 'Subordinate Women,'" in Felder, *Stony the Road We Trod*, 206–31.
20. Ibid., 225.
21. Ibid., 228.

gaze on her and her narrative, I will draw attention to John's own imperialistic and patriarchal ideology, thereby challenging the general African American notion that John stands fully over and against empire. Instead of a minority report, I argue that John presents a *masculinist* minority report. A minority report at the expense of a woman is not inclusive of women at all.

Building upon traditional historical-critical scholarship on Revelation, my thesis will be argued through an interdisciplinary effort consisting of two newer approaches: womanist criticism—specifically, Martin's liberationist womanist approach—and postcolonial criticism, which draws on extrabiblical postcolonial theory. This combined interpretive effort will fill a void in Revelation scholarship. To the best of my knowledge, these two approaches have only been employed individually in Revelation scholarship and never in tandem.

Postcolonial analysis complements a womanist biblical analysis by offering analytic terminology to describe and account for the colossal realities of colonialism and imperialism. Postcolonial biblical criticism—the critical analysis of empire, imperialism, colonialism, and other related phenomena as they pertain to the biblical texts and their reception history—has largely developed from and within liberation theology.[22] Postcolonial biblical criticism analyzes biblical

---

22. This development is especially evident from two further studies of Revelation: Vitor Westhelle, "Revelation 13: Between the Colonial and the Postcolonial, a Reading from Brazil," in Rhoads, *From Every People and Nation*, 183–99; and Jean-Pierre Ruiz, "Taking a Stand on the Sand of the Seashore: A Postcolonial Exploration of Revelation 13," in *Reading the Book of Revelation: A Resource for Students*, ed. David L. Barr (Atlanta: Society of Biblical Literature, 2003), 119–35. The number of works that engage postcolonial theory or criticism (beyond biblical studies) in their analyses of Revelation's relationship to empire is rather scarce. For example, Jean K. Kim's 1999 article, "'Uncovering her Wickedness': An Inter(con)textual Reading of Revelation 17 from a Postcolonial Feminist Perspective," is informed by postcolonial studies (*Journal for the Study of the New Testament* 73 [1999]: 83–112). Steven J. Friesen (*Imperial Cults and the Apocalypse of John: Reading Revelation in the Ruins* [Oxford: Oxford University Press, 2001]) and Christopher A. Frilingos (*Spectacles of Empire: Monsters, Martyrs, and the Book of Revelation* [Philadelphia: University of Pennsylvania Press, 2004]) employ the postcolonial

texts in their original relation to empire, and in their relation to empire from the fourth century to the present.[23] It focuses not only on how biblical texts were being legitimized as part of colonial and imperial enterprises, but also how they have been used to resist and interrogate such enterprises. Such resistance can be fraught with complexity. Moore, for example, employing the postcolonial theory of Homi Bhabha, illustrates how Revelation simultaneously resists and mimics essential aspects of Roman imperial ideology,[24] Postcolonial analysis, therefore, helps to highlight the blurred borders of Rome and John's imperial agendas.

A womanist analysis of Revelation can refocus a postcolonial critique of Revelation in powerful ways, especially when one seeks to determine the implications of such a text for African American women today—one of the goals of this book. The womanist principles that serve as a foundation for Martin's liberationist approach prove helpful for my project. In conjunction with other womanist biblical scholars and theologians,[25] she foregrounds the experiences of African American women, centers on issues of race, gender, and class, and places the interpreter in solidarity with the

theory of Edward Said in their work. Additionally, Catherine Keller performs a feminist and postcolonial analysis of Revelation and contemporary US imperialism in her *God and Power: Counter-Apocalyptic Journeys* (Minneapolis: Fortress Press, 2005).

23. This is more than just an intensification of a task that was always already part of the historical-critical project. Biblical scholars have analyzed the biblical text's relations to the Assyrian, Babylonian, Persian, Seleucid, and Roman empires. There is an interestedness in postcolonial biblical criticism that surpasses a false sense of neutrality.

24. Stephen D Moore, *Empire and Apocalypse: Postcolonialism and the New Testament*, Bible in the Modern World 12 (Sheffield, UK: Sheffield Phoenix, 2006), 97–121.

25. See, for example, Raquel A. St. Clair, *Call and Consequences: A Womanist Reading of Mark* (Minneapolis: Fortress Press, 2008); Stacey M. Floyd-Thomas, "'I am Black and Beautiful, O Ye Daughters of Jerusalem . . . ': African American Virtue Ethics and a Womanist Hermeneutics of Redemption," in *African American Religious Life and the Story of Nimrod*, ed. Anthony B. Pinn and Allen Dwight Callahan (New York: Palgrave Macmillan, 2008), 35–51; Katie Geneva Cannon, *Katie's Canon: Womanism and the Soul of the Black Community* (New York: Continuum, 1995); and Delores Williams, *Sisters in the Wilderness: The Challenge of Womanist God-Talk* (Maryknoll, NY: Orbis, 1993).

oppressed. Taken together, the interpretive sensibilities of both postcolonial and womanist inquiry help to compose a postcolonial womanist hermeneutics with which to engage Revelation: what I call a hermeneutics of ambi*veil*ence.

A hermeneutics of ambi*veil*ence begins with the experiences of African American women and, therefore, analyzes concepts of gender, race, and class (three interlocking systems of oppression), but also political elements of language and empire. It combines African American intellectual W. E. B. Du Bois's notion of the "veil," as outlined in *The Souls of Black Folk*,[26] with postcolonial theorist Homi K. Bhabha's analytic category of colonial ambivalence, as posited in *The Location of Culture*.[27] The "veil" is suggestive of a metaphorical covering that prohibits and hinders African Americans—women, in this case—from seeing themselves as they truly are. Instead, they perceive themselves through the eyes of white America or black men, causing them to either deny or ignore their racial heritage or gender. Du Bois's assertion that this veil is forcibly positioned is evidenced today, as there are instances when African American women must comport themselves to a certain preconceived and established Euro-American or black male standard. Added to this, however, is the fact that there are times when the veil may be personally positioned as a means of protection—a critical interpretive strategy similar to the use of cryptic messages in slave songs—or to perpetuate one's supposed ignorance of the suffering of others to maintain one's seat at the imperial table. Both uses of the veil, involuntary or voluntary, occur in the academy and the church.

The "ambivalence" part of the hermeneutics reflects the tension—the simultaneous attraction to and repulsion from a

---

26. Du Bois, *The Souls of Black Folk* (New York: Library of America, 1986; originally published 1903).
27. Bhabha, *The Location of Culture* (New York: Routledge, 1994).

particular object or person—that exists within a single individual, not least in the colonial or postcolonial arena. In this book, such tension is generated by the ambivalent characterization of the woman Babylon, whose veil—the line that separates both aspects of her identity—is made evident in her dual representation as both colonizer and colonized. This veil reflects back to me the particularized veil in my own life. Weems captures this ambivalence in her captivating reflection on the paradox of being a minority in a capitalistic society, but also being privileged when in the company of other minorities—even those of the same race. As an educated and professionally employed African American woman, Weems is "painfully aware" of her difference when she notices the black janitress who cleans the floor that Weems traverses on the way to an executive meeting.[28] The paradox in my reading of the *simultaneously* brothel slavewoman *and* empress/imperial city is that it becomes an experience of looking in an "unclouded" mirror.[29] I come face to face with the veil in my own identity. The line has been drawn. Although I do not benefit from the consumption of blood as the woman Babylon, in her empress persona, does from her victims (17:6), I must be forever aware that I benefit from the blood, sweat, and tears that were shed and continue to be shed by the many women and men, so many of them African American, who work at menial tasks to make my (imperial) life comfortable. With a hermeneutics of ambi*veil*ence, the marks of empire that signify both my victimization by, and my participation in, empire are unveiled before me. And the mantra begins again: "I love her. I love her not."

Chapter 1 establishes the postcolonial womanist hermeneutics that I employ to analyze the woman Babylon in Revelation. I begin with

---

28. Renita J. Weems, *Just a Sister Away: A Womanist Vision of Women's Relationships in the Bible* (Philadelphia: Innisfree, Inc., 1988), 11.
29. Martin, "Polishing the Unclouded Mirror," 83.

an overview of womanist theology and its relationship to biblical hermeneutics, as the former is the foundation of my interpretive lens. A discussion of the origins of womanist thought, and an examination of its appropriation by African American female scholars in various fields such as theology, ethics, and biblical studies, will help determine the criteria that are needed for the development of a womanist approach to Revelation. Next, I discuss the second component of my approach, postcolonial theory. An overview of postcolonial studies and its relevance for biblical studies will illustrate how the tools and analytic categories of extrabiblical postcolonial theory help to more accurately analyze phenomena such as colonialism and imperialism. The last section of this first chapter is intended to have a cumulative effect. I explain the need for an interdisciplinary venture between womanist hermeneutics and postcolonial studies by briefly explicating the lack of a central focus on the experiences of black women in the two disciplines of African American studies and postcolonial studies. I also discuss the benefits of the interpretive venture between womanist hermeneutics and postcolonial studies by illustrating how they complement each other. Finally, I bring everything together from the chapter by outlining the womanist tenets and postcolonial premises that I employ to formulate my postcolonial womanist hermeneutics of ambi*veil*ence.

In chapter 2, I introduce two scholarly conversations that my work engages because they focus on issues that affect some aspect of my identity as an African American woman. First, I present a survey of the work of Elisabeth Schüssler Fiorenza and Tina Pippin with regard to the figure Babylon in Revelation—a scholarly conversation known as the "Great Whore" debate. As a *woman*, I am interested in their focus on issues such as the text's use of gendered language, imperial rhetoric, and their implications for women today. More specifically, however, I am concerned with how they interpret Babylon—as a woman or as a city—and the implications of such readings. As a *black* woman, however, I am also interested and culturally invested in what is posited in African American scholarship about Revelation; namely, the overall interpretive message that John writes a minority report representing his solidarity with marginalized peoples against oppression. My self-identification as a simultaneously privileged and oppressed black woman causes me to read Revelation a bit differently. By providing a little history of these conversations, it will help illustrate not only *how* my work builds upon the scholarship presented, but also *why* my work is such an important undertaking.

Chapter 3 discusses Revelation in its historical, religious, and cultural contexts. Specifically, I state my working assumptions regarding authorship and dating, and discuss in some detail the social setting of Revelation that has led to various arguments for the occasion of its writing, in order to establish the historical context that informs my interpretation. I understand Revelation to be written by a Christian[30] prophet named John, although not the apostle, during the latter years of Emperor Domitian's reign (81–96 C.E.), when the persecution of Christians in the Roman province of Asia was local and sporadic.

Chapter 4 is a postcolonial womanist analysis of the woman Babylon, in which I apply my hermeneutics of ambi*veil*ence. I will discuss sealing and marking as they are understood in the context of Revelation. I will also examine the practices of tattooing and branding in the Roman world as set forth by classicist C. P. Jones, in order to make sense of the inscription on the forehead of the woman

---

30. In the ancient context of Revelation, there were no "Christians" per se, only Jews, some of whom were followers of Jesus Messiah. The term *Christian* is not even found in the text. There is no "Christianity" in this period, at least not in the sense of an independent religion separate and distinct from Judaism. It emerged within Judaism, is intimately bound up with it, and is still a fledgling development in this period. The use of the word *Christian* in this book is strictly for the purpose of convenience.

Babylon as a slave tattoo and to connect her with African American history and experience.[31] Next, I will analyze the woman Babylon as an at once brothel slavewoman and empress/imperial city, noting her ambivalent characterization. I will then interpret the text with a hermeneutics of ambiveilence, while foregrounding the experiences of African American women.

My analysis extends and complicates the Revelation scholarship of both African Americans and feminists. First, by adding postcolonial analysis to a reading that privileges African American female culture and experience, I am able to illustrate that what John presents, through his reinscription of empire and its imperial and patriarchal ideologies that subjugate women, is a *masculinist* minority report, contrary to the minority report suggested by African American biblical scholars. Second, my reading helps to identify and emphasize the ambivalent characterization of the woman Babylon; she reflects both sides of the colonial divide. This argument, grounded in my particular sociocultural context, disrupts the either/or (woman or city) dichotomy of the "Great Whore" debate by incorporating an analysis of the categories of race, ethnicity, and class.

The implication of my reading of the woman Babylon's text with a hermeneutics of ambiveilence, however, is not just for me and other African American women. As I will discuss in the conclusion, my approach is not bound to any particular gender, race, or class distinction. Its application is also not confined solely to the text of Revelation. When we—as readers of biblical texts—employ a hermeneutics of ambiveilence in the task of biblical interpretation we may be confronted with an image that is intimately familiar. The veil that highlights the opposing characteristics of our identity may be revealed in the reflection of the text, and we may begin to sense the

---

31. Jones, "Tattooing and Branding in Graeco-Roman Antiquity," *The Journal of Roman Studies* 77 (1987): 139–55.

tension it elicits. Do not run from it; rather, embrace the revelation. Certainly, this veil can be rent, and we can behold a fuller awareness of our beautiful complexity, if we are willing to admit and embrace the seemingly conflicting aspects of our identity. "I love me. I love me not."

1

Critical Convergences

Toward a Postcolonial Womanist Hermeneutics

A postcolonial inflection of a womanist hermeneutics is necessary to analyze the figure of the woman Babylon because this combined interpretive lens helps to highlight the dual aspects of her identity as both a slavewoman *and* as an empress/imperial city. To be sure, both womanist and postcolonial interpretations of Revelation have previously been done by other scholars. To the best of my knowledge, however, no one has yet engaged in a *combination* of these two lenses, which is the task of this book.

Although the interests of these two approaches have overlapped—womanist concerns have included issues of empire, and postcolonial concerns have included countering structures that oppress racial, ethnic women—I still find it necessary to combine the trajectories of these two lenses in a more self-conscious, systematic fashion. They complement each other well, each filling in the gaps where the other is found lacking. A womanist hermeneutics helps to position the experience of African American women as a starting point for biblical interpretation and offers ways to name that experience, while postcolonial theory provides a vocabulary that helps identify the various, interlocking structures of domination and the psychological states caused by them.

For my approach to Revelation, I appeal to postcolonial theory, specifically the work of postcolonial theorist Homi K. Bhabha, and to African American thought, through the work of black intellectual W. E. B. Du Bois. In particular, I employ two of their terms: Bhabha's notion of *ambivalence*—the simultaneous attraction to and repulsion from a particular object or person, which exists within a single individual, not least in the colonial or postcolonial arena—and Du Bois's notion of the *veil*—a metaphorical covering that hinders and prohibits African Americans from seeing themselves as they truly are. My reason for doing so is because together, the meanings of their terms capture my experience as an African American when I engage the text of the woman Babylon. They call to mind both the negative impact of capitalist systems on oppressed peoples, as well as one's ability to strategically comport oneself to those very same systems in order to survive, and in some cases, to excel.

It is important to note that I did not say that Bhabha and Du Bois's terms help to capture my experience as an African American *woman*. Although the work of Bhabha and Du Bois are foundational to the way in which I read Revelation, something is missing. Neither of these two intellectuals discusses the implications of what it means to be colonized, to be racially discriminated against, or how to endure such oppression, *as a woman*. My point is not to suggest a lacuna in their respective work, although a discussion of the possible reasons for such an omission is quite tempting. Their terminology thus only helps to capture my experience as I encounter the woman Babylon *in part*. Once I bring their work into critical dialogue with womanist thought—which has the experiences of black women at the *start* of any biblical exploration, the interests and love of black women at its *core*, and the liberation and advancement of black women as the *result* of its work—then and only then, do I begin to comprehend that experience *in full*.

By complementing womanist biblical inquiry with postcolonial theory, my aim is to build upon and extend their distinctive trajectories in an effort to posit a hermeneutics of ambi*veilence*—a combination of both Du Bois's notion of the veil and Bhabha's notion of ambivalence. However, before explicating this new term, and in an effort to fully and concisely articulate why and how I see these two trajectories working together, it is important to discuss them separately. I will begin with womanist theology and biblical hermeneutics, as this is the foundation of my analysis—following the womanist protocol of beginning with black women's experience. I will present a broad overview of womanist biblical interpretation by examining the origins of womanist thought, its appropriation by African American female scholars in theology, ethics, and biblical studies, and begin to explore the prospect of developing a womanist approach to the text of Revelation based on my analysis.[1]

Womanist Theology and Biblical Hermeneutics

The twentieth century will be ushered out by a prophecy similar to the one by which it was introduced. In the preface to his famous book of 1903, *The Souls of Black Folk*, W.E.B. Du Bois wrote: "The problem of the Twentieth Century is the problem of the colour line . . ." The

---

1. It is necessary that I include the work of womanist theologians and ethicists in my discussion of womanist *biblical* hermeneutics because womanist work is not categorized according to academic disciplines. What is important to note is that the ways in which these women discuss the implications of their work in the lives of African American women in church and society correspond to the aims of womanist biblical scholarship.

problem of the twentieth-first century is the problem of the color line, the gender line, and the class line.

—*Katie Geneva Cannon*[2]

Womanism emerged in the 1980s not only "in response to sexism in black liberation theology and racism in the feminist movement,"[3] but also "independently out of women's culture and experience."[4] Although womanism recognized the contribution of black liberation theology's analysis of historical and political systems of oppression and feminist theology's analysis of sexist oppression, the fact of the matter is that the concerns of the black woman in both theologies remained an afterthought. "In the '60s and '70s, besides ignoring the African diaspora, the overwhelming majority of black male liberation scholars and white feminist scholars failed to address the spiritual and social reality of black women in the continental United States."[5]

---

2. Katie Geneva Cannon, *Katie's Canon: Womanism and the Soul of the Black Community* (New York: Continuum, 1995), 25, emphasis added, citing W. E. B. Du Bois, *The Souls of Black Folk* (New York: Library of America, 1969), xi.

3. Wilda Gafney, "A Black Feminist Approach to Biblical Studies," *Encounter* 67 (2006): 393.

4. Karen Baker-Fletcher, *A Singing Something: Womanist Reflections on Anna Julia Cooper* (New York: Crossroad, 1994), 160. Womanist theologian Jacquelyn Grant notes that "the possibly irreparable nature of the tension between White women and Black women necessitates a completely different word to describe the liberative efforts of Black women: 'womanist'" ("Womanist Theology: Black Women's Experience as a Source for Doing Theology, with Special Reference to Christology," in *African-American Religious Studies: An Interdisciplinary Anthology*, ed. Gayraud S. Wilmore [Durham: Duke University Press, 1989], 212–13). Grant also includes the tension between black men and black women in this assertion. Womanist thought helps black women not only fill in the gap between black theology and feminist theology, but also "challenges Black male and White feminist theologians to be more inclusive in their understanding of freedom and equality, liberation and wholeness" (Baker-Fletcher, *A Singing Something*, 160–61).

5. Gafney, "A Black Feminist Approach," 393. Delores S. Williams also notes that womanist theology has an "organic relation" both to black liberation theology and feminist theologies, connecting them at vital points: however, "the distinct and sometimes hostile differences that exist between them are precipitated, in part, by the maladies afflicting community life in America—sexism, racism, and classism" (*Sisters in the Wilderness: The Challenge of Womanist God-Talk* [Maryknoll, NY: Orbis, 1993], 178). "Feminist theologies" is plural in order to reflect the various strands of feminist theology: Asian, Hispanic, Jewish, Anglo-American, etc.

Black women suffered from "double jeopardy"—African American women's experience with racism and sexism—and needed a theology that reflected their entire being, one that only they could express.[6] However, the creation of a space that African American women could call their own, and the task of maintaining their whole identities, did not involve a definite isolation from white feminists or black theologians, but rather became more and more solidified through their interaction. African American theologian James Cone notes that as black feminist theology began to emerge, black women were not only in dialogue with other minority women, both in the United States and in places such as Africa, Asia, and Latin America, but also white feminists.[7] For example, Cone notes that black women were able to build upon, and particularize some of white feminists' beliefs and values, such as their resistance to gender inequality, and their "terminology . . . in response to women's subordination, such as patriarchy, misogyny, and sexism."[8] Thus, womanist hermeneutics should not be read as "wholly other and ideologically distinct from other forms of feminist discourse."[9] Before turning to a discussion of

6. James Cone, "Black Theology, Black Churches, and Black Women," in *Out of the Revolution: The Development of Africana Studies*, eds. Delores P. Aldridge and Carlene Young (Lanham, MD: Lexington, 2000), 410.

7. Ibid., 418. Interestingly, in Cone's list of the black women seminarians and professors who began to develop a black feminist theology, he includes those who today are identified as womanists: Jacquelyn Grant, Katie Cannon, Delores Williams, Kelly Brown Douglas, and Cheryl Townsend Gilkes (ibid., 417). Hebrew biblical scholar Wilda Gafney notes that the shift from these women identifying themselves as black feminists to womanists occurred over time. "Early African American feminists, later womanists, disenchanted with the white supremacist ideologies perpetuated by the feminist movement soon began to question its methodologies and motivations" ("A Black Feminist Approach," 395). This conflict resulted in various identifiable differentiations between the two groups. "One clear point of demarcation from the feminist movement in general and from feminist theology in particular: a deep valuation of ancestral, nonacademic, oral discourses, knowledge and coping skills. Another point of departure is the relationship that womanist theologians have with the institutional church—they are more likely to critique it from within, rather than from a distance" (ibid., 395–96).

8. Cone, "Black Theology, Black Churches," 411.

9. Gafney, "A Black Feminist Approach," 396.

contemporary womanist hermeneutics, however, let us reflect on the roots of womanist discourse.

Wilda Gafney reminds us that the "task of negotiating the intersection of gender and ethnicity within the context of the divine-human encounter," was being performed by women of color well before the twentieth century.[10] Black women such as Sojourner Truth, Anna Julia Cooper, Jarena Lee, Harriet Tubman, and Ida B. Wells-Barnett insisted on "being recognized as the sole legitimate arbitrators of their knowledge and experiences," and advocated strongly for the right of black women to articulate their whole identity, "without being forced to choose between being a woman and being of African descent."[11]

Sojourner Truth, the self-given name of African American abolitionist and women's rights activist Isabella Baumfree, addressed the issue of male superiority and privilege based on the manhood of Christ in her famous speech, "Ain't I a Woman?" (1851). Her famous argument against this claim is that Christ came from God and a woman. "Man had nothing to do with him."[12] Anna Julia Cooper, a spokeswoman for the feminist and suffrage movements, believed that "black women were created equal in intelligence to women and men of all races, and employed her religious belief and education to interpret the social message of the bible."[13] In

---

10. Ibid. Renita Weems notes that "Anglo women like Margaret Fuller (*Woman in the Nineteenth Century* [New York: Greeley & McElrath, 1845]) and Elizabeth Cady Stanton (*The Woman's Bible* [New York: European Publishing Company, 1895–1898]) were not the only women in the nineteenth century thinking, writing, and strategizing on behalf of women" ("Womanist Reflections on Biblical Hermeneutics," in *Black Theology: A Documentary History*, vol. 2: *1980–1992*, ed. James H. Cone and Gayraud S. Wilmore [Maryknoll, NY: Orbis, 1993], 219).
11. Gafney, "A Black Feminist Approach," 393.
12. James Loewenberg and Ruth Bogin, eds., *Black Women in Nineteenth-Century American Life* (University Park: Pennsylvania State University Press, 1976), 236. See also Hertha Pauli, *Her Name Was Sojourner Truth* (New York: Camelot/Avon, 1962), 177.
13. Karen Baker-Fletcher, "Anna Julia Cooper and Sojourner Truth: Two Nineteenth-Century Black Feminist Interpreters of Scripture," in *Searching the Scriptures*, vol. 1: *A Feminist Introduction*, ed. Elisabeth Schüssler Fiorenza (New York: Crossroad, 1993), 42. In Baker-

her essay, "Womanhood a Vital Element in the Regeneration and Progress of a Race," Cooper argues that based on the ideals that Christ gave to be comprehended by civilization, black women were to be given equal education and economic opportunities.[14] Karen Baker-Fletcher, in her article, "Anna Julia Cooper and Sojourner Truth: Two Nineteenth-Century Black Feminist Interpreters of Scripture," compares the biblical hermeneutics of both women, and powerfully argues that "age, class, literacy, and region of origin" were irrelevant in determining the effectiveness and potency of black women who were adamant in their fight for equal rights.[15] Although Cooper has been described as "a black woman intellectual and Truth as an illiterate, itinerant preacher," Baker-Fletcher states that both were "highly intelligent, self-possessed, and irrepressible black feminists and social reformers, who publically challenged whites who questioned their humanity because they were black, and whites and blacks who questioned their authority to speak because they were women."[16]

Added to this list of nineteenth-century black women who advocated for women's rights are itinerant preacher and autobiographer Jarena Lee, African American abolitionist Harriet Tubman, and journalist Ida B. Wells-Barnett. Lee, whose preaching ministry in the African Methodist Episcopal (AME) church was blocked for eight years, argued that it should not be thought of as "impossible, heterodox, or improper for a woman to preach, seeing

Fletcher's *A Singing Something*, she notes, however, that "Cooper's concept of a God of freedom and equality whose spirit is within humankind," must be extended to include the notion of human complicity. African Americans help to perpetuate their own oppression "through practices such as classism, political apathy, and intra-community violence" (175). Still, much is to be learned from Cooper's social ethic of equality and freedom for all peoples.

14. Anna Julia Cooper, "Womanhood a Vital Element in the Regeneration and Progress of a Race," in *A Voice from the South*, ed. Mary Helen Washington (New York: Oxford University Press, 1988), 9–47.

15. Baker-Fletcher, "Anna Julia Cooper and Sojourner Truth," 41.

16. Ibid., 41, 49.

the Savior died for the woman as well as the man."[17] Harriet Tubman, the "Moses" of her people because she helped more than three hundred slaves attain freedom, attended "several women's suffrage conventions and became involved in the National Federation of Afro-American Women."[18] Ida B. Wells-Barnett individually led a campaign against lynching and was involved in the "work of black club women."[19] Baker-Fletcher asserts that "the voices of the silenced have the power to challenge and the potential to change social patterns that are racist, sexist, heterosexist, or ethnocentric."[20] All of the aforementioned nineteenth-century women recognized the power of voice, and advocated unyieldingly for the right for black women to assert their full humanity. Clearly, this is why many black women scholars view them as protowomanists.[21]

Some of the twentieth-century African American women outside the fields of theology and biblical studies who have been critical contributors to the womanist discourse are Alice Walker, Audre Lorde, bell hooks, and Angela Davis (to name a few). Alice Walker provides a definition of the term *womanist* in her 1980 essay "Coming Apart," stating that it "encompasses 'feminist' [which she equated with a white women's movement] . . . , means *instinctively* pro-woman . . . , and has a strong root in Black women's culture."[22] Gafney expounds, "Womanists were 'pro-women,' which meant that

17. Jarena Lee, *The Life and Religious Experience of Jarena Lee: A Colored Lady Giving an Account of Her Call to Preach the Gospel* (Philadelphia, 1836), 129. Reprinted in Dorothy Porter, ed., *Early Negro Writing 1760–1837* (Boston: Beacon, 1971). This text is Lee's self-recorded story of her conversion and call to preach.
18. Cone, "Black Theology, Black Churches," 409.
19. Ibid.
20. Baker-Fletcher, *A Singing Something*, 181–82.
21. Baker Fletcher notes that although the term *black feminist* is probably the more accurate term to use to describe these historical black women, since *womanist* is a contemporary term, "they share something in common with contemporary womanist interpretations of reality," that is, "their historical and traditional values, ideas, self-understanding, and social outlook" (ibid., 154–55).
22. Alice Walker, "Coming Apart," in *Take Back the Night: Women on Pornography*, ed. Laura Lederer (New York: William Morrow and Company, 1980), 100, emphasis original.

womanist discourse was intentionally antiracist, anticlassicist, antielitist, antiheterosexist, and antidiscriminatory in every particularity."[23] A fuller definition of *womanist* is found in Walker's, *In Search of Our Mothers' Gardens: Womanist Prose*,[24] and includes four parts:

1. From *womanish*. (Opp. of "girlish," i.e., frivolous, irresponsible, not serious.) A black feminist or feminist of color. From the black folk expression of mothers to female children, "You acting womanish," i.e., like a woman. Usually referring to outrageous, audacious, courageous or *willful* behavior. Wanting to know more and in greater depth than is considered "good" for one. Interested in grown-up doings. Acting grown up. Being grown up. Interchangeable with another black folk expression: "You trying to be grown." Responsible. In charge. *Serious.*

2. *Also:* A woman who loves other women, sexually and/or nonsexually. Appreciates and prefers women's culture, women's emotional flexibility (values tears as natural counterbalance of laughter), and women's strength. Sometimes loves individual men, sexually and/or nonsexually. Committed to survival and wholeness of entire people, male *and* female. Not a separatist, except periodically, for health. Traditionally universalist, as in: "Mama, why are we brown, pink, and yellow, and our cousins are white, beige, and black?" Ans.: "Well, you know the colored race is just like a flower garden, with every color flower represented." Traditionally capable, as in: "Mama, I'm walking to Canada and I'm taking you and a bunch of other slaves with me." Reply: "It wouldn't be the first time."

---

23. Gafney, "A Black Feminist Approach," 393–94.
24. Alice Walker, *In Search of Our Mothers' Gardens: Womanist Prose* (Orlando, Florida: Harcourt, 1983). In this work, Walker establishes womanist thought and practice by appealing to the words and actions of historical African American women.

3. Loves music. Loves dance. Loves the moon. *Loves* the Spirit. Loves love and food and roundness. Loves struggle. *Loves* the Folk. Loves herself. *Regardless.*

4. Womanist is to feminist as purple to lavender.[25]

The usage of the term *womanist*, however, goes beyond Walker's definition. In a roundtable discussion on the topic of "Christian Ethics and Theology in Womanist Perspective," which focused on the development, variations, and "potential impact of womanist theological scholarship upon the life of the academy, the church, and the community," Christian ethicist Cheryl J. Sanders argues that womanists have subjected Walker's definition to their "own editing and interpretation," and wonders whether their appropriation and adaptation has "misconstrued the womanist concept and its meaning."[26] Sanders argues that Walker's original definition of the term "'womanist' carries the connotation of black *lesbian*, and in the second [in *In Search of Our Mother's Gardens*] it denotes black *feminist*, a designation that includes women who love women and those who love men."[27] In both instances, Walker "names the experience of audacious black women with a word that acknowledges their sensibilities and traditions in ways that the words *lesbian* and *feminist* do not."[28] Perhaps womanists gravitated to Walker's "celebration

25. Ibid., xi–xii, emphasis original. The comparison of womanist to feminist as purple to lavender "expresses in vivid terms the conclusion that womanist has a deeper and fuller meaning than feminist" (Cheryl J. Sanders, "Roundtable Discussion: Christian Ethics and Theology in Womanist Perspective," *JFSR* 5, no. 2 [1989]: 84).

26. Sanders, "Christian Ethics," 85, 111. The various perspectives presented about what *womanist* means suggested to Sanders that "we are far from uniform even in some of our basic assumptions" (ibid., 112). This is not to be viewed as a problem, however, but rather serves as an indication of the need for further dialogue, or, perhaps, it may simply reflect the multiplicity of African American female experience.

27. Ibid., 84–85, emphasis original. Sanders states that Walker's original use of *womanist* is found in Walker's review of Rebecca Jackson's *Gifts of Power: The Writings of Rebecca Jackson (1795–1871), Black Visionary, Shaker Eldress* (Amherst: University of Massachusetts Press, 1981), *Black Scholar* 12 (1981): 64–67.

of the black woman's freedom to choose her own labels," because language and the power of naming is viewed as an act of autonomy, resistance, and self-love.[29] Employed as a symbol of African American experience, "womanist" has been adopted to "point to the richness and complexity of being black and female in a society that tends to devalue both Blackness and womanhood."[30]

bell hooks, born Gloria Jean Watkins, does not take on the term *womanist*, but rather self-identifies as feminist. She is, nevertheless, included here, because her work overlaps with, and speaks to, womanist concerns. In her 1981 work *Ain't I a Woman: Black Women and Feminism*, she analyzes the black female experience and our "relationship to society as a whole by examining both the politics of racism and sexism from a feminist perspective."[31] hooks furthers feminist dialogue by asserting that the feminist movement must be broadened to include issues of race, sex, and class as its starting point. "If women want a feminist revolution, then we must assume responsibility for drawing women together in political solidarity, by eliminating all the forces that divide women."[32] She concludes that the black woman's "struggle for liberation has significance *only* if it takes place *within* a feminist movement that has as its fundamental goal the liberation of all people."[33]

Employing Walker's definition of *womanist*, ethicist Katie Geneva Cannon was the "first [theological] scholar to articulate a specifically womanist theology."[34] In her 1995 work, *Katie's Canon: Womanism*

28. Sanders, "Christian Ethics," 85, emphasis original.
29. Ibid., 85.
30. Kelly Delaine Brown Douglas, "Womanist Theology: What Is Its Relationship to Black Theology," in Cone and Wilmore, *Black Theology*, 290.
31. bell hooks, *Ain't I a Woman: Black Women and Feminism* (Boston: South End, 1981), 13.
32. Ibid., 157.
33. Ibid., 13, emphasis added.
34. Gafney, "A Black Feminist Approach," 394. Cannon, Jacquelyn Grant, and Renita Weems are referred to as the "initial triumvirate" of womanist scholars (Monica A. Coleman, "Roundtable Discussion: Must I Be Womanist?" *JFSR* 22, no. 1 [2006]: 93).

and the Soul of the Black Community, Cannon argues that the black womanist tradition is an "interpretive principle" that informs the black woman's practice of critically interpreting Scripture in order to understand the divine word from the perspective of her own situation, one that has been shaped by her experience with white supremacy and male superiority.[35] Cannon is careful to note that "black life is more than defensive reactions to oppressive circumstances; it is the rich, colorful creativity that emerged and reemerges in the Black quest for human dignity."[36] Therefore, the function of womanism is not to replace one set of "elitist, hegemonic texts" with another set of Afrocentric texts, but to challenge those domineering traditions, encourage the oppressed to overcome their oppressive situations, and "put forth critical analysis in such a way that the errors of the past will not be repeated."[37] These practices that Cannon explicates were performed by African American women before the term *womanist* was coined, and they continue to be employed even beyond the fields of theology and ethics, as indicated by African American female scholars in the field of biblical studies.

35. Cannon, *Katie's Canon*, 56. See also Cannon, "The Emergence of Black Feminist Consciousness," in *Feminist Interpretation of the Bible*, ed. Letty M. Russell (Philadelphia: Westminster John Knox, 1985), 30.

36. Cannon, *Katie's Canon*, 56. Biblical scholar Clarice Martin similarly notes that "a womanist worldview is as concerned with activist moral agency as it is with resistance to oppression" (Clarice J. Martin, "Polishing the Unclouded Mirror: A Womanist Reading of *Revelation* 18:13," in *From Every People and Nation: The Book of Revelation in Intercultural Perspective*, ed. David Rhoads [Minneapolis: Fortress Press, 2005], 85).

37. Cannon, *Katie's Canon*, 23–24. Elsewhere Cannon writes, "For those of us who read and subscribe to the *Journal of Feminist Studies in Religion*, 'womanist' is the methodological framework that the vast majority of African American women have been using for the past twenty years to challenge inherited traditions of androcentric patriarchy, and as a method of engaging in revolutionary acts of resistance as members of the American Academy of Religion and the Society of Biblical Literature" (Coleman, "Must I Be Womanist?" 96; Cannon's response is included in Coleman's roundtable discussion). Cannon also states that Walker's four-part definition of womanist is a "critical, methodological framework [that is used] for challenging inherited traditions for their collusion with androcentric patriarchy as well as a catalyst in overcoming oppressive situations through revolutionary acts of rebellion" (*Katie's Canon*, 23).

As Weems notes, "Our participation in certain realms of discourse is recent, [but] our demands are ancient."[38]

Womanist theologian Jacquelyn Grant, in her *White Women's Christ and Black Women's Jesus: Feminist Christology and Womanist Response*, builds on the womanist conversation by speaking about the differences between the sociohistorical experiences of black women and white women, and the ways they respond to oppression, and argues that it leads to distinctions between feminist and womanist theological discourse.[39] Feminist Christology, Grant asserts, fails to speak for the concerns of nonwhite, non-Western women, by privileging the white woman's experience and subsuming the experiences of all other women within it. She, therefore, proposes a womanist theology and Christology to account for the reality of black women's lives.[40] Because of the possible racist character of feminist Christology, and more generally, of the feminist movement, many black women are apprehensive about feminism, and, therefore, "believe that Black feminism is a contradiction of terms"; it is also why Grant self-identifies as a womanist.[41]

New Testament scholar Clarice J. Martin contributes to the womanist conversation by expanding the notion of the threefold interlocking system of oppression (that is, race, gender, and class) to include the concern of "linguistic sexism."[42] In her article, "Womanist

---

38. Weems, "Womanist Reflections," 219.
39. Jacquelyn Grant, *White Women's Christ and Black Women's Jesus: Feminist Christology and Womanist Response* (Atlanta: Scholars, 1989).
40. Grant refers to "feminist" theology as "White feminist" theology because of the "*nature of the sources* they use for the development of their theological perspectives," and because oftentimes the concerns and issues pertinent to feminists of color are not considered (ibid., 195, emphasis original).
41. Ibid., 201. Grant does not, however, suggest that "because feminist theology is White it is also racist," nor does she state that all white feminists are racist because of their skin color (ibid., 199).
42. Clarice J. Martin, "Womanist Interpretations of the New Testament: The Quest for Holistic and Inclusive Translation and Interpretation," *JFSR* 6 (1990): 42.

Interpretations of the New Testament: The Quest for Holistic and Inclusive Translation and Interpretation," Martin asserts that this "quadruocentric interest" of womanist biblical interpretation is important because the way words are translated and interpreted has a profound effect on how the historical experiences of oppressed peoples are viewed.[43] For this reason, Martin asserts that the challenge for womanist biblical interpreters is to "clarify whether potential 'texts of terror' for black people, can in any way portend new possibilities for our understanding of what actually constitutes the radicality of the Good News of the Gospel."[44]

Renita Weems, in her essay, "Reading *Her Way* through the Struggle: African American Women and the Bible," turns the womanist conversation to focus on the paradoxical relationship between the Bible and African Americans—specifically, African American women.[45] She examines the ways in which black women read the Bible in order to determine the rationale by which they continue to regard the Bible as significant. Weems achieves this by examining "the social-cultural location of African American women against the backdrop of American history," and by assessing the voices and values that black women hear expressed within biblical texts. [46] She concludes that the only way for African American

43. Ibid., 42. For example, Martin argues that the term *doulos* should be translated as "slave" in most New Testament texts because "a widescale translation of *doulos* as 'servant' would promote an unrealistic and naively 'euphemistic' understanding of slavery," which, according to the womanist biblical interpreter, "risks 'masking' socioeconomic or political verities that are of fundamental significance in assessing historical and symbolic meaning" (ibid., 45, 55).

44. Ibid., 60. This task entails the retrieval of not only marginalized female voices, but all persons (including children and slaves) that have been excluded by the biblical traditions, their writers, and the interpreters of those traditions (ibid., 51).

45. Renita J. Weems, "Reading *Her Way* through the Struggle: African American Women and the Bible," in *Stony the Road We Trod: African American Biblical Interpretation*, ed. Cain Hope Felder (Minneapolis: Fortress Press, 1991), 57–77. Weems finds it ironic that the Bible is "extremely influential in the African American religious life," despite its frequent use as a tool of marginalization and subjugation (ibid., 57).

46. Ibid., 59, 76.

women to read the Bible in a way that liberates them, and does not devalue them, is to seek to recapture the voice of the oppressed in the Bible. This is accomplished when black women are able to "read and hear the text for themselves, with their own eyes and with their own ears."[47] They must learn to read the Bible with caution and resistance—being careful not to internalize those things that offend them or threaten their dignity.[48]

Biblical scholar Koala Jones-Warsaw takes the womanist critique of feminist biblical interpretation's "one-dimensional" focus on gender, and applies it to the Hebrew Scriptures. In her article, "Toward a Womanist Hermeneutic: A Reading of Judges 19–21," Jones-Warsaw highlights the differences between a womanist and a feminist reading by comparing her interpretation of Judges 19–21 with that of feminist scholar Phyllis Trible.[49] She argues that Trible's reading, although groundbreaking in that she brings "the reader in solidarity with the female victims in the text" like never before, does not account for the diverse types of victimization found in the text, and therefore, has "limited use for women of color who experience multivariate victimization."[50] Thus, black women, like the Levite in Judges 19–21, must not only be cautious in the "retelling of our story to others," but also, like the Benjaminites, must "distinguish whether it is better to stand in solidarity with our brothers or not, and at what cost."[51] Being both black and female, we must "fight for liberation and equality of both aspects of ourselves," making certain not to be a "pawn" for either movement.[52]

47. Ibid.
48. Ibid., 63–64.
49. Koala Jones-Warsaw, "Toward a Womanist Hermeneutic: A Reading of Judges 19–21," *Journal of the Interdenominational Theological Center* 22 (1994): 18–35. See also Phyllis Trible, *Texts of Terror: Literary-Feminist Readings of Biblical Narratives* (Philadelphia: Fortress Press, 1984).
50. Jones-Warsaw, "Toward a Womanist Hermeneutic," 18.
51. Ibid., 32–33.
52. Ibid., 31.

Theologian Kelly Brown Douglas directs the gaze of womanist scholarship away from issues of racism and sexism, toward the womanist task of theological and biblical interpretation in her article, "Marginalized People, Liberating Perspectives: A Womanist Approach to Biblical Interpretation."[53] One of her most powerful arguments is that the idea that "a singular or universal approach to the biblical witness" does not exist applies to African American women as well.[54] She argues that black women in our professional positions must acknowledge that we are in a position of privilege, and therefore, must bear witness to the voices of "the least of these" in our task of biblical interpretation.[55] She posits that a womanist approach to the Bible, if it is to be liberating for *all* persons must include the following: (1) naming our own points of privilege in order to "free us to appreciate the perspectives of the underside, [(2)] approaching the text from the perspective of the most marginalized, and [(3)] recognizing the impact that our use of the Bible can have on people's lives."[56] Certainly, the tenets of Douglas's threefold approach to the Bible can and should be adopted by all theological and biblical interpreters.

In 2008, womanist biblical interpretation expanded with the introduction of two new hermeneutical approaches, a "hermeneutics of wholeness" by New Testament scholar Raquel St. Clair, and a "hermeneutics of redemption" by ethicist Stacey M. Floyd-Thomas. Raquel St. Clair's *Call and Consequences: A Womanist Reading of Mark*

---

53. Kelly Brown Douglas, "Marginalized People, Liberating Perspectives: A Womanist Approach to Biblical Interpretation," in *Anglican Theological Review* 83, no. 1 (2001): 41–48.

54. Ibid., 41.

55. Ibid., 44. Douglas notes the importance of this task because she asserts that "the least of these," that is, the "underside of marginal realities who experience unjust systems of privilege in their rawest, vilest forms," are "better situated to see the radical and revolutionary change required to ensure that *all* human beings have access to what is needed to live and to fulfill our human potential" (ibid., emphasis original).

56. Ibid., 46–47.

is the first full-blown monograph of a womanist interpretation of a biblical text.[57] A hermeneutics of wholeness, which is based on four tenets of womanist Christology,[58]

> must promote the wholeness of African American women without prohibiting the wholeness of others. Stated negatively, a womanist biblical hermeneutic cannot aid or abet the oppression of African American women or anyone else. Womanists recognize the interrelatedness of all people. Therefore, African American women will not accomplish individual or community wholeness by the destruction or bondage of others. Womanists are "committed to the wholeness of an entire people." This commitment extends across racial, gender, and class lines.[59]

It combines the womanist focus on countering the tridimensional reality of racism, sexism, and classism, with the notion of God's solidarity with, and commitment to, black women's survival and wholeness, a commitment that womanists already uphold in their "theological formulations and praxis."[60] In essence, what St. Clair does

---

57. Raquel A. St. Clair, *Call and Consequences: A Womanist Reading of Mark* (Minneapolis: Fortress Press, 2008). In this work, St. Clair analyzes the triple interplay of the cross, suffering (what she calls agony), and discipleship. She identifies the pain of the cross with the pain that black women experience today. She argues that this pain, which Jesus has overcome with his resurrection, affords African American women the opportunity to triumph over their pain. To follow Jesus is to experience pain; it is a consequence, and not a condition of discipleship.

58. These four precepts are: (1) to seek the wholeness of African American women without prohibiting the wholeness of others; therefore, to be committed to the wholeness of an entire people, male *and* female (which she directly draws from Walker's definition of "womanist"); (2) to take seriously the intersection between African American women's experience and biblical interpretation; (3) God, through Jesus Christ, supports African American women in their commitment and struggle for wholeness; and (4) Jesus' life and ministry, and suffering and death are significant (the first two leading to the last two) (ibid., 59–60).

59. Ibid., 82. As we will see, my book, which places postcolonial theory in conversation with womanist thought, differs from St. Clair's concept of wholeness. Whereas St. Clair focuses on God and Christ's commitment to support black women in their struggle for wholeness, I focus not only on what may be prohibiting this wholeness from being realized—namely, the possible conflicting characteristics within a black woman that need to be identified and held in a necessary tension—but also on a specific process on how to attain it.

60. Ibid. St. Clair's hermeneutics of wholeness builds on the work of theologian Kelly Brown Douglas, who states that a womanist theology "engages in a social-political analysis of 'wholeness,' that seeks to eliminate anything that prevents Black people from being whole,

is present an explicitly Christian womanist interpretation of the Bible that she uses to analyze the Gospel of Mark.

Floyd-Thomas's "hermeneutics of redemption" that she posits in her article, "'I am Black and Beautiful, O Ye Daughters of Jerusalem . . .': African American Virtue Ethics and a Womanist Hermeneutics of Redemption," is connected to, or logically precedes St. Clair's hermeneutics of wholeness.[61] Also based on four tenets, a hermeneutics of redemption helps black people to "chart within the biblical scripture the genealogy of black moral wisdom of surviving and thriving in the face of oppression and the coping strategies that emerge out of their struggle for a politics of respectability/public decorum, social mobility, self-realization, and civilized progress."[62] After this has occurred, then the Scriptures that were used to associate blackness with vice can instead be used to highlight the "multivalent survival mechanisms used and developed by the blackest people of the Bible" and be redeemed as virtuous.[63] Building on this insight, I suggest that in order to seek the type of "wholeness" indicated by St. Clair, black people, and more specifically, black women must

liberated people, and from living as a whole, unified community" (Douglas, "Womanist Theology," 295).

61. Stacey M. Floyd-Thomas, "'I am Black and Beautiful, O Ye Daughters of Jerusalem. . .': African American Virtue Ethics and a Womanist Hermeneutics of Redemption," in *African American Religious Life and the Story of Nimrod*, ed. Anthony B. Pinn and Allen Dwight Callahan (New York: Palgrave Macmillan, 2008), 35–51.

62. Ibid., 49. What follows are the four tenets of Floyd-Thomas's hermeneutics of redemption. Radical subjectivity traces the process of how black people gained moral agency to "defy forced subjugation, and to incite resistance against marginality through the audacious act of naming and claiming voice, space, and knowledge" (44). Traditional communalism highlights the ways in which black people "act as moral conveyors for their communities through acts of inclusivity, mutuality, reciprocity, and self-care" (44–45). Redemptive self-love seeks to "demystify racial stereotypes and monolithic assumptions of black identity, in order to transform their sense of who they can be while still being black" (45). Critical engagement is the articulation not only of black peoples' "value systems and heritage, but also their racial-ethnic embodiment and culture" (44–45).

63. Ibid., 49. For an elaborate analysis of the use of blackness as political invective in early Christian literature, see womanist biblical scholar Gay Byron's *Symbolic Blackness and Ethnic Difference in Early Christian Literature* (New York: Routledge, 2002).

embrace and love their blackness, and be able to identify the virtues of blackness in the authoritative Scriptures we hold so dear.

The above survey indicates that womanist theology has a deep and rich *her*story. The foundational theological material for womanist thought and womanist biblical hermeneutics can be traced back to the nineteenth century with protowomanists such as Jarena Lee and Sojourner Truth. This assertion is unequivocally made due to these women's struggle for equality for women of color, their fight for the creation of a (discursive) space where black women can maintain both aspects of their identity—race and gender—as well as their commitment to the survival and well-being of all peoples. Regardless of their education, or supposed lack thereof, these women are considered womanists because of their audacious tenacity to proclaim their place and God-given right to practice their full humanity.

In womanist biblical studies, the above characterization is also ever-present. Differences in womanist hermeneutical approaches to the task of biblical interpretation exist because the experiences of black women are not uniform. This is not a negative observation. Womanist biblical interpretation "varies as widely as do the contexts in which women of color live, work, read, write, reflect, and worship."[64] There are commonalities between them, however.

1. Womanist hermeneutical approaches are regularly multidimensional; they can be interdisciplinary, collaborative, and multicontextual.

2. They emphasize and prioritize women's experience in general and the social location of the reader and interpreter in particular.

3. A goal (if not *the* goal) of womanist discourse is the eradication of all forms of human oppression.

---

64. Gafney, "A Black Feminist Approach ," 391–92.

4. The fruit of womanist scholarship must be accessible to the wider nonspecialist worshiping community.[65]

These are some of the tenets that make up the womanist lens that I use to analyze the woman Babylon in Revelation. I also take the experience of some black women's issues with oppression due to their race, sex, and class as my starting point, and find resonances and dissonances with the woman Babylon. I consider the ways in which the text is used and interpreted, and how it affects the manner in which the historical experiences of black women may be perceived. I am particularly referring to African American women's experience with slavery, either firsthand or through generational reverberations. Since the Bible is a text of significance for many African American women, I also aim to change the effects of the narrative of the woman Babylon—which I consider a text of terror—by suggesting a new interpretive possibility. I also bring with me the womanist notion of choosing one's own labels—the black woman's "self-determination and right to identify and name the parameters and character of [her] experience."[66] For this reason, I not only intentionally refer to Babylon as a woman instead of a whore,[67] but I also coin the term *ambiveilence*—a new postcolonial womanist hermeneutics, which is explicated in the final section of this chapter.

Lastly, my analysis is tempered by the acknowledgement of my privilege as an educated black woman. Delores S. Williams, in her 1993 monograph *Sisters in the Wilderness: The Challenge of Womanist God-Talk*, writes that "womanist theologians (who are among the

---

65. Ibid., 392, emphasis added.
66. Lorine L. Cummings, "A Womanist Response to the Afrocentric Idea: Jarena Lee, Womanist Preacher," in *Living the Intersection: Womanism and Afrocentrism in Theology*, ed. Cheryl J. Sanders (Minneapolis: Fortress Press, 1995), 58.
67. Certainly, I am not the first to do this. I join the ranks of biblical scholars such as Tina Pippin and Caroline Vander Stichele, neither of whom is African American. A discussion of their work is found in chapter 2.

educated elite) must also dialogue with the poor, uneducated women of all colors in order to discern where womanist definitions, concepts and practices oppress poor women."[68] Throughout my project, I try to be cognizant of the fact that my experience, although distinct from any other African American woman, may differ most especially from African American women less fortunate than myself. In summation, the womanist framework—the set of ideas, values, beliefs, practices, and concerns that formulate my perception of reality—that I employ in this book is rooted in the black woman's experience, and informs the questions that I bring to the text of Revelation. This framework also guides my use of other approaches, such as postcolonial theory, which adds a further dimension to my womanist lens. Let us now turn to an overview of postcolonial studies and its connection to biblical hermeneutics.

Postcolonial Studies and Biblical Hermeneutics

Postcolonial studies, simply stated, is the critical analysis of colonialism and its aftermath. The term postcolonial does not suggest that a "clean . . . break from the colonial 'past'" has occurred.[69] Although it refers to the "formal" end of imperialism—"the practice, the theory, and the attitudes of a dominating metropolitan center ruling a distant territory," and colonialism—the practice of acquiring the land, or, stated differently, the "consequence" of imperialism, both phenomena continue to effectively operate today in new and more subtle forms.[70] Postcolonial studies reflects not only on the concrete practice of these phenomena, but also on the discourse about them.[71]

68. Williams, *Sisters in the Wilderness*, 186.
69. Stephen D. Moore, *Empire and Apocalypse: Postcolonialism and the New Testament* (Sheffield, UK: Sheffield Phoenix, 2006), 5, 4, respectively. For a clear and succinct explanation of the term *postcolonial/post-colonial*, that is, its understanding with and without the hyphen, see ibid., 4–5. Moore notes, however, that the unhyphenated form is presently preferred (ibid., 5).

Nevertheless, the areas of interest for postcolonial studies extend beyond what Moore refers to as "the twin phenomena of colonialism and postcolonialism."[72]

> A series of other, interrelated realia also fall comfortably within its orbit: imperialism, Orientalism, universalism, expansionism, exploration, invasion, slavery, settlement, resistance, revolt, terrorism, nationalism, nativism, negritude, assimilation, creolization, cosmopolitanism, colonial mimicry, hybridity, the subaltern, marginalization, migration, diaspora, decolonization, neocolonialism, and globalization—all intersected by the ubiquitous determinants of language, gender, race, ethnicity, and class.[73]

The last five determinants of language, gender, race, ethnicity, and class, along with the varied experiences, reactions, and contexts (social, historical, and cultural, etc.) of the many persons affected by colonial systems, speak to the multiplicity of postcolonial studies. It is certainly an academic phenomenon.

With the inclusion of numerous violent and oppressive texts in the Bible, as well as the hegemonic ideologies and structures of ancient Near Eastern and Mediterranean empires, Moore asserts that "the relevance of many of these [postcolonial] concepts to the biblical texts . . . hardly needs arguing."[74] He continues, "So much biblical

---

70. Edward Said, *Culture and Imperialism* (New York: Knopf, 1994), 9. See also Moore, *Empire and Apocalypse*, 4. These new and more subtle forms are neoimperialism and neocolonialism. They describe superpowers such as the United States who have replaced their "former imperial powers" with a more "dominant role in establishing a global capitalist economy" (Bill Ashcroft, Gareth Griffiths, and Helen Tiffin, *Post-Colonial Studies: The Key Concepts*, 2nd ed.[New York: Routledge, 2001], 163).

71. Fernando F. Segovia, "Biblical Criticism and Postcolonial Studies: Toward a Postcolonial Optic" in *The Postcolonial Biblical Reader*, ed. R. S. Sugirtharajah (Malden, MA: Blackwell, 2006), 43n3.

72. Ibid., 9.

73. Ibid.

74. Moore, *Empire and Apocalypse*, 9. "That hallowed gateway to biblical criticism, for instance, the 'Old' or 'New' Testament introduction (whether the textbook or the course), derives much of its efficacy and allure from its ability to summon 'exotic' empires from the shadows of the biblical texts and parade them before the student: Egypt, Assyria, Babylon, Persia, Greece, Rome" (ibid.). Asian theologian Kwok Pui-Lan alleviates any uncertainties about the

scholarship is already a reflection on imperialism, colonialism, and the resistance they inevitably elicit."[75] Although biblical studies has, to a degree, been able to analyze the above topics without any debt to postcolonial studies, the latter "would offer significant conceptual and practical resources for focusing, sharpening, and nuancing such analyses."[76] A multimethodological approach must be used, however, when analyzing such colossal realities as imperialism and colonialism because, as Segovia asserts, postcolonial criticism "is *an* optic, not *the* optic, in full engagement and dialogue with a host of other models and other optics."[77]

In biblical studies, postcolonial criticism works along with the tools of historical criticism. Kwok Pui-Lan states that "postcolonial criticism does not reject the insights of historical criticism, because much of the work of the historical critics contributes to the understanding of the 'worldliness' of the text, that is, the material and ideological backgrounds from which the texts emerged and to which the texts responded."[78] Postcolonial criticism complements these findings by asking new questions about such matters as the interconnectedness between the biblical text and empire, which influenced "the literary production and redaction of biblical texts,"

---

applicability of postcolonial analysis (having "developed largely from the experiences of *modern* colonialism") to the examination of *ancient* situations and texts ("Making the Connections: Postcolonial Studies and Feminist Biblical Interpretation" in Sugirtharajah, *The Postcolonial Biblical Reader*, 46, emphasis added). She asserts that "since the 1970s, biblical scholars using social scientific methods, including those with a Marxist bent, have not shied away from employing 'modern' theories to illuminate ancient societies" (ibid., 47).

75. Moore, *Empire and Apocalypse*, 9.

76. Ibid., 9–10. This assertion serves as the basis for my use of a postcolonial inflection of a womanist lens. Although a womanist lens can effectively analyze issues of empire, an added postcolonial lens allows for a clearer, more concise evaluation and investigation. See Martin's "Polishing the Unclouded Mirror," for her use of a womanist approach to Revelation that is used to present a notable social critique of Roman slavery.

77. Segovia, "Biblical Criticism and Postcolonial Studies," 42, emphasis added.

78. Kwok, "Making the Connections," 46.

impacted the production of the canon, and "shaped the collective memory of Jewish people" (to name a few examples).[79]

In addition to the new lines of inquiry that postcolonial studies brings to the interdisciplinary engagement with biblical studies, it also helps biblical critics keep the imperial origins of the biblical texts to the fore. Thus, instead of simply adding to the number of investigative analyses and questions already associated with historical criticism, postcolonial criticism adds a decolonizing, liberative, and ethical element—one that will hopefully lead the biblical critic to seek a means of transformation as an interpretive end. Segovia writes,

> Even as one among equals, [postcolonial studies] proves most incisive and most telling, for it reminds us all . . . that the discipline of biblical criticism as we know it and have known it must be seen and analyzed, like all other discourses of modernity, against the much broader geopolitical context of Western imperialism and colonialism. . . . The goal is not merely one of analysis and description but rather one of transformation: the struggle for "liberation" and "decolonization."[80]

Be that as it may, postcolonial studies might also benefit from an interdisciplinary venture with biblical studies. In his essay, "Mapping the Postcolonial Optic in Biblical Criticism: Meaning and Scope," Segovia notes that two major lacunae in postcolonial studies that can be directly addressed are its minor consideration of the realm of antiquity—namely, the historical trajectory of the imperial-colonial formation—and religious discourse, such as the influence of religious

---

79. Ibid.
80. Segovia, "Biblical Criticism and Postcolonial Studies," 42. Segovia's argument for the confluence of biblical studies and postcolonial studies is made from "within the paradigm of cultural studies in biblical criticism, with its distinctively ideological mode of discourse" ("Mapping the Postcolonial Optic in Biblical Criticism: Meaning and Scope" in *Postcolonial Biblical Criticism: Interdisciplinary Intersections*, ed. Stephen D. Moore and Fernando F. Segovia [New York: T & T Clark International, 2005], 23). Within cultural studies, the postcolonial studies model "can address at one and the same time the various interrelated and interdependent dimensions of criticism: the analysis of texts—the world of antiquity; the analysis of 'texts'—the world of modernity; the analysis of readers of texts and producers of 'texts'—the world of postmodernity" (Segovia, "Biblical Criticism and Postcolonial Studies," 42).

texts on cultural production, and the position of religious institutions within imperial systems.[81] Thus, as Segovia and Moore assert, "The application of the postcolonial angle of vision to biblical criticism emerges as entirely warranted," and if "readily formulated and executed," it can result in a "properly grounded and properly informed postcolonial biblical criticism."[82]

As noted earlier, biblical scholarship is not oblivious to the concepts of colonialism or imperialism, as evident in the fact that a major interest of scholars is empire. Moore notes, however, that any interdisciplinary attempts have tended to draw on fields other than postcolonial studies, such as that of classics.[83] The boundaries of postcolonial biblicalcriticism, that is, where it begins or ends, however, are not readily identifiable. [84] Moore and Segovia note three different trajectories for its emergence: liberation hermeneutics, extrabiblical postcolonial studies, and historical biblical criticism.

With regard to liberation hermeneutics, the version from which postcolonial biblical criticism seems to have emerged is contextual or cultural hermeneutics. Contextual hermeneutics focuses on the "local, the indigenous, the ethnic, and the culturally contingent, with the aim of recovering, reasserting, and reinscribing identities, cultures, and traditions that colonial Christianity had erased, suppressed, or pronounced 'idolatrous.'"[85] Moore and Segovia illustrate the

---

81. Segovia, "Mapping the Postcolonial Optic," 72–75. Segovia is careful to note that "by lacunae, . . . I do not mean to say that there is no discussion whatsoever, only that such discussions are, comparatively speaking, rather minor in character" (ibid., 72).

82. Moore and Segovia, "Postcolonial Biblical Criticism: Beginnings, Trajectories, Intersections" in Moore and Segovia, *Postcolonial Biblical Criticism*, 11.

83. Moore, *Empire and Apocalypse*, 9.

84. Moore and Segovia, "Beginnings, Trajectories, Intersections," 5.

85. Ibid., 6. This is in lieu of a "(frequently Marxist-driven) focus on economics and the universal plight of the poor typical of classic liberation theology" (ibid.). The first monograph on the topic of how "biblical land traditions have been pressed into service for colonial ends" was *The Bible and Colonialism: A Moral Critique* by Irish Roman Catholic priest Michael Prior (Sheffield, UK: Sheffield Academic, 1997), followed by R. S. Sugirtharajah's *Asian Biblical Hermeneutics and Postcolonialism* (Maryknoll, NY: Orbis, 1998). See Moore, *Empire and Apocalypse*, 16.

connection between contextual and postcolonial hermeneutics by noting the distance between two collections, each edited by R. S. Sugritharajah: *Voices from the Margin: Interpreting the Bible in the Third World* (1991) ("an early landmark of contextual hermeneutics"), and *The Postcolonial Bible* (1998) ("an early landmark of postcolonial biblical criticism").[86] Most of the contributors to both collections write out of their own sociocultural locations. A change is noted, however, in the fact that *Voices from the Margin* only occasionally focuses on the "lingering specter of colonialism," while *The Postcolonial Bible* centers firmly on the colonial and postcolonial, with some of its contributors employing some of the analytical concepts of extrabiblical postcolonial studies to study these phenomena as they pertain to biblical texts.[87]

Interestingly, the switch in the above-noted collections from the use of a liberation approach to that of postcolonial inquiry is indicative of a change in the perspective of their editor, R. S. Sugirtharajah—the most prolific and most influential exemplar of postcolonial biblical criticism. Formerly one of the leading liberationist exegetes, Sugirtharajah engages in an "extensive *internal* critique of the liberationist tradition from a 'postcolonial perspective.'"[88] Moore succinctly summarizes Sugirtharajah's lengthy (seventy-plus page) critique found in the latter's *The Bible and the Third World*.[89]

Liberation hermeneutics, for Sugirtharajah, is largely prevented by its

---

86. Moore and Segovia, "Beginnings, Trajectories, Intersections," 15. See R. S. Sugritharajah, ed., *Voices from the Margin: Interpreting the Bible in the Third World* (Maryknoll, NY: Orbis Books, 1991), and R. S. Sugritharajah, ed., *The Postcolonial Bible* (Sheffield, UK: Sheffield Academic, 1998).

87. Moore, *Empire and Apocalypse*, 15.

88. Ibid., 16, emphasis added.

89. Sugirtharajah, *The Bible and the Third World*, 203–75. See also Sugirtharajah, *Postcolonial Criticism and Biblical Interpretation* (Oxford: Oxford University Press, 2002), 103–23.

Christian presuppositions and investments from seeing the Bible as at once a source of emancipation and a source of oppression, and from respecting the truth claims of other religious traditions, even when those traditions are the characteristic religious expressions of the poor; while it conceives of oppression in turn in terms that are too exclusively economic, neglecting other forms of it based on gender, sexuality, or race/ethnicity.[90]

Essentially, what Sugirtharajah does is accuse classic liberationist theology and theologians of romanticizing the poor and idealizing the Bible. Sugirtharajah advocates for postcolonial criticism because, when used as an oppositional tool, it can examine biblical texts for their colonial entanglements by "unmask[ing] the past textual production of colonialism and . . . dislodge its legitimizing strategies. . . . [It also] provides a location for other voices, histories and experiences to heard," and frees people of the Third World from "interpretive cages"—focused on ethnicity, religion, or nationalism—from which they are oftentimes encouraged to speak.[91]

The second trajectory of postcolonial biblical criticism—the field of extrabiblical postcolonial studies—is due to a profound engagement with works mostly in the field of literary studies that focused on phenomena such as colonialism, imperialism, postcolonialism, and neocolonialism.[92] Extrabiblical postcolonial studies offers "a fresh conceptual vocabulary and analytic apparatus with which to treat those themes in relation to biblical texts and their histories of interpretation and appropriation."[93] The collection commonly said to mark the origins of postcolonial biblical criticism (although not the first to appear: see *Postcolonial Literature and the Biblical Call for Justice*, edited by Susan VanZanten Gallagher),[94] was *Postcolonialism*

90. Moore, *Empire and Apocalypse*, 16.
91. Sugirtharajah, *The Bible and the Third World*, 272.
92. Moore and Segovia, "Beginnings, Trajectories, Intersections," 8.
93. Ibid., 6.

and Scriptural Reading, edited by Laura E. Donaldson.[95]It should be noted, however, that not all of the contributors in this work are "thoroughly rooted in extra-biblical Postcolonial Studies."[96]

Historical biblical criticism, the third trajectory, has always employed an exegetical lens that focused on the theme of empire "through which to reframe and reread selected New Testament texts."[97] Part of the reconstruction of "various 'backgrounds' against which the historical critic's Bible becomes visible is, in part at least, to conjure up a succession of empires, beginning . . . with the Assyrian Empire and ending with the Roman."[98] This third trajectory represents an intensification of such efforts. Some of the resulting works have the word *empire* in their titles, such as *Paul and Empire: Religion and Power in Roman Imperial Society* (ed. Richard A. Horsley, 1997) and *Matthew and Empire: Initial Explorations* (Warren Carter, 2001), while others sharing the same thematic focus do not, such as *Liberating Paul: the Justice of God and the Politics of the Apostle* (Neil Elliott, 1994) and *Paul and Politics: Ekklesia, Israel, Imperium, Interpretation: Essays in Honor of Krister Stendahl* (ed. Horsley, 2000).[99]

94. Susan VanZanten Gallagher Jackson, ed., *Postcolonial Literature and the Biblical Call for Justice* (Jackson, MS: University Press of Mississippi, 1994).

95. Moore and Segovia, "Beginnings, Trajectories, Intersections," 8–9. Laura E. Donaldson, ed., *Postcolonialism and Scriptural Reading*, Semeia, 75 (Atlanta: Scholars, 1996).

96. Moore and Segovia, "Beginnings, Trajectories, Intersections," 8–9.

97. Ibid., 7.

98. Ibid.

99. Ibid.; Richard A. Horsley, ed. *Paul and Empire: Religion and Power in Roman Imperial Society* (Harrisburg, PA: Trinity Press International, 1997); Warren Carter, *Matthew and Empire: Initial Explorations* (Harrisburg, PA: Trinity Press International, 2001); Neil Elliott, *Liberating Paul: the Justice of God and the Politics of the Apostle* (Sheffield, UK: Sheffield Academic, 1994); and Richard A. Horsley, ed. *Paul and Politics: Ekklesia, Israel, Imperium, Interpretation: Essays in Honor of Krister Stendahl* (Harrisburg, PA: Trinity Press International, 2000). Warren Carter also has a later work that fits into the "X and Empire" category entitled, *John and Empire: Initial Explorations* (New York: T & T Clark, 2008). This text, which fills the gap on empire studies of John's Gospel, differs from Carter's *Matthew and Empire* by using a more interdisciplinary approach, such as drawing on the work of James C. Scott (*Domination and the Arts of Resistance: Hidden Transcripts* [New Haven: Yale University Press, 1990]). Additionally, Carter's former work makes no mention of postcolonial studies.

Still, the distinction among these empire-critical scholars is the fact that some of them are only interested in the ancient imperial contexts in which the texts emerged, while others are focused on maintaining a "tensive dialogue" between ancient imperial and contemporary contexts.[100] Despite this distinction, "empire studies" best characterizes the work of these "X and Empire" authors, since only a few label their work "postcolonial."[101]

As stated above, postcolonial biblical criticism's task of examining the biblical texts in relation to their ancient imperial contexts is a task already assumed in the historical-critical project. Moore cites this as the one of three tasks of postcolonial biblical criticism. A second task is to analyze biblical texts in their relation to empire from the fourth century to the present. One attempts to understand how biblical texts have, for example, been legitimized as colonial and imperial enterprises,[102] but also how they have been used by the colonized to resist and interrogate such enterprises. "The colonized 'read back' to the empire with equal creativity, causing 'the white man's book' to turn and convict him in African, Indian, or Caribbean accents."[103] Biblical texts have been used both ways, but overwhelmingly on the side of empire. The third task is to "trac[e] the affiliations and correlations" between critical biblical scholarship and European colonial empires.[104] It is the case that "critical biblical scholarship was being invented in Europe—principally, [in] the eighteenth,

---

100. Moore and Segovia, "Beginnings, Trajectories, Intersections," 8.
101. Moore, *Empire and Apocalypse*, 19.
102. R. S. Sugirtharajah refers to the use of the "Great Commission" in the Gospel of Matthew (28:19-20) in Baptist missionary pioneer William Carey's 1792 pamphlet, *An Enquiry into the Obligations of Christians to Use Means for the Conversion of the Heathen* ("A Postcolonial Exploration of Collusion and Construction in Biblical Interpretation," in Sugirtharajah, *The Postcolonial Bible*, 91–116 [96–100]). "The *Enquiry*, . . . resembles the prospectus of a modern-day multinational company, with elaborate statistical details reminding Christians [using 'the Matthean commission as the proof text'] of their inescapable obligation to preach the gospel to distant lands" (ibid., 96–7).
103. Moore, *Empire and Apocalypse*, 10.
104. Ibid., 10–11.

nineteenth, and early twentieth centuries"—during the long ascent of the European colonial powers.[105]

Postcolonial biblical criticism is understood as oscillating between two poles: the reading of the biblical text as "unequivocal and exemplary anti-imperial and anti-colonial resistance literature," and the reading of it as "literature that, irrespective of the conscious intentionality of its author, insidiously reinscribes imperial and colonial ideologies even while appearing to resist them."[106] Although Moore cites Richard Horsley's *Hearing the Whole Story: The Politics of Plot in Mark's Gospel* (2001)[107] as indicative of the first reading, Horsley later alters his position in his edited volume *In the Shadow of Empire: Reclaiming the Bible as a History of Faithful Resistance* (2008).[108] Instead of arguing that biblical texts are undeniably anti-imperial/colonial, he highlights their complexity by noting their ambivalent nature—a noted task of postcolonial studies. In his introductory essay, "The Bible and Empires," Horsley states that "biblical books are not unanimously and unambiguously anti-imperial or pro-imperial. They speak with different and sometimes ambivalent voices."[109]

The future of postcolonial biblical criticism in North America is undoubtedly and, in a sense, unfortunately, quite promising.[110] This

---

105. Ibid., 10.

106. Moore, *Empire and Apocalypse*, 13–14.

107. Richard Horsley, *Hearing the Whole Story: The Politics of Plot in Mark's Gospel* (Louisville: Westminster John Knox, 2001).

108. Moore, *Empire and Apocalypse*, 11–14. Richard A. Horsley, ed. *In the Shadow of Empire: Reclaiming the Bible as a History of Faithful Resistance* (Louisville: Westminster John Knox Press, 2008). The nine contributors to *In the Shadow of Empire* offer a "basic survey of key issues and passages [of both the Hebrew Bible and the Christian Testament] focused on the political-religious rule of empires and the people's accommodation or resistance to imperial rule" (ibid., 7). Since "the issue of American imperial power and behavior have come to the fore in public discussion," Horsley asserts that it is time that religious leaders gain some "acquaintance with issues of Empire in the Bible, which has been so influential in shaping the American identity" (ibid.).

109. Horsley, "The Bible and Empires" in Horsley, *In the Shadow of Empire*, 7.

110. Moore states that the "'X and Empire' brand of postcolonial biblical criticism seems poised for widespread dissemination within biblical studies—certainly within New Testament

is because, as Sugirtharajah rightly asserts, "As long as there are empires, dominations, tyrannies and exploitations—either rising or resurfacing—postcolonial [biblical] criticism will continue to have its vigilant role to play."[111] I suggest that a good assessment of the world in which we live negates any foreseeable change in this imperial climate. Sugirtharajah goes on to state that there is also "unfinished or unstarted textual work [that] postcolonial criticism has to undertake within the discipline of biblical studies"; the "hermeneutical horizons" of postcolonial biblical criticism need to be expanded.[112]

In the same year of publication as Sugirtharajah's essay, Elisabeth Schüssler Fiorenza, in *The Power of the Word: Scripture and the Rhetoric of Empire*, notes a gap in anti-imperial and postcolonial studies. She asserts that in their attempt to "analyze imperial domination of the 'generic' citizen, or the 'generic' colonized and oppressed," they paid

studies"—because it "represents the smoothest, least taxing, and least threatening extension of traditional historical criticism" (*Empire and Apocalypse*, 22). He envisions, however, that the liberationist trajectory of postcolonial biblical criticism will prevail in the two-thirds world, and continue to "counter postcolonial biblical criticism's inherent inclination as an academic enterprise to coagulate into an esoteric discourse herme(neu)tically sealed off from the extra-academic world" (ibid., 22–23).

111. R. S. Sugirtharajah, "Postcolonial and Biblical Interpretation: The Next Phase," in *A Postcolonial Commentary on the New Testament Writings*, ed. Fernando F. Segovia and R. S. Sugirtharajah (New York: T & T Clark, 2007), 455. The text in which Sugirtharajah's essay is found, *A Postcolonial Commentary on the New Testament Writings*, is described by Segovia as "a landmark achievement in the trajectory of postcolonial biblical criticism" (Segovia, "Introduction: Configurations, Approaches, Findings, Stances," in *A Postcolonial Commentary*, 1). He states that this book is critical for postcolonial biblical criticism in three ways: in terms of its "integrative critical analysis" of all the New Testament writings, the "highly diverse representation of critical faces and voices," and the inclusion of a "highly expansive deployment of critical frameworks and responses (ibid., 1). This compilation of "contending definitions and contrasting paths, [and] varying findings and diverging encounters" helps to "organize and scrutinize the past as well as to inform and guide the future" of postcolonial biblical criticism (ibid., 68).

112. Sugirtharajah, "Postcolonial and Biblical Interpretation: The Next Phase," 455. Sugirtharajah suggests three ways that the "hermeneutical horizons" of postcolonial biblical criticism can be expanded: (1) by embracing diverse texts such as the early Christian literature found at Nag Hammadi in Egypt that were excluded from the Christian canon; (2) by "look[ing] beyond the limitations of the Jewish-Hellenistic context [of the milieu of early Christianity]" to include the Jewish-Aramaic context; and (3) by investigating the "ritual practices in the lives of the biblical Jews or in the formative years of early Christianity"—an important "outward manifestation of faith" for the majority of Asian and African communities (ibid., 455, 457, 459–60).

little attention "to a critical feminist analytics and the workings of gender in biblical texts."[113] She, therefore, posits a critical feminist decolonizing approach, which includes a critical feminist hermeneutics of liberation, and has a twofold purpose: (1) to identify and highlight wo/men's situation in imperial contexts of domination; and (2) to find places in the biblical text that present "thorough-going egalitarian spiritual visions," which can be used to create a "biblical

---

113. Elisabeth Schüssler Fiorenza, *The Power of the Word: Scripture and the Rhetoric of Empire* (Minneapolis: Fortress Press, 2007), 11. Feminist biblical criticism, especially in its analysis of imperial structures, has been critiqued. Musa W. Dube, in her *Postcolonial Feminist Interpretation of the Bible*, examines the "interconnection between biblical texts and the ideology and practices of imperialism," (St. Louis: Chalice, 2000), 157. Examining the works of white Western male and feminist scholars who have interpreted the Canaanite woman of Matthew 15, for example, she critiques their analyses for failing to account for certain factors such as race, ethnicity, imperialism, and colonialism. Dube, therefore, asserts that there is a "need to depatriarchalize *as well as* to decolonize texts before any attempt is made to reclaim them. They show that the patriarchal category of analysis does not necessarily translate into imperial criticism" (ibid., 184, emphasis added). Dube, therefore, insists on a *postcolonial* feminist approach to the Bible because "Western feminist discourses have inscribed themselves within the Western imperialist parameters in order to point the way forward toward postcolonial readings of the Bible" (ibid., 23).In a later essay, "Rahab is Hanging Out a Red Ribbon: One African Woman's Perspective on the Future of Feminist New Testament Scholarship" (in *Feminist New Testament Studies: Global and Future Perspectives*, ed. Kathleen O'Brien Wicker, Althea Spencer Miller, and Musa W. Dube [New York: Fortress Press, 2005], 177–202), Dube continues to critique the shortsightedness and exclusiveness of feminist New Testament scholars' work. By identifying with the Hebrew Bible/Old Testament character of Rahab, Dube frames the relationship of feminist New Testament studies (FNTS) with liberative and contemporary concerns. Itemizing her critiques, she not only states what is lacking in this particular field, but also offers suggestions on how it can improve. For example, she proposes that FNTS foster grassroots reading in the church and the academy, alter the feminist commentary style, and develop a scholarship fund for two-thirds world students. She also suggests that feminist New Testament scholars embrace "world scriptures," since "the New Testament, as a Christian text, now exists with many other world scriptures and cultures as a direct consequence of modern imperialism" (ibid., 192). Additionally, Dube recommends that scholarly dialogue be turned into action. Similar to Rahab, FNTS should also commit "'cultural treason' against hegemonic structures . . . to bring liberation through transformation rather than reforming oppressive structures" (ibid., 197).Kwok Pui-Lan recommends that "postcolonial feminist critics not only recover the insights of ordinary women readers but also unmask the myriad ways in which biblical scholars, feminists among them, have been complicit with or oblivious to colonialism and neocolonialism" ("Making the Connections," 45–46). The postcolonial feminist project, Kwok continues, explores "the interstices of different forms of oppression under the shadow of the empire," thus making up for those male postcolonial critics who omit gender in their analysis, and those feminist critics who "isolate gender from the larger economic and colonial context" (ibid., 48). (Kwok's essay was first printed in her *Postcolonial Imagination and Feminist Theology* [Louisville: Westminster John Knox, 2005], 77–99).

ethos of radical democracy and human rights as an alternative to the imperial ethos of domination and subordination."[114] For example, with regard to the text of Revelation, Schüssler Fiorenza notes the problematic nature of Revelation's "co-optation" and reinscription of "Roman imperial language and imagery" for the purpose of "shap[ing] Christian imagination in terms of empire."[115] As such, Schüssler Fiorenza is right to assert that both liberationist and decolonizing readings of texts such as Revelation are important, especially when Christians who are in power turn to the ways in which the imperial language of biblical texts functions in order to guide and buttress their agendas.[116]

I suggest that a future trajectory for postcolonial biblical studies is its engagement with womanist biblical hermeneutics, a task I undertake in this book. Sugirtharajah calls for the postcolonial biblical critic to adopt a "new vocation," which includes the continual formulation of new scholarship about issues that "attract media attention," because the interpreter has both a "discursive and interventionist function that is ethically and ideologically committed."[117] Heeding this call, I propose a postcolonial womanist hermeneutics with which to engage Revelation in particular, and biblical texts in general. This hermeneutics, by the very inclusion of a womanist framework—which includes an intentional focus on the experiences of black women and the development of practical strategies that help them either to maintain their present condition, if

114. Schüssler Fiorenza, *The Power of the Word*, 12. "Wo/men" with a slash is an inclusive generic term used to refer to both female and male, in order to counter "the linguistic violence of so-called generic male-centered language"(ibid., 6).
115. Ibid., 211.
116. Ibid., 212.
117. Sugirtharajah, "Postcolonial and Biblical Interpretation: The Next Phase," 460, 465. Sugirtharajah proposes that postcolonialism and postcolonial biblical criticism move past its traditional focus on "ritualized theoretical negotiations and niceties," and to the work of "recover[ing] practical projects" that address the "crises that affect the contemporary world" (ibid., 455).

favorable, or to help them overcome and prevail over their oppressive situations—goes beyond a solely discursive function and includes an interventionist one. The hermeneutical horizons of postcolonial biblical criticism, therefore, is about to be expanded not simply through womanist talk, but also through womanist praxis.

A Postcolonial Womanist Convergence:
A Hermeneutics of Ambive*ile*nce

One might question whether my interdisciplinary interpretive venture is necessary—redundant even—since African American studies and postcolonial studies, each in its own way, address issues of race and empire. One might also wonder if my approach is needed because womanist thought already considers these very same issues. Such inquiries would be valid. Nevertheless, I maintain that my work is not in vain. Not only is there a distinction between disciplines of African American studies and postcolonial studies with regard to race and empire as central interests, but there is also a major deficiency in both disciplines as it pertains to the experiences of African American women. In addition, I assert that the hermeneutical lens of womanist inquiry can also be enhanced with a complementary postcolonial lens. Before you raise an eyebrow, let me explain.

African American studies and postcolonial studies may share a similar interest in countering various forms of oppression, giving voice to the marginalized, and critiquing dominant discourses; however, in terms of *central* concerns, the issues of race and empire are not equally weighted. A direct concern of African American studies is racial discrimination and its continuing effects within the United States. This continues to be a major issue for African Americans, despite the insistence by some individuals that it no longer exists. Certainly, prejudicial acts and ways of thinking still exist; they have only become, in most cases, more implicit in nature, which is a more dangerous form. Michelle Alexander highlights this very point in her provocative and influential book, *The New Jim Crow: Mass Incarceration in the Age of Colorblindness*, which emphasizes the use of the criminal justice system, in lieu of overt racial language, to perpetuate discrimination.[118]

Race is also a focus for postcolonial studies, but in a generalized way, because of the power relations associated with it. "Race continues to be relevant to post-colonial theory for two reasons: first, because it is so central to the growing power of imperial discourse over the nineteenth century, and second, because it remains a central and unavoidable 'fact' of modern society that race is used as a dominant category of daily discrimination and prejudice."[119] This interest in racial concerns is a result—a consequence—of a better understanding of the more subtle workings of imperial dominance.

As discussed earlier, the study of empire is at the core of postcolonial studies. However, for African American studies, an understanding of imperial systems has been a concern because it is a context *within which* racial discrimination is experienced.[120] A

118. Michelle Alexander writes, "What has changed since the collapse of Jim Crow has less to do with the basic structure of our society than with the language we use to justify it. In the era of colorblindness, it is no longer socially permissible to use race, explicitly, as a justification for discrimination, exclusion, and social contempt. So we don't. Rather than rely on race, we use our criminal justice system to label people of color 'criminals' and then engage in all the practices we supposedly left behind" (*The New Jim Crow: Mass Incarceration in the Age of Colorblindness* [New York: The New Press, 2012], 2).
119. Bill Ashcroft, Gareth Griffiths, Helen Tiffin, "Introduction to the Second Edition," in *The Key Concepts*, 5. The editors continue: although "race is a flawed and self-defeating category that traps its users in its biological and essentialist meshes . . . , in practical terms race remains a ubiquitous social category that needs to be addressed as a reality in contemporary personal and social relations even when ethnicity might offer a more nuanced understanding of cultural identity. Ethnicity, with its emphasis on symbolic, social and cultural markers of difference provides a useful extension and complication of analyses of race" (ibid.).
120. Supporters of African American culture with postcolonial interests, more often than not, appealed to the work of classic postcolonial theorists such as Frantz Fanon, although "not always in an uncritical way" (Ashcroft, Griffiths, and Tiffin, *The Key Concepts*, 6). Fanon, himself of black African descent, published works that focused on the psychological effects of racism and

displaced people, African Americans share a commonality with other peoples who have been forcefully relocated in order to "serve the economic needs of empire . . . [during] European expansion from the sixteenth century onwards."[121] Thus, a major focus for African American studies has been the ways in which Africans suffered under the condition of slavery, and how they were able—if indeed they were—to maintain aspects of their culture in their new oppressive environments.[122] Despite the "civilizing *rhetoric* of imperialism," violence was the means that was used to achieve the desired control of African peoples.[123] Indeed, actions spoke louder than, and contradicted, words. The connection between the institution of slavery and the practices of imperialism thus becomes apparent, because both have at their root racial discrimination.

Other scholars who have advocated for a joint venture between postcolonial studies and African American studies precede me. For example, Malini Johar Schueller, in her *Locating Race: Global Sites of Post-Colonial Citizenship*, "link[s] the project of race with that of anti-imperial resistance and, theoretically, . . . suggests tactical ways in which postcolonial theory and critical race studies can come

colonialism. Both *Black Skin, White Masks* (trans. Charles Lam Markmann [New York: Grove, 1991, French original 1952]) and *The Wretched of the Earth* (trans. Constance Farrington [New York, Grove, 1963, French original 1961]) investigate "the nature of colonialism and racism, and the psychological damage they caused in colonial peoples and in the colonizer" (*Black Skin*, vii). Fanon also wrote about "the role of violence in the anticolonial struggles of the mid-twentieth century" (ibid., vii–viii). He weaves three interrelated themes in his writing: "a critique of ethnopsychiatry (which aimed to provide an account of the mental life, in sickness and in health, of colonized peoples) and of the Eurocentrism of psychoanalysis; a dialogue with Negritude, then the dominant system of thought among black francophone intellectuals, in which he challenges its account of the mental life of black people; and the development of a political philosophy for decolonization that starts with an account of the psychological harm that colonialism had produced" (ibid., viii).

121. Ashcroft, Griffiths, and Tiffin, *The Key Concepts*, 6.
122. "The fact that the bulk of African peoples were shipped under conditions of slavery makes the relationship between that institution and the wider practices of imperialism central to an understanding of the origins of African American culture" (ibid., 7).
123. Ibid., emphasis added.

together."[124] Schueller notes that bringing together postcolonial theory and critical race studies (a focus of African American studies) may appear contradictory, because "postcolonial theory in its *universalist* and *globalist* guises simply absorbs the *specific* functioning of racism into a narrative of diaspora and migration."[125] However, she asserts that "these two forms of oppositional knowledge" need not be defined in such a subsuming manner: "Postcolonial analyses at the local level . . . can challenge or provincialize the putative universality of (European) modernity. And critical race studies itself . . . might be witnessing a global turn."[126]

Black female deconstructionist Sandra Adell helps to counter the likely critique that my combined lens of "black" and "European" analysis signifies racial border crossing or contamination. In her 1994 work, *Double-Consciousness/Double Bind: Theoretical Issues in Twentieth Century Black Literature*, Adell provides a unique voice in the ongoing debate in African American literary studies regarding the relationship between black literary theory and practice and the European philosophical tradition.[127] She argues that the often "ignored or forgotten" association between black literary theory and Western philosophy is impossible to dissociate, because black literary critics "must *supplement* their critical discourses by appropriating terms and concepts from the methodologies they call into question . . . [namely those from] within the Western metaphysical tradition."[128] Ann DuCille, a self-identified African Americanist, in

124. Malini Johar Schueller, *Locating Race: Global Sites of Post-Colonial Citizenship* (Albany: SUNY, 2009), 2.
125. Ibid., 3, emphasis added.
126. Ibid.
127. Sandra Adell, *Double-Consciousness/Double Bind: Theoretical Issues in Twentieth Century Black Literature* (Urbana, IL: University of Illinois Press, 1994). This work also includes a critique of African American academic feminism and an analysis of other black literature such as that of Maya Angelou and Henry Louis Gates Jr.
128. Adell, *Double-Consciousness*, 1, 4, emphasis original. To illustrate her argument regarding the use of European philosophical traditions in the literary works of African Americans, Adell

similar fashion, states that "although [Afrocentricity] acknowledges blacks in the Americas as an African-derived people with their own cultural legacies, it does not adequately consider the degree to which Euro-American culture is intertwined with those around it."[129] Lastly, Kenneth Mostern, in his essay, "Postcolonialism after W. E. B. Du Bois," also notes that the parallels between contemporary postcolonial discourse and that of the African American intellectual tradition have been ignored.[130] For example, he finds it problematic that Du Bois's name has been absent from almost all postcolonial discourse, despite the fact that there are striking similarities between the African American intellectual tradition that he presents and the kind of postcolonial theory that contemporary postcolonial theorists Homi K. Bhabha and Gayatri Chakravorty Spivak employ.[131] An explicit interdisciplinary effort between postcolonial studies and African American studies thus would prove to be essential.

points to W. E. B. Du Bois's *The Souls of Black Folk*. She notes that although Du Bois "posits a founding metaphor, that of the Veil, and a founding concept, *double consciousness*, for an ontology of blackness upon which is grounded the Black American literary tradition," his critical discourse is not free from European influence (*Double Consciousness*, 11, emphasis original). *Souls* most effectively shows "that in African-American critical discourses, [the] textual system is from the beginning strongly Eurocentric" (ibid., 5). She avers that Du Bois's "famous formulation of 'double-consciousness' [for example] . . . emerges from the philosophy of Hegel as it is articulated in the *Phenomenology of Spirit*" (ibid., 8). Georg Wilhelm Friedrich Hegel, *Phenomenology of Spirit*, trans. A. V. Miller (Oxford: Oxford University Press, 1952). "Like most late nineteenth-century New England intellectuals, Du Bois would have been fairly well acquainted with Hegel's major philosophical texts" (Adell, *Double Consciousness*, 12).

129. Ann DuCille, *Skin Trade* (Cambridge, MA: Harvard University Press, 1996), 132.

130. Kenneth Mostern, "Postcolonialism after W. E. B. Du Bois," in *Postcolonial Theory and the United States: Race, Ethnicity, and Literature*, Amritjit Singh and Peter Schmidt (Jackson, MS: University Press of Mississippi, 2000), 258.

131. Mostern writes, "It is my contention that the absence of Du Bois' name from the contemporary discourse of 'postcolonialism' helps to circumvent various issues that term ought to bring about: the genesis of the ambivalences said to be postcolonial, but which in fact have to do with 20th century colonialism in only the broadest sense; the rewriting of anti-imperialist history in a way that sidesteps Marxism; and most strikingly, for me, how theorists of the contemporary academy continue to presume that the intellectual history of the African diaspora (and perhaps all non-European diasporas) is marginal to the task of theory construction" (ibid., 258).

A postcolonial womanist hermeneutics is also warranted because in African American and postcolonial studies the investigation of systems of racial and imperial oppression excludes the way they affect black women.[132] Our experiences are omitted, neglected, glossed over, or subsumed under the experiences of either black men—denying our sex, as in African American studies, or under a racially neutral category of women—denying our race, as in postcolonial studies. The identities of black women are, once again, fractured. Thus, my defense in support of my postcolonial womanist hermeneutics with respect to an issue of disciplinary redundancy is matter-of-fact: the (con)texts of black women matter.

To those who may argue that a womanist lens already studies the issue of empire, I assert that a postcolonial inflection of a womanist biblical hermeneutics—the task of this book—has its benefits because the two disciplines complement each other's endeavors well. Womanist thought has a specific interest in the lives of black women, and thus, contributes a *particularized* analysis of the history and implications of various forms of oppression. Postcolonial studies offers analytical categories and terminology that provide an even sharper view and clearer evaluation of imperial relationships. A *combined* womanist andpostcolonial investigation of empire, therefore, can only be a more powerfully effective undertaking.

Furthermore, my interdisciplinary effort should not be understood as an indication of a deficiency in womanist biblical hermeneutics.

132. Kwok Pui-Lan writes, "Although the works of postcolonial male critics may include some discussion of women's scholarship, gender remains a marginal issue in their overall analysis" ("Making the Connections," 47). The same could be said about African American male intellectuals. I am not the first female scholar to make note of the lack of a gendered focus in African American studies and postcolonial studies. See, for example, Gina Wisker's *Post-Colonial and African American Women's Writing: A Critical Introduction* (New York: Palgrave Macmillan, 2000), in which she "aims to unite a concentration on twentieth-century post-colonial and African American writing, with a *gendered* focus on women's writing, its contexts, forms, and concerns," as well as a focus on feminist critical practice (ibid., 1, 2, emphasis added).

It simply buttresses the fact that the experiences of black women in America and in the African Diaspora vary greatly, from the types of oppressions they experience to the ways that they confront and write about them. Since "experience is the starting point for the scholarly reflection of African American women engaged in the study of religion and society," there are sure to be various types of hermeneutics developed and employed by womanist theologians, ethicists, and biblical scholars to help make sense of the situations and texts that plague black women.[133]

A Hermeneutics of Ambiveilence

The hermeneutics that I propose is a hermeneutics of ambiveilence. Although derived from terminology posited by men—Homi K. Bhabha's analytical category of ambivalence and W. E. Du Bois's notion of the "veil"—it is deeply rooted in a womanist framework.[134] With the insertion of one term into the other, ambi-veil-ence, I understand myself to be creatively interrupting the discourse of these men with each other, thereby creating and claiming a discursive space for women. In the midst of this literary pause, the voices of

---

133. Kelly Brown Douglas and Cheryl J. Sanders, "Introduction" in *Living the Intersection: Womanism and Afrocentrism in Theology*, ed. Cheryl J. Sanders (Minneapolis: Fortress Press, 1995), 13. Kwok Pui-Lan notes how the efforts of "women from all over the world [with different histories and cultures]," that is, their "claiming [of] the power and authority to retell, rewrite, and reinterpret" the biblical text in a way that "challenge[s] patriarchal readings and articulate[s] their faith and understanding of God," has become "a global movement" (Kwok, "Making the Connections," 60.) There does not have to be a limit to the number of biblical hermeneutics proposed and espoused by women. Female biblical critics especially have the task of uniting their efforts to confront, reject, and pose new questions to the task of biblical interpretation.

134. A womanist framework keeps the experiences of African American women as the starting point of interpretation. This is similar to the work of Musa W. Dube, who advocates for a postcolonial feminist interpretation of the Bible. In her explication of the interrelatedness between biblical texts and the practice and ideology of imperialism, Dube exemplifies how one can read with a framework that is based on one's cultural context. See *Postcolonial Feminist Interpretation of the Bible*.

women begin to be heard—and they will. However, I must first "play" the tunes of Du Bois and Bhabha, that is, explain what they mean by the terms *veil* and *ambivalence*, respectively, and how I employ them in my analysis.

W. E. B. Du Bois's "Veil"

Du Bois's *The Souls of Black Folk*—a compilation of fourteen essays—presents an account of the nature of racial identity in America. He captures the experience of black Americans in the early moments of Reconstruction, when the nation was attempting to redefine itself.[135] During this time, Du Bois writes, "life amid free Negroes was simply unthinkable, the maddest of experiments."[136] Although he captures a gamut of black experience in America, from the cruelty of racism to the exuberance of cultural significance and aspirations of black America, Du Bois's most significant insight is the state of "double consciousness" of African American life.

> After the Egyptian and Indian, the Greek and Roman, the Teuton and Mongolian, the Negro is a sort of seventh son, born with a veil, and gifted with second-sight in this American world,—a world which yields him no true self-consciousness, but only lets him see himself through the revelation of the other world. It is a peculiar sensation, this double-consciousness, this sense of always looking at one's self through the eyes of others, of measuring one's soul by the tape of a world that looks on in amused contempt and pity. One ever feels his two-ness,—an American, a Negro; two souls, two thoughts, two unreconciled strivings; two

135. Despite the successes of the Freedman's Bureau during the early Reconstruction, such as setting up "a system of free labor, establish[ing] a beginning of peasant proprietorship, secur[ing] the recognition of black freedmen before courts of law, and found[ing] the free common school in the South," it was also plagued with failures (Du Bois, *Souls*, 31). It "failed to begin the establishment of good-will between ex-masters and freedmen, to guard its work wholly from paternalistic methods which discouraged self-reliance, and to carry out to any considerable extent its implied promises to furnish the freedmen with land" (ibid.).

136. Ibid., 26.

warring ideals in one dark body, whose dogged strength alone keeps it from being torn asunder.[137]

This double consciousness is not a form of weakness, but rather leads to double aims—the attempt to please both the self and the "other"—and only makes for an unsuccessful individual, because one's efforts are spent, divided, and contradicting.[138] It is this double consciousness, which results from racial segregation and other-ing, that Du Bois seeks to free the Negro, bringing about the "end of [the Negro's] striving."[139]

Du Bois' metaphor of the "veil" illustrates his notion of double consciousness, which causes blacks to see themselves through the eyes of another, that is, white America. It is his concept of the veil that I extend and employ in my postcolonial womanist hermeneutics. Wimbush explicates the notion of the veil thusly:

> All black folks, [Du Bois] argued, had been placed, no, forced, behind the "veil." Referred to (by my count) more than thirty times, the metaphor of the veil in *Souls of Black Folk* is Du Bois's attempt to define the existence of black folks in the United States as those forced into divided consciousness. Thus we have the poignant significance of the plural term *souls*—not *many* souls, as in *many* persons, but two "souls" in the one representative black body, or in each black body, warring

137. Ibid., 8–9. Du Bois's notion of the veil has affinities with Frantz Fanon's idea of the mask in *Black Skin, White Masks*. Both of them, each in his own way, reflect on the ways in which blacks are "othered" by whites. However, a difference between the two, in this regard, is that for Du Bois, the veil is forced (blacks are born with it), whereas for Fanon, the mask seems to be personally situated due to a black person's interaction with white culture. Suffering from an inferiority complex, which results from blacks internalizing the negative racist stereotypes issuing from whites, blacks ignore or reject their black culture (black skin) and embrace the dominant culture (white masks).

138. "The black man's turning hither and thither in hesitant and doubtful striving has often made his very strength to lose effectiveness, to seem like absence of power, like weakness. And yet it is not weakness,—it is the contradiction of double aims. The double-aimed struggle of the black artisan—on the one hand to escape white contempt for a nation of mere hewers of wood and drawers of water, and on the other hand to plough and nail and dig for a poverty-stricken horde—could only result in making him a poor craftsman, for he had but half a heart in either cause" (Du Bois, *Souls*, 9).

139. Ibid.

against each other. This division was for Du Bois the deep internal psychologically felt reflection of the external social-political existence of black folks as the chronic persistent other, as the subaltern, as the enslaved/colonized living next to, and reduced to looking at themselves through the gaze of, the enslaver/colonizer.[140]

According to Du Bois, true self-consciousness is something for which blacks are always striving, and the only way for it to be attained is for this veil to be rent. This joining of both consciousnesses—as a Negro and as an American—does not subtract from the essence of either identities, but rather is a realization and acceptance of the two.[141] It includes a move from being both black and *also* American to being a (unified) black American—without criticism or rebuke from blacks or whites.

Although Du Bois refers to this process as attaining "self-conscious *man*hood" (thus, excluding women), his concept of the veil, that is, the metaphorical covering that is placed over the eyes of blacks in order to prevent them from truly seeing themselves as they are, is quite relevant to black women.[142] It is even more appropriate when coupled with Toni Morrison's further development of the term. In an essay titled "The Site of Memory,"[143] Morrison

expands the Du Boisian notion of the attendant/resultant divided consciousness [represented by the veil] into an argument about a type

---

140. Vincent L. Wimbush, "'We Will Make Our Own Future Text': An Alternate Orientation to Interpretation," in *True to Our Native Land: An African American New Testament Commentary*, ed. Brian K. Blount (Minneapolis: Fortress Press, 2007), 45, emphasis original.

141. Du Bois, *Souls*, 9. In this "merging" of the self, the individual constituents of the Negro's identity are not lost, because each has something to offer. "He would not Africanize America, for America has too much to teach the world and Africa. He would not bleach his Negro soul in a flood of white Americanism, for he knows that Negro blood has a message for the world. He simply wishes to make it possible for a man to be both a Negro and an American, without being cursed and spit upon by his fellows, without having the doors of Opportunity closed roughly in his face" (ibid.).

142. Ibid., emphasis added.

143. Toni Morrison, "The Site of Memory," in *Inventing the Truth: The Art and Craft of Memoir*, ed. William Zinsser (Boston: Houghton Mifflin, 1987), 101–24.

of shutting off, occlusion, and silencing of the interior life/self [by blacks]. . . . With special attention to the autobiographical works that were the slave narratives of the eighteenth and nineteenth centuries she identifies what is for black folk the perduring poignant problem of uniting the divided consciousness and accessing and probing and articulating the movements of the interior life.[144]

Morrison notes that in the attempt to get "the fair appraisal of literary critics, . . . writers of these narratives [had to] appear as objective as possible."[145] Thus, "in shaping the experience to make it palatable to those who were in a position to alleviate it, they were silent about many things, and they 'forgot' many other things."[146] Morrison extends Du Bois's understanding of the veil by adding the notion of agency. The veil, therefore, is not only forced upon blacks, resulting in their state of double consciousness—at times preventing us from realizing our true potential and true selves—but is also oftentimes personally and purposely positioned as a means of protection.[147]

144. Wimbush, "We Will Make Our Own Future Text," 47.
145. Morrison, "The Site of Memory," 105, 106.
146. Ibid., 110. Wimbush elucidates that "although it is clear that in the slave narratives the phenomenon of the silencing, hiding, and forgetting about which Morrison argues was much in evidence, it is less clear that in every instance of the narration of the experiences of slavery the term *veil* was referenced as euphemistic registration of or allusion to the phenomenon. Not all of Morrison's examples [of slave narratives] . . . include the term itself. Yet there is no doubting their support of her general argument. She used the pointed metaphor of the veil as a way to think and make the point about the occlusion" ("We Will Make Our Own Future Text," 48).
147. Du Bois speaks of the use of the veil in a manner of protection when referring to the slave songs. "In these songs, . . . the slave spoke to the world. Such a message is naturally veiled and half articulate. Words and music have lost each other and new and cant phrases of a dimly understood theology have displaced the older sentiment.. . . The music is distinctly sorrowful. . . . [They] tell in word and music of trouble and exile, of strife and hiding; they grope toward some unseen power and sigh for rest in the End. The words that are left to us are not without interest, and, cleared of evident dross, they conceal much of real poetry and meaning beneath conventional theology and unmeaning rhapsody. . . . Over the inner thoughts of the slaves and their relations one with another the shadow of fear ever hung, so that we get but glimpses here and there, and also with them, eloquent omissions and silences" (*Souls*, 185–86). Wimbush notes that "these songs seemed to have been for Du Bois evidence of a serious grappling with the 'veil' of the other negative valence, the veil that was to be overcome. The point seems to have been that a certain kind of veiling—or critical interpretive strategy—was needed by those forced behind the veil. Such folk thought that for the sake of safety—physical and psychological—they had to express their deepest sentiments in veiled terms,

I extend Du Bois's meaning of the veil by engaging it with womanist and postcolonial thought. This allows me to add an analysis of the categories of gender and empire to Du Bois's focus on race. This broader investigative lens not only captures the various forces by which black women are oppressed, but also explains the increase in the frequency of the use of a veil, whether forced or personally situated. Thus, while I maintain the understanding of a "forced" veil, I also agree with Morrison's assertion about agency. The veil can be personally positioned as a means of protection, and, I would add, as a way to maintain one's supposed ignorance of the suffering of others. This will be further explicated below, when I discuss the tactics taken by some who benefit from imperial structures.

Another distinction between my understanding of the veil and that of Du Bois's concerns the process of its rending. Du Bois asserts that the rending of the veil, resulting in the joining of a black person's double consciousness, is a personal transformation that depends on external acceptance. My rending of the veil also includes the realization and acceptance of two conflicting characteristics within an individual, but not a joining of the two *per se*. Instead, these two characteristics remain in a necessary fluctuating tension—a notion that differs from Raquel St. Clair's womanist hermeneutics of wholeness, as we shall see. The personal transformation that results also does not depend on *external* acceptance, as in Du Bois's understanding, but on the *individual's* acceptance of her or his duality.

indirectly, 'in other words'" ("We Will Make Our Own Future Text," 46). Wimbush makes note of the fact, however, that Morrison views slave songs as a "continuing part of the veiling, needing to be ripped. The veiling here is that which keeps black folks from probing their interiority—on their own terms" (Ibid., 49). Morrison, in an interview, states, "The music kept us alive, but it's not enough anymore. My people are being devoured. Whenever I feel uneasy about my writing, I think: what would be the response of the people in the book if they read the book?" (Thomas Leclair, "'The Language Must Not Sweat': A Conversation with Toni," in *Toni Morrison: Critical Perspectives Past and Present*, ed. Henry Louis Gates Jr. and K. A. Appiah, Amistad Literary Series [New York: Amistad, 1993], 371).

The rending of the veil also moves beyond the individual being transformed, by hopefully inciting within them the will to act on behalf of others. It is outreach(ing).

Homi K. Bhabha's "Ambivalence"

Bhabha is considered one of three main scholars whose work is ascribed special importance in contemporary postcolonial studies.[148] He seeks to do justice to the complexity of colonial situations, by taking the work of contemporary postcolonial theorist Edward Said and of Frantz Fanon (a North African psychoanalyst and freedom fighter based in Algeria, who focused on decolonization and the psychopathology of colonization) a step further.[149] Bhabha focuses on both entities in the colonial relationship, unlike Said, who gravitates more to the colonizer, or Fanon, who centers more on the colonized. According to Bhabha, the colonial relationship is very complex, and therefore, a focus on one entity within it is not sufficient.[150] Thus,

148. The other two contemporary postcolonial critics are Edward Said and Gayatri Chakravorty Spivak, who, together with Bhabha are commonly regarded as the "postcolonial trinity." Said's 1978 work, *Orientalism* (New York: Vintage Books, 2003 [original 1978]), which served as a catalyst in the development of postcolonial studies as an academic discipline, analyzes and critiques the production of cultural stereotypes in Western discourse. Spivak focuses on the marginalization of the subaltern's discourse in official narratives or histories, arguing in her groundbreaking article, "Can the Subaltern Speak? Speculations on Widow Sacrifice," that the subaltern inhabits a discursive space that is completely outside of dominant discourse (*Wedge* 7, no. 8 [1985]: 120–30; reprinted in much expanded form, and without the subtitle, in *Marxism and the Interpretation of Culture*, ed. Cary Nelson and Lawrence Grossberg [Urbana: University of Illinois Press, 1988], 271–313).It should be noted, however, that"Contemporary histories of postcolonial studies… customarily trace its intellectual roots to a disparate group of post–World War II critics and literary authors, each of whom lived the transition from colonialism to postcolonialism in his particular cultural context and engaged in sustained reflection on colonialism and its complex legacies, notably Frantz Fanon, Aimé Césaire, Chinua Achebe, C. L. R. James, Albert Memmi, and Ngũgĩ wa Thiong'o" (Moore, *Empire and Apocalypse*, 5).
149. In his *Black Skins, White Masks*, , Fanon investigates "the nature of colonialism and racism, and the psychological damage they caused in colonial peoples and in the colonizer" (vii).
150. Bhabha argues that the tensions within colonial relations in Said's *Orientalism* were resolved due to his (Said's) "assertion of the unidirectionality and intentionality of colonial knowledge as will

because Said and Fanon fail to consider the mutual responsibility of each party within the colonial relationship, they are led to assume that "the identities and positionings of colonizer and colonized exist in stable and unitary terms which are also absolutely distinct from, and necessarily in conflict with, each other."[151] Contrarily, Bhabha, who uses a poststructuralist theory of identity throughout his work, states that identity is not conceived as a given or preexisting, but rather is constructed, fluid, unstable, shifting, and mobile.[152] It is a product of culture. Bhabha, therefore, advocates for three analytic categories that he asserts help to explicate and illustrate the intricacies of the colonial relationship: colonial ambivalence, mimicry, and hybridity.[153] I will

to power. . . . [This] re-establishes the very division between colonizer and colonized which Said deplores in colonial discourse itself" (Bart Moore-Gilbert, *Postcolonial Theory: Contexts, Practices, Politics* [London: Verso, 1997], 116). With respect to Fanon, Bhabha avers that due to "the increasing pressure of political exigencies (particularly the Algerian war of independence), Fanon reinstates models of colonial identity which are psychically and phenomenologically fixed in a similar way to *Orientalism*" (ibid.).

151. Ibid.
152. In my project, I do not necessarily embrace a classic poststructuralist theory of identity. I appropriate certain of Bhabha's analytic categories (particularly ambivalence and hybridity), but without buying completely into Bhabha's theory of the subject or identity. I do, however, choose to deal with the tension, the disjunction, within the African American subject, which I assert is separated by a metaphoric veil.
153. Bhabha explains these three terms in depth in *The Location of Culture* (New York: Routledge, 1994); however, I will give a very brief treatment of mimicry and hybridity here. Mimicry is the outworking or expression of ambivalence evident in the colonial relationship. Both the colonized and the colonizer can employ mimicry, albeit in different ways and for different purposes. For the colonized, it can be used as a form of active resistance by reinterpreting "the foundational narratives and texts of Western culture…and us[ing] them for purposes which were not foreseen by the colonizer" (Moore-Gilbert, *Postcolonial Theory*, 131–32). For the colonizer, "mimicry is the desire for a reformed, recognizable Other, as a subject of a difference that is almost the same, but not quite" (Bhabha, *Location*, 122). The colonized subject is to imitate the colonizer's customs, beliefs, and ways of living, but without becoming exact replicas as this could lead to an undercutting of the colonizer's superiority. Bhabha's concept of hybridity reflects a shared space between the colonized and the colonizer. This does not reflect "a simple synthesis or syncretic fusion of two originally discrete cultures," but rather is where cultures collide and interact, and where the colonized and colonizer reside in their shared ambivalence regarding identity (Moore, *Empire and Apocalypse*, 110–11). This "Third Space," as Bhabha calls it, is where both the colonizer and the colonized share the experience of identity formation that develops from the presence of differences that emerge from the interaction of their cultures (*Location*, 55). Hybridity thus has the potential to dismantle "the structures of domination in the

only provide an explication of the first one here, however, since it comprises a major aspect of my proposed hermeneutics.

Colonial ambivalence has its roots in psychoanalytic theory, and was adapted by Bhabha for colonial theory.[154] His employment of the word *ambivalence* differs slightly from its original use in psychoanalysis because of his application of it to the colonial experience. In psychoanalysis, ambivalence "describe[s] a continual fluctuation between wanting one thing and wanting its opposite. It also refers to a simultaneous attraction toward and repulsion from an object, person, or action."[155] What Bhabha does is apply this understanding to the relationship between the colonized and the colonizer, and to colonial discourse itself. Bhabha asserts that in lieu of suggesting polarized groups of colonized persons, that is, those who are "complicit" and those who are "resistant" (as Said does), there is, in fact, a combination of both characteristics in every colonized subject in varying degrees.[156] In other words, the binary of the colonial relation is broken. The colonized person experiences an internal conflict in her relation to the colonizer.

This ambivalence, or as it has been phrased, "*ambi-valent* or 'two-powered[ness]' . . . (the simultaneous attraction and repulsion)," enables the colonized subject to undercut the authority of the colonizer or colonial discourse.[157] Bhabha illustrates ambivalence at work in chapter 6 of his *Location of Culture*, "Signs Taken for Wonders: Questions of Ambivalence and Authority under a Tree outside Delhi, May 1817."[158] He speaks of the process in which the

colonial situation," by diminishing or confusing any concept of identity (Ashcroft, Griffiths, and Tiffin, *The Key Concepts*, 120).

154. Ashcroft, Griffiths, and Tiffin, *The Key Concepts*, 12.
155. Ibid.
156. Bhabha draws his concept of ambivalence from Sigmund Freud, who sees ambivalence as occurring everywhere in the human psyche.
157. Ashcroft, Griffiths, and Tiffin, *The Key Concepts*, 13.
158. Bhabha, *Location*, 145–74.

"book," the English Bible—which Bhabha refers to as "an insignia of colonial authority and a signifier of colonial desire and discipline"[159]—gets transformed when it is used by the natives in India. Bhabha argues that the native's reception and selective adaptation of the "book" is what occurs when colonial discourse enters a colonized subject's space. He writes, "But the institution of the Word in the wilds is also an *Entstellung*, a process of displacement, distortion, dislocation, repetition—the dazzling light of literature sheds only areas of darkness."[160] Moore concisely captures this selective assimilation: "Bhabha's conception of colonial discourse and colonial power conjures up a rather different Bible, . . . which, as it permeates the cultural space of the colonized, effortlessly adapts to its contours, is rewritten in the process of being reread, and thereby subverts the colonizer's claims on its behalf of univocity and universality."[161] According to Bhabha, the reshaping of the text by the natives not only allows them to use it according to their own standards, but also undercuts colonial power. Bhabha understands this reconfiguring of the "book" not only as a form of resistance, but also as taking place in an ambivalent space—the space where colonial power is emptied of its effectiveness. Thus, while colonial discourse attempts to persuade the colonized subject to adapt to its ideologies, "instead it produces ambivalent subjects whose mimicry is never very far from mockery."[162]

---

159. Ibid., 146.

160. Ibid., 149. There is something lost in translation: either in the colonized subject's adaptation of it, or the colonizer's desire for the creation of replicas—similar, but not exact. This is evident in the natives' partial acceptance of the "book." For example, in a conversation regarding baptism and the sacrament (i.e., the Eucharist) between an elderly native man and an Indian catechist named Anund Messeh, the native responds, "We are willing to be baptized, but we will never take the Sacrament. To all the other customs of Christians we are willing to conform, but not the Sacrament, because the Europeans eat cow's flesh, and this will never do for us" (ibid., 147–48).

161. Moore, *Empire and Apocalypse*, 90.

162. Ashcroft, Griffiths, and Tiffin, *The Key Concepts*, 13. Although Bhabha believes that the natives' acceptance of the "book" is an example of how "the colonized are engaged in active subversion

As an African American female biblical scholar with a commitment to identifying and countering oppressive elements in the biblical text that are oftentimes used to inform and buttress oppressive ideologies and situations in contemporary society, I find Bhabha's analytic category of colonial ambivalence quite valuable. Along with Moore, I too, have "discover[ed in this critical category] analytic tools that enable [me] to reconceptualize [my] own relationships to [my] frequently complex socio-cultural locations in ways that [I] experience as transforming and even empowering."[163]

With regard to the goals of this book, Bhabha's analytic category of ambivalence provides an important aspect in the formation of my postcolonial womanist biblical hermeneutics. It enables me to get past the impasse whereby one part of the biblical text appears to be purely anti-imperialistic literature, and the other—or in the case of the woman Babylon, the same—part is like holding up a mirror in which the text reflects empire. As we shall see, the woman Babylon represents the colonial relationship itself; her imperial attire signifies empire (the colonizer), yet the punitive writing on her forehead and the manner in which she is destroyed are reminiscent of the

of the colonizer's discourse, in this case the colonizer's Scripture," the implications of such an act are not always positive (Moore, *Empire and Apocalypse*, 93). Despite their rejection of the sacrament, "all [the natives (Brahmins)] united to acknowledge the superiority of the doctrines of this Holy Book to every thing which they had hitherto heard or known" (Bhabha, *Location*,147). They conformed to everything of the Christian culture except the sacrament (ibid., 148). There is no reference to physical force in the telling of this story, so perhaps the Brahmins' automatic (and joyful) assimilation of European culture is in fact, a reflection of their "ignorance and simplicity" (ibid., 147). The rejection of the sacrament appears to be more of a maintenance of dietary restrictions than active resistance to colonial authority. Thus, the identification of the events outside Delhi as "a moment of 'civil disobedience' enacted openly under the eye of colonial power by means of the subtle strategy that [Bhabha] terms 'sly civility'" may not be a form of active(conscious) resistance at all (Moore, *Empire and Apocalypse*, 94). Moore-Gilbert also interrogates this supposed form of resistance: "Bhabha seems to see the subaltern as actively and purposively 'hybridizing' the 'English Book.' But the peasants' questions to the catechist are based as much on category mistakes or misunderstandings as on a considered challenge to his teachings. Is this kind of response a mode of resistance and, if so, is it then conscious or unconscious, transitive or intransitive?" (*Postcolonial Theory*, 133).

163. Moore, *Empire and Apocalypse*, 85.

colonized. She embodies ambivalence. Her simultaneous suffering from, and participation in, empire reflects my own experience, and thus, stirs up tension within me. The concept of ambivalence captures the presence of both complicity and resistance within a single individual, and thus, helps me to navigate between two poles, and create a more nuanced, more adequate, reading.

Womanist Tenets and Postcolonial Premises

Although Du Bois provides a thorough treatment of the experience of racial discrimination from a black man's perspective, and Bhabha imparts his wisdom regarding the complexities of the colonial relationship, neither of these *men* include gender as an analytical category. Therefore, I have resolved to bring a particular kind of concreteness andrelevance to their work by placing it in dialogue with womanist biblical hermeneutics. The following are the womanist tenets and postcolonial premises that inform and guide my approach. Appealing to the work of womanist biblical scholar Clarice J. Martin, who outlines a womanist critical method for approaching Revelation, I propose the following:

1. A hermeneutics of ambi*veilence* "foregrounds the hermeneutical lenses, epistemic assumptions, and cultural matrices of African-American people in general and of African American women in particular."[164] As womanist theologian M. Shawn Copeland states, "Womanist theology claims the experiences of Black women as proper and serious data for theological reflection."[165]

2. A hermeneutics of ambi*veilence* "seek[s] to dissolve and to

164. Martin, "Polishing the Unclouded Mirror," 84.
165. M. Shawn Copeland, "'Wading through Many Sorrows': Toward a Theology of Suffering in Womanist Perspective," in *A Troubling in My Soul: Womanist Perspectives on Evil and Suffering,* ed. Emilie M. Townes (Maryknoll, NY: Orbis, 1993), 111.

dismantle the three-fold tyrannies of gender, race, and class as among the overarching and interlocking structures of domination in [the] lives [of African American women]."[166] It also necessitates a critical analysis of issues of language and empire due to the power dynamics therein.

3. A hermeneutics of ambi*veil*ence "interrogates [the text] from within an extended community" that includes "a . . . Black feminist and womanist community of activism," and "Africana women."[167] Although one speaks collectively of "black women's experience," one must remember that the texts (both oral and written), contexts, and experiences of women of African descent differ greatly.

4. A hermeneutics of ambi*veil*ence "places the interpreter in solidarity with the oppressed and marginalized."[168] As this book illustrates, one can be in solidarity with a character in the text or an actual individual or group.

5. A hermeneutics of ambi*veil*ence promotes not only the well-being of African American women, but of all peoples, despite one's race, gender, or class. African American female experience may be the starting point of the interpretive task, but the result of one's analysis should be for the benefit of all, and not at the expense of any.

6. A hermeneutics of ambi*veil*ence "allow[s] one to discern with more nuanced hermeneutical insight and to relumine with more theoretical precision" the ways in which a text employs imperial ideology, through its rhetoric and imagery, to exploit, abuse, and oppress.[169]

166. Martin, "Polishing the Unclouded Mirror," 85.
167. Ibid., 86.
168. Ibid., 104.
169. Ibid., 105.

7. A hermeneutics of ambi*veil*ence helps to highlight the ways in which one's own "historical [and contemporary] experiences of subjectivity" or one's aiding and abetting in the subjectivity of others may be reflected by the text.[170]

8. A hermeneutics of ambi*veil*ence intends that the recollection or realization of one's subjected experience or participation in another's subjectivity will lead the interpreter to engage in honest self-reflection, with the goals of coming to a fuller understanding of the self, and the desire to help others prevail over their oppressive conditions.

A postcolonial womanist hermeneutics of ambi*veil*ence is a powerful tool of interpretive inquiry. In this book, the use of this combined lens in my examination of the narrative of the woman Babylon has an unexpected outcome. My engagement with the ambivalent characterization of the woman Babylon incites tension within me, with which I struggle deeply. I am repulsed by her imperial practices and yet drawn to her because of the violence that she experiences. However, the more I consider her text, the more *both* aspects of her character become unsettlingly familiar. Her text functions as, what Martin calls, an "unclouded mirror" that reflects the conflicting characteristics within me.[171] The veil that masks my own ambivalent characterizations is exposed or forced to reappear (perhaps, but I am not ready to admit it), and I begin my own process of self-realization, giving birth to my hermeneutics of ambi*veil*ence. The very name of this approach is also an illustration of its concept; there is a veil that separates the two sides of my ambivalent characterization.

170. Ibid.

171. Martin, "Polishing the Unclouded Mirror," 82. "Mirrors . . . exhibit an incomparable capacity to reflect, distort, and reproduce . . . reality" (ibid.). Martin argues that Revelation 18:11–13—the reference to "slaves and human lives" in the cargo list—"*functions* for African American readers as a 'mirror' or 'looking glass' into their own history" (ibid., 83, emphasis added).

With regard to Revelation, "it takes no 'daring hermeneutical leap' ['for those who have experienced racial or colonial oppression, marginalization, and domination'] to recognize" the ways in which the woman Babylon has suffered under the discursive command of the author of Revelation.[172] "The stark, refracted reflections of the mirror flash out" certain experiences of African American history and those we face today.[173] The tension that the text elicits, the stirring of emotions based on an attraction to, and repulsion from, various warring situations in our lives is the everyday reality for many oppressed peoples, not just black women. Being both victims of empire through various forms of oppression, as well as—at times—beneficiaries of imperial privilege, we find ourselves as potential mirror images of the woman Babylon.

A hermeneutics of ambiveilence exposes the veil that prevents one from coming into a full awareness of oneself. It removes the metaphorical covering that hides the complex reality of one's identity, and hopefully leads to a decision to rend the veil. Wholeness is achieved not by the sum of one's characteristic "parts," since there is almost never a full representation of each aspect at one time. Context matters; it determines which characteristic reaches maximal expression. Wholeness is attained when one acknowledges and embraces one's differing internal characteristics, and effectively functions while negotiating one's surrounding culture. This is a different, not contradicting, understanding of wholeness than what is posited by St. Clair. She focuses on God and Jesus'—through his saving work on the cross—solidarity with black women in their attempt to attain wholeness, whereas I focus on a specific process on

172. Ibid., 105. To be sure, Martin was referring to the ways in which the author of Revelation presents a minority report in his critique of slavery, resonant with the activism and resistance of African American women to racial oppression.

173. Ibid., 84. Martin states that the "mirror" of Revelation 18:11-13 "flashes out [through various events in African American history in America] . . . a continuing story of liberation" (ibid.).

how to attain it. Nevertheless, I think St. Clair would agree that God assists with this process as well. "Intrinsic to [this new] understanding of wholeness are both survival and liberation," which are "affirm[ed by] God's solidarity with and commitment to [all]."[174]

The benefits of a hermeneutics of ambi*veil*ence are multiple. In the process of self-reflection, we not only better ourselves, but being the relational creatures that we are, we also ultimately improve the lives of others. For example, the benefits that some African American women, particularly those who are educated and employed, receive from the capitalist system, such as access to scholarship, healthcare, and a discursive platform, and so on, does not have to be a source of tension, especially when considering underprivileged women of the same race. Instead, their privilege can be used to draw attention to the sufferings of other marginalized and oppressed peoples, in order to evoke change. The field of biblical studies can also be transformed by the employment of this hermeneutics, because a fuller understanding of the self leads to a more honest and accurate biblical interpretation. The interpretive process, properly understood, is based on an *interaction* between the reader and the text.

The positive effects of this hermeneutics, therefore, trickle down. "Knowledge [of one's 'veiled' characteristics], [a positive] attitude, and responsible action [to rend the veil] will not only enhance the quality of life for individuals, but also invariably enhance the quality of life for all people."[175] This is what a postcolonial womanist hermeneutics of ambi*veil*ence sets out to do. Being rooted in the womanist understanding of seeking the well-being of all people, this hermeneutics cannot simply be for the benefit of the advancement

174. St. Clair, *Call and Consequences*, 82.
175. Raymond A. Winbush, *The Warrior Method: A Parents' Guide to Rearing Healthy Black Boys* (New York: Amistad, 2001), 2.

of biblical scholarship, but also for the improvement of the lives of interpreters.

2

Interpretive Foundations

Furthering Two Scholarly Conversations

My analysis pertaining to the woman Babylon did not develop out of nothing. It was not a matter of immaculate scholastic conception. Rather, what I have constructed has its foundations in two scholarly conversations from which I have learned a great deal and whose participants I greatly respect and admire. It is important to note this because too often the advancement of scholarship seems to be accomplished at another academic's expense. The very scholars by whom we are trained, on whose learned shoulders we stand to gain knowledge, we cut off at the erudite knees with a bladed critique. This is not what I set out to do. My work engages and builds upon two scholarly conversations: The "Great Whore" debate—basically, the academic discussion pertaining to the interpretation of the figure of Babylon as either a woman or a city and the implications of such an interpretation—and on African American interpretations of Revelation in general. While my work extends, and may go in a different direction than the scholarship included this section, my aim is not to discount, disregard, or decrease the impact that it has in Revelation scholarship, but rather to further the conversation, inspiring others in the process.

I did not randomly or painstakingly choose to engage these two scholarly conversations; it was rather instinctive and effortless. What I mean by this is that in my reading of Revelation as an African American, and the woman Babylon's text as an African American *woman*, I was drawn to the arguments that asked the "So what?" question pertaining to both aspects of my identity: race and gender. However, my womanist instincts kicked in and I realized that neither of these conversations incorporated both my race *and* my gender in their analysis. In addition, there is the issue pertaining to class. I could have researched and engaged a third set of scholarship that focused on the issue of class in Revelation, but this illustrates the same issue and impetus that led to the formation of womanist thought, as I said earlier in chapter 1. In lieu of having to express one part of my identity while veiling the others, I decided to make a space—to write a book—in which I could bring all of me to the interpretive work. Instead of being all over the place, and hence, nowhere, I decided to simply be. What follows is a survey of the two conversations that guided my footsteps on the path to discovery.

The "Great Whore" Debate:
Elizabeth Schüssler Fiorenza and Tina Pippin

When I think about the figure of Babylon and the interpretations thereof, I immediately think about the work of, and the debate between, two prominent scholars, Tina Pippin and Elisabeth Schüssler Fiorenza.[1] Certainly, others have also contributed to this conversation; however, the scholarly interactions between Pippin and

Schüssler Fiorenza will be the focus of this section, because their work most clearly and most pointedly highlights one of two major aspects of my project; namely, the issue of the identification of Babylon as either a woman or a city.[2] (The other major aspect is how the text has been interpreted by African American biblical scholars, but I will discuss that in the next section.) It is the issue of the city/ woman binary that my work seeks to dismantle. Informed by my contextual identity as a privileged African American woman who is both a victim and a participant in empire, I must keep these two understandings of Babylon in tandem. Indeed, the juncture of Pippin and Schüssler Fiorenza's scholarship is precisely where my work takes off.

At first blush, one might surmise that the issue at hand in Pippin and Schüssler Fiorenza's work—the former focusing on the destruction of a feminine-gendered character and the latter on the persuasive power of the text's symbolic language—pertains to the

---

1. See, e.g., Tina Pippin, *Death and Desire: The Rhetoric of Gender in the Apocalypse of John* (Louisville: Westminster John Knox, 1992); and Elisabeth Schüssler Fiorenza, "A Decolonizing Interpretation of the Book of Revelation," in *The Power of the Word: Scripture and the Rhetoric of Empire* (Minneapolis: Fortress Press, 2007), 130–47.

2. Although for the purposes of my project, I concentrate on what the characterization of the metaphor of the figure Babylon *means*, Lynn R. Huber moves beyond this focus to a detailed discussion of how metaphors *function*—a task she says has only been done in a general fashion. In *Like a Bride Adorned: Reading Metaphor in John's Apocalypse,* Emory Studies in Early Christianity (New York: T & T Clark International, 2007), 45, 81, Huber argues that metaphors function to get Revelation's audience to "imagine along with the text"). Huber exemplifies the use of conceptual metaphor theory by employing it in an analysis of the nuptial imagery in this text, and then to the image of the 144,000 virgins in her 2008 article, "Sexually Explicit? Re-reading Revelation's 144,000 Virgins as a Response to Roman Discourses," *Journal of Men, Masculinities and Spirituality* 2, no. 1 (2008): 3–28. See also Huber's article, "Unveiling the Bride: Revelation 19.1-8 and Roman Social Discourse," in *A Feminist Companion to the Apocalypse of John,* ed. Amy-Jill Levine and Maria Mayo Robbins, Feminist Companion to the New Testament and Early Christian Writings, vol. 13 (New York: T & T Clark International, 2009), 159–79. Huber continues her analysis of the rhetorical power of Revelation's imagery in her most recent work, *Thinking and Seeing with Women in Revelation* (New York: Bloomsbury/T & T Clark, 2013). She looks at the ways in which Revelation's imagery "participate[s] within the discourses of John's day to construct and evoke attitudes and actions," and she surveys "later visionary appropriations of the text's metaphors" to see "how the text's metaphorical language simultaneously limits and invites new meaning" (ibid., 5, 7).

question, do metaphors matter? However, that is not the case at all. As we will see, both of these writers speak about the negative implications of the use of such gendered metaphors, especially that of the "Great Whore." The issue at hand, however, is which methodology one employs and what one feels is at stake. Let us begin with Schüssler Fiorenza, since Pippin's work builds on her scholarship.

Elisabeth Schüssler Fiorenza

Elisabeth Schüssler Fiorenza performs a rhetorical analysis of Revelation in her 1991 commentary, *Revelation: Vision of a Just World*.[3] She argues that this approach helps to highlight "the persuasive power of Revelation's symbolic language" not only within the overall meaning of the text itself, but also within the sociohistorical context out of which it emerged.[4] Although she asks the question, "What does a reading of Revelation *do* to someone who submits to its world of vision?" her inquiry is rooted in the fact that biblical texts have negatively influenced "not only the perceptions, values, and imagination of Christians but also those of Western cultures and societies on the whole."[5] Thus, she argues that "theo-ethical and rhetorical-political criticism" be used not only to analyze the text of Revelation in order to identify whether its "language and

---

3. Elisabeth Schüssler Fiorenza, *Revelation: Vision of a Just World*, Proclamation Commentaries (Minneapolis: Fortress Press, 1991). This book is a thoroughgoing revision of her *Invitation to the Book of Revelation: A Commentary on the Apocalypse with Complete Text from the Jerusalem Bible* (Garden City, NY: Image Books, 1981), and as such, can be treated as a new work. I am discussing Schüssler Fiorenza's *Revelation: Vision of a Just World* before her *The Book of Revelation: Justice and Judgment*, 2nd ed. (Minneapolis: Fortress Press, 1998), despite the fact that the first edition of the latter work was published in 1984. My decision is motivated largely by the fact that the second edition includes a substantial epilogue, "The Rhetoricality of Apocalypse and the Politics of Interpretation," which features prominently in my summary.

4. Schüssler Fiorenza, *Vision of a Just World*, 20.

5. Ibid., 4, emphasis original.

composition" help to perpetuate "stereotypical images and linguistic violence," but also to recognize whether one's interpretations of the text and other biblical writings, interpretations that are influenced by one's own sociopolitical contexts, do the same.[6]

This type of rhetorical approach goes beyond the feminist reading strategy that Schüssler Fiorenza states "takes the androcentric, linguistic-cultural, sex/gender system as a self-contained, closed system signifying reality."[7] For example, this strategy critiques Revelation for its "oppositional dualism" with regard to its feminine symbolism that is based on male characterizations: women are either "'the whore' [representing 'female desire for power'] or 'the good woman' [signifying controlled sexuality, powerlessness, and passivity]" such as the Bride and the Woman Clothed with the Sun.[8] Although Schüssler Fiorenza states that this feminist reading

---

6. Ibid.
7. Ibid., 13. Theologian Catherine Keller, in her *Apocalypse Now and Then: A Feminist Guide to the End of the World*, "defers sex/gender analysis," which highlights gender dualism in the text, and rather allows "the feminist construction of gender [to] refract through the lens of apocalypse as one 'configural zone' among others" (Boston: Beacon , 1996), xiii. She admits that the very use of the term *feminist* in the title of her work may imply that it seeks to put an end to patriarchy, or an attempt to create a type of forthcoming utopia for women; however, in efforts to move beyond these associations, Keller argues that "perhaps feminism is in its own apocalypse" (ibid., xii). The problematic teleology that Keller perceives in these feminist visions is that in its attempt to create a "messianic unity of sisterhood" to achieve these goals, the differences between women (as pertaining to "race . . . , economics, class, and in some circumstances sexual orientation") were being overlooked (ibid., 215–16). She therefore asserts that a "critically sharpened mutuality," one in which "difference . . . is not . . . uncritically celebrated but negotiated, discerned, [and] transformed," leads to an enhanced "capacity to *connect*, 'to use each other's differences to enrich our visions and our joint struggles'" (ibid., 215–16).
8. Ibid. Barbara R. Rossing, in her published dissertation, *The Choice between Two Cities: Whore, Bride, and Empire in the Apocalypse* (Harrisburg, PA: Trinity Press International, 1999), also analyzes this oppositional dualism. She employs a rhetorical approach to analyze John's use of a "'sapiential' or wisdom" two-women *topos*, which she asserts is "for the purpose of political critique and exhortation" (ibid., 164, 15 respectively). John sets up a contrast between an evil-woman figure (Babylon/Rome) and a good-woman figure (New Jerusalem) in order to present "ethical alternatives" or "allegiances" to his audience (ibid., 14). The stark dissimilarity between these two figures is to help persuade the audience "to come out of Rome in order to participate in God's New Jerusalem" (ibid., 15). Rossing argues that the destruction of the Babylon figure in Rev. 17:16 should not be read as a sexual assault on the female body (as argued by Pippin,

THE WOMAN BABYLON AND THE MARKS OF EMPIRE

strategy helps to highlight the "all-pervasive androcentric ideology of Western culture" that is often used to interpret texts such as Revelation, it does not "challenge this cultural androcentric perspective of reality," but rather, "reinscribes this system as a self-contained totality," thus, making it difficult for readers to "reclaim cultural texts and traditions for women."[9]

As such, Schüssler Fiorenza posits an alternate feminist reading approach—a rhetorical reading strategy that "understands androcentric language as a conventional tool creating and negotiating meaning in specific contexts."[10] Thus, when properly understood as conventional language, the metaphors of whoring and fornication are seen as indicative of the "prophetic-apocalyptic tradition."[11]

as we will see), but rather as a critique, punishment, and annihilation of the Roman Empire, followed by the arrival of the New Jerusalem (ibid., 163). Rossing brings a dual focus on ecology and empire to the text of Revelation in "For the Healing of the World: Reading *Revelation* Ecologically," in *From Every People and Nation: The Book of Revelation in Intercultural Perspective*, ed. David Rhoads (Minneapolis: Fortress Press, 2005), 165–82. See also "Prophecy, End-Times, and American Apocalypse: Reclaiming Hope for Our World," *Anglican Theological Review* 89, no. 4 (Fall 2007): 549–63.

9. Schüssler Fiorenza, *Vision of a Just World*, 13. "Valoriza[tion of] the sex/gender system and grid of reading . . . risk[s] magnifying the androcentric marginalization, objectification alienation, and negation of women inscribed in the text" (ibid., 14). Adela Yarbro Collins also seeks to counter the reinscription of Revelation's androcentric perspectives in contemporary society in her essay, "Feminine Symbolism in the Book of Revelation," in Levine and Robbins, *A Feminist Companion to the Apocalypse of John*, 121. This is a reprint of an article of the same title that appeared in *Biblical Interpretation* 1, no.1 [Fall 1993]: 20–33). She pairs psychological analysis in the tradition of Carl Jung with feminist analysis, in order to assert that the ambiguity of the feminine figures in Revelation calls for a rethinking of the restricted roles of men and women. "All the feminine symbols of Revelation are ambiguous when viewed from the point of view of the desirability of mutuality between men and women, and of flexibility in the definition of male and female roles" (ibid., 130). Although she gives Revelation credit for employing "both masculine and feminine symbols to describe the heavenly world," she also notes that the "particular forms of the feminine symbols . . . are limited and limiting for women" (ibid.).

10. Schüssler Fiorenza, *Vision of a Just World*, 12. This rhetorical reading strategy rejects "sexist assumptions such as centricity (male as central, female as peripheral), exclusivity (male as focal point, female as marginal), isolation (male as self, female as other), and subjectification (male as agent and subject, female as passive object)" (ibid., 13). Additionally, this rhetorical lens helps to understand the grammatically masculine language not as associated with "'natural' sex," but functioning as both "gender-specific and as generic language" (ibid., 14).

11. Ibid.

John ... uses the image of woman to symbolize the present murderous reality of the imperial world power. .... It must not be overlooked, however, that such female imagery for cities utilizes conventional language because then, as today, cities and countries were grammatically construed as feminine. .... The female imagery of Revelation, therefore, would be completely misconstrued if it were understood as referring to the actual behavior of individual women.[12]

Schüssler Fiorenza affirms that these symbols must be subjected to feminist critique; however, their "gendered meaning can not be assumed as primary within the narrative contextualization of Revelation."[13] Lastly, her rhetorical reading strategy extends the twofold sex/gender lens to include the other interlocking systems of oppression such as racism, sexism, classism, and colonialism, to name a few.[14] Thus, it allows one to view the woman Babylon not only in sexualized terms, but also "in terms of high status, ruling power, egregious wealth, and divine aspirations," leading to "a feminist-liberationist strategy of rhetorical reading."[15]

12. Ibid., 95–96.
13. Ibid., 14. David L. Barr, in his essay, "Towards an Ethical Reading of the Apocalypse: Reflections on John's Use of Power, Violence, and Misogyny," also affirms the importance of a gender critique; however, he also notes its limitations. Specifically naming Pippin, he agrees that she is "absolutely right to confront the way women are portrayed in this text," as misogynist readings of the text do occur; however, her literal reading of the gendered inscriptions in the text causes her to miss their ambiguity (Barr, "Towards an Ethical Reading of the Apocalypse: Reflections on John's Use of Power, Violence, and Misogyny," in *Society of Biblical Literature 1997 Seminar Papers*, Society of Biblical Literature Seminar Papers Series, no. 36 [Atlanta: Scholars, 1997], 364–65). Instead of viewing the figure of Babylon as a woman, Barr insists that the very fact that she is also characterized as a city "changes the moral equation that comes from the Whore's destruction" (ibid., 365). Based on a narrative and social reading of Revelation, he states that the text suggests that "those who seek to dominate others [such as Babylon over the kings of the earth (17:18)] will themselves be devoured by the process ... While the image of violence is problematic ..., the understanding of violence is not" (ibid., 366). Thus, in the depiction of Babylon's demise, "human brutality ... is portrayed," not violence simply toward women (ibid.). Barr's essay reappears as "Doing Violence: Moral Issues in Reading John's Apocalypse," in *Reading the Book of Revelation: A Resource for Students*, ed. David L. Barr (Atlanta: Society of Biblical Literature, 2003), 97–108.
14. Schüssler Fiorenza, *Vision of a Just World*, 14.
15. Ibid., 14–15.

Schüssler Fiorenza maintains her argument in *The Book of Revelation: Justice and Judgment* concerning both the value and the limitations of a strict gender-critical approach to Revelation. A gender-critical approach is beneficial because it draws attention to the gender inscriptions in the text; however, "by establishing a one-to-one relationship between female/feminine language and symbol on the one hand and actual wo/men on the other, [it] does not destabilize but rather literalizes the gender inscriptions of Revelation."[16] What she adds in this work, in which she employs a liberationist feminist reading, is an understanding of Revelation as "subaltern rhetorical discourse," which is a "'fitting response' [expressed through the use of 'multivalent language, mythic images, and visions of doom and bliss,' that is specific] to its socio-political 'rhetorical situation.'"[17] John creates an alternative world, in order to encourage Christians of Asia Minor who are experiencing harassment and persecution to persevere, and to refrain from any participation in the imperial religion.[18]

Schüssler Fiorenza argues that Revelation's response remains "fitting" only "wherever a social-political-religious 'tension' generated by oppression and persecution persists or re-occurs."[19] In a different rhetorical situation, such as our present one, in which

16. Schüssler Fiorenza, *Justice and Judgment*, 217. For the purposes of this chapter, I will highlight Schüssler Fiorenza's assertions that focus centrally on gender, though she discusses other matters too.

17. Ibid., v, 6. "While the poetic work seeks to create or organize imaginative experience, the rhetorical seeks to 'persuade' or 'motivate' people 'to act right'" (ibid., 187). The portion of this book that focuses on a rhetorical-political reading of the woman Babylon is also presented as an essay ("Babylon the Great: A Rhetorical-Political Reading of Revelation 17–18") in *The Reality of Apocalypse: Rhetoric and Politics in the Book of Revelation*, ed. David L. Barr, Symposium Series, no. 39 (Atlanta: Society of Biblical Literature, 2006), 243–69.

18. *Justice and Judgment*, 196. It should be noted, however, that Schüssler Fiorenza finds John's reinscription of imperial language for God and Christ in his alternative world problematic because of its ethos of domination. (In her work, Schüssler Fiorenza uses the term *G*d* with an asterisk to denote the insufficiency of human language to name the divine.) See also Schüssler Fiorenza, *The Power of the Word*, 207–213.

19. *Justice and Judgment*, 199.

we are more cognizant of "androcentric language and its socializing function," not only do we perceive a different rhetorical function and effect of the symbols in the text, but also "the dramatic action of Rev. will [not] have the same cathartic effects it had in its original situation."[20] Although she admits that for the contemporary reader, the images employed in Revelation may aid in continuing prejudice and injustice, she also states that this occurs when the "symbolic action of Rev. . . . is not 'translated' into a contemporary 'rhetorical situation' to which it can be a 'fitting' rhetorical response."[21]

This misappropriation, Schüssler Fiorenza asserts, can be seen in a strict gender reading of Revelation, such as of the feminine symbols. One may perceive from the feminine symbols that there are only two types of women—good or evil, pure or impure, wife or whore, and son on. However, such contained dualism "does not allow for ambiguity and change in meaning but only for an 'either/or' dualistic alternative."[22] Thus, the rhetorical situation of Revelation—in which cities are personified as women, and terms like "whoring" and phrases like "defilement with women" refer to idolatry in the "prophetic and cultic language of Israel"—is not "translated," or gets lost in a strict gender approach.[23] She, therefore, concludes that instead of solely focusing on "woman" in the text, one should also focus on Revelation's rhetorical-historical situation, which can help one "investigate and critically assess its power of persuasion,"[24] and prevent one from "reduc[ing] 'the reader' to a timeless, ideal reader, because in so doing we essentialize and dehistoricize the book."[25]

---

20. Ibid.
21. Ibid.
22. Ibid., 217.
23. Ibid., 199.
24. Ibid., 209.
25. Ibid., 199.

Finally, in *The Power of the Word: Scripture and the Rhetoric of Empire*, Schüssler Fiorenza extends her own trajectory to complement her analysis of the power of Scripture with an analysis of the rhetoric of empire.[26] In accomplishing this task, Schüssler Fiorenza not only underscores the limitations of a gendered analysis, but also of postcolonial critique. By employing a feminist rhetorical-political analysis, Schüssler Fiorenza asserts that one can move beyond a narrow gendered analysis to a political one, which helps to highlight John's critique of empire.[27] "Feminism . . . cannot be concerned only with gender injustice and gender marginalization but must also address other forms of domination, such as racism, poverty, religious exclusion, heterosexism, and colonialism, all of which are inflected by gender and themselves inflect gender."[28]

For example, with regard to the figure of Babylon (chapters 17–18), Schüssler Fiorenza preserves the idea that the feminine symbol, despite the "sexually charged language" of the text, is "the conventionally coded feminine language for a city," but adds that this rhetoric "uses gender for constructing power."[29] John's intention is to deliver the most scathing presentation of empire possible. Schüssler Fiorenza further buttresses her argument by stating that the "feminine figuration of Babylon is not a metaphor but a steno-symbol which is to be read as having a one-to-one meaning. Babylon equals imperial city."[30]

26. She maintains her claim that misogynist readings based on the negative depictions of women in Revelation can occur, and she continues to argue against the notion that Revelation's feminine symbolism conveys any information about actual women. "My argument is not that the feminine images of Revelation have not and do not produce misogynist readings because they have done so and continue to do so. Rather, I stress that one must avoid absolutizing gender as an essentializing category of analysis and cease to identify gendered figurations with actual wo/men" (*The Power of the Word*, 143).

27. Ibid., 131–32. This type of reading also "enable[s] contemporary interpreters to read 'against the grain' of their own cultural religious assumptions or prejudices as well as against those of the grammatically and symbolically kyriocentric text" (ibid., 131).

28. Ibid., 13.

29. Ibid., 136; cf. 130–47 passim.

Schüssler Fiorenza states that further textual evidence suggests that the proper understanding of Babylon is as a city and not an actual woman.

> Whereas in chapter 17, Babylon is seen primarily as a feminine figure (17:1-7, 9, 15-16) and secondarily as a city (17:5, 18), in chapter 18, Babylon is primarily characterized as an imperial city (18:2, 4, 10, 16, 18-19, 21) and only three times as a "woman" (18:3, 7, 16). This reversal in emphasis indicates that the rhetorical argument shifts from feminine figuration to that of imperial city. The author's explanatory identification of "the woman" vision, as that of the "great city which has dominion over the kings of the earth" in 17:18, serves as a rhetorical directive telling readers that they should understand this sequence of visions in terms of imperial Rome. [31]

Schüssler Fiorenza notes the references to woman in chapter 17, but suggests that they are strictly a means to an end, which is the identification of the Babylon figure with the city of Rome. She concludes that a feminist reading of Babylon's text must include an understanding of "Revelation's arguments as well as . . . one's own frames of meaning and understanding of language 'as a reality-generating system.'"[32] Failure to do so could result in an understanding of Babylon not as an imperial city, but as "representing an historical wo/man."[33]

Before we turn to the work of Tina Pippin, it is important to reiterate that Schüssler Fiorenza remains one of the main feminist scholars who notes the effects of biblical texts on contemporary readers. It is an argument that she maintains in each of her works discussed above. The interpretations of Schüssler Fiorenza and Pippin contrast greatly; however, as we will see, this is due more to the choice of methodological approaches than to a difference in an

---

30. Ibid., 134.
31. Ibid.
32. Ibid., 133.
33. Ibid.

interest in the implications of Revelation for women. In the words of Schüssler Fiorenza, "Competing interpretations of Revelation are not simply either right or wrong, but they constitute different ways of reading and constructing socio-historical and theo-ethical meaning."[34] Let us now turn, then, to Tina Pippin, whose competing interpretations of Revelation "explicit[ly] articulat[e]" the "interested perspectives [and] ethical criteria" that Schüssler Fiorenza states are needed for "critical public discussion."[35]

Tina Pippin

Feminist scholar Tina Pippin is best known for pioneering the use of a gender-critical approach in her analysis of Revelation. She is also one of the first biblical scholars to deal with the spectacle of the destruction of the woman Babylon in chapter 17. Countering the interpretations of feminist scholars who dismiss, or reduce via explanation, the use and implications of gendered metaphors, Pippin argues that these metaphors are not unintentional, or simply conventional, but rather precisely reflect an androcentric perspective. As such, Revelation entails a direct relationship between the fantastic world of the text and reality.

In her 1992 book, *Death and Desire: The Rhetoric of Gender in the Apocalypse of John*, Pippin builds on the work of both Adela Yarbro Collins—her notion of Revelation's cathartic and emotive dimensions[36]—and Schüssler Fiorenza—her feminist-liberationist

---

34. Schüssler Fiorenza, *Vision of a Just World*, 3.
35. Ibid. "What is appropriate in such a rhetorical paradigm of biblical scholarship is not detached value-neutrality, but an explicit articulation of one's rhetorical strategies, interested perspectives, ethical criteria, theoretical frameworks, religious presuppositions, and sociopolitical locations for critical public discussion" (ibid.).
36. Adela Yarbro Collins, *Crisis and Catharsis: The Power of the Apocalypse* (Philadelphia: Westminster, 1984).

rhetorical reading strategy—and reads Revelation from a Marxist/ materialist-feminist perspective.[37] This enables her to read "the desire for and death of the Whore of Babylon along gender, racial/ethnic, and economic lines."[38] This reading runs counter to dominant Revelation scholarship by challenging the notion that Babylon is a city.[39] Pippin "unanchors [the symbol of Babylon] from any specific historical context," affording her the ability to detect, highlight, and critique the sexual language of the text and the negative implications for both women characters and "real" women.[40] In this way, she diverges from the scholarship of those, such as Schüssler Fiorenza, who insist that the text be read in light of its sociohistorical context, in order to transcend misogynist readings based on gendered dualisms.

> Schüssler Fiorenza wants to transcend . . . gender assumptions. When she states that "interpreters must adopt methods and approaches that

---

37. Pippin, *Death and Desire: The Rhetoric of Gender in the Apocalypse of John* (Louisville: Westminster John Knox, 1992).
38. Ibid., 58–59.
39. Others have also undermined the argument that the whore metaphor refers solely and simply to a city. Jean K. Kim, in her article, "'Uncovering Her Wickedness': An Inter(con)textual Reading of Revelation 17 from a Postcolonial Feminist Perspective" compares the plight of the figure of Babylon to Korean women who were forced into sex labor during the Japanese occupation, and argues that the sociohistorical context of Revelation, that is, the fact that "in the Roman period, prostitution was a very necessary trade for which there was a great demand," indicates that this feminine metaphor also "stands for women sexually involved in a colonizing context" (*JSNT* 73 [1999]: 68–69). Caroline Vander Stichele, in her essay "Re-membering the Whore: The Fate of Babylon According to Revelation 17:16" (in Levine and Robbins, *A Feminist Companion to the Apocalypse of John*), compares the predicament of the woman Babylon to women in the "red light district of Amsterdam who were "lured to Western Europe . . . and forced into prostitution" (117). She argues that the violence done to these women-turned-slaves should not occur and is not justified, but seems validated when Rev. 17:16 is read without considering the social reality of prostitution; for some it is a trade, but it is not always a choice (ibid., 118-119). (See also an earlier version of this essay under the title, "Just a Whore: The Annihilation of Babylon According to Revelation 17:16," *Lectio Difficilior* 1 [2000]: 1–14.) Avaren Ipsen reads Revelation with sex workers in the Sex Worker Outreach Project (SWOP-USA) in her *Sex Working and the Bible* (London: Equinox Publishing, 2009), and states that while SWOP readers felt that the critique of Rome was valid, the use of their identities (as "whores") as a negative was a problem" (190).
40. Pippin, *Death and Desire*, 16.

undermine the androcentric-reality construction of the text" (1991:14),
I could not agree more. But first the text must be allowed to speak. The
inscribed negation of women is not something that can be worked out
or generalized; oppression is always specific and specific females in the
text are targeted, and this violence has impact on the specific lives of
women readers by promoting an extreme hatred of women.[41]

Pippin argues that feminine characters in the text[42]—such as Jezebel,[43]
Babylon, the woman clothed with the sun, and the bride—whether
depicted as good or evil, are never identified in their own
subjectivity, but rather always as objects of male desire: "erotic images
with erotic power over men."[44] Hence, all the females in the text are
to be viewed as victims. Additionally, women with power, who act
independently of men, such as Jezebel and the woman Babylon, are
viewed as evil, and therefore, must be violently destroyed; whereas
women such as the Woman Clothed with the Sun and the Bride,
who are dependent on men and who behave according to established
patriarchal norms, are saved and established as that to which women
should aspire.[45]

41. Ibid., 52–53.
42. Pippin also focuses on the absence of women in the text—for example, with regard to the
144,000 (those "who have not defiled themselves with women" [Rev. 14:4]). "The 144,000
represent the whole number of the faithful, and they are all men" (ibid., 70). Although crediting
Collins with the argument that the text suggests that the model of Christian is male, Pippin
states that Collins "fails to make full use of the logical inference—that the New Jerusalem, God's
future world, will exclude females! For the candidates for heaven to remain 'spotless'—indeed
for heaven itself to remain spotless—women are displaced" (ibid., 70–71).
43. The name "Jezebel" is in quotations because the general assumption is that it is a symbolic name.
"Jezebel" is a name that retained a negative connotation from the Hebrew Bible. She is the
daughter of King Ethbaal of the Sidonians (1 Kgs. 16:31) and is said to have encouraged her
husband to worship idols.
44. Ibid., 73. Pippin states that the materialist-feminist lens she employs "reveals [the] textual/sexual
strategies for dividing the woman symbol in the narrative" (ibid., 60). In *Apocalyptic Bodies: The
Biblical End of the World in Text and Image*, Pippin returns to her focus on sexual and erotic desire
as it pertains to gendered characters of Revelation (New York: Routledge, 1999). She maintains
her assertion that all of the female figures of the text, whether depicted as good or evil, are the
objects of the male gaze that focuses on their sexual activity (ibid., 121).
45. "Females with autonomous power bring death. Only those females who are connected with
God—adorned for the honeymoon or with wombs for use by God—that is, brides and mothers
(men-identified women), are safe. These are women who are controlled by men and who do

Pippin's detailed analysis of the figure of Babylon's demise in Revelation 17—the first of its kind—helps to illustrate how such sexualized textual violence can perpetuate negative stereotypes of, and violence toward, women. Although explored in *Death and Desire*, Pippin returns to this gruesome account, as well as other arguments from *Death and Desire*, in her essay, "The Heroine and the Whore: The Apocalypse of John in Feminist Perspective."[46] She writes that her issue is "not with whatthe image of the woman Babylon symbolized [that is, 'all the evil of the Roman Empire, and in particular, the city of Rome']," but rather "with the way in which this image of a prostitute is portrayed and used as a female symbol."[47] In the tradition of the Hebrew Bible, the harlot is either characterized

not exercise their powers independently. Still, they too lure men; they are also highly erotic images of desire" (Pippin, *Death and Desire*, 74).New Testament scholar Stephen D. Moore, in *God's Beauty Parlor: And Other Queer Spaces in and around the Bible*, asserts that the detriment and subjugation of femininity helps God achieve hypermasculinity—representing power and dominion—in Revelation and other biblical texts (Stanford, CA: Stanford University Press, 2001), 1–2. This elevation of hegemonic masculinity at the expense of its gendered counterpart is explored in the context of Revelation in Moore's fourth essay, "Revolting Revelations" (ibid., 173–99). Keeping in mind that war language in ancient times was extremely masculine and inextricably linked to sexual violence (ibid., 6), Moore suggests that in Revelation, "Jesus is not so much God become *man* as God become *masculine*" (ibid., 190, emphasis original), and feminine imagery, and the sexual violence associated with it, is reserved for the enemy (ibid.). For an earlier discussion about this hypermasculine God, see Moore's *God's Gym: Divine Male Bodies of the Bible* (New York: Routledge, 1996). In a later essay, "Metonymies of Empire: Sexual Humiliation and Gender Masquerade in the Book of Revelation," Moore employs both masculinity studies and queer theory to illustrate how both the rhetoric and the imagery used to describe the figure Babylon is intended to subvert the hypermasculine identity of the Roman Empire (in *Postcolonial Interventions: Essays in Honor of R. S. Sugirtharajah*, ed. Tat-siong Benny Liew [Sheffield, UK: Sheffield Phoenix, 2009], 71–97).

46. "The Heroine and the Whore," in *From Every People and Nation: The Book of Revelation in Intercultural Perspective*, ed. David Rhoads (Minneapolis: Fortress Press, 2005), 127–45. The essay was adapted from *Death and Desire*. For practical reasons, it will not be possible to deal in this survey with all of Pippin's articles and essays that discuss gender or sex in Revelation. See in addition, for example, "Eros and the End: Reading for Gender in the Apocalypse of John," *Semeia* 59 (1992): 193–210; "The Revelation to John," in *Searching The Scriptures*, vol. 2: *A Feminist Commentary*, ed. Elisabeth Schüssler Fiorenza (New York: Crossroad, 1994), 109–30; and "Revelation/Apocalypse," co-authored with J. Michael Clark, in *The Queer Bible Commentary*, ed. Deryn Guest, Robert E. Goss, Mona West, and Thomas Bohache (London: SCM, 2006), 753–68.

47. Pippin, "The Heroine and the Whore," 137.

as the "heroine" or the "whore"; certainly, the woman Babylon is depicted as the latter.[48] According to Pippin, the woman Babylon exudes power, has control over her sexuality, and thus "will not be tolerated."[49] Because the woman Babylon has "stepped out of her place," her destruction, which is described in horrific detail, is "violent and total."[50] By the end of the Apocalypse, all of the female figures, whether depicted as good or evil, are entirely absent in the narrative world of the text: Jezebel will be thrown upon a bed and her children will be killed (2:22-23), the Women Clothed with the Sun is "'banished' for protection and safekeeping to the wilderness" (12:14), and the Bride "alone is left standing, but only briefly, for she is replaced by the imagery of the city."[51]

This is not surprising to Pippin, however, because throughout Revelation, John is adamant about overturning the political realities of Rome, and yet persistent in maintaining the hierarchical structures that relegate women to marginal status. "While the political realities represented by these images are subverted and reversed, the stereotypes of female figures in themselves remain unchanged and unchallenged."[52] Pippin notes that the stereotypes of women in the text and their implications "may remain obscure to readers noticing

---

48. Ibid., 137–38. Pippin makes reference to Tamar (Genesis 38) and Rahab (Joshua 2 and 6) as representative of harlots who are heroines.

49. Ibid., 138.

50. Ibid., 138.

51. Pippin, "The Heroine and the Whore," 132. In "'And I Will Strike Her Children Dead': Death and the Deconstruction of Social Location," Pippin explores the ideology of death in Revelation (in *Reading from this Place*, vol. 1: *Social Location and Biblical Interpretation in the United States*, ed. Fernando F. Segovia and Mary Ann Tolbert [Minneapolis: Fortress Press, 1995], 191–98). She considers not only the political implications of death as expressed in Revelation, but also the different conclusions and ethical implications that might be drawn if one does a gender-critical reading of the text (ibid., 191). Death in Revelation is "governed by a political and gender-based discourse that is anticolonial (desiring the death of imperialism) and misogynist (desiring the death/eternal silencing of the female)" (ibid.). With regard to the effects of this text on "real" women, Pippin asserts that "participating in the Apocalypse means saying no on many levels: no to this story as liberating for women; no to the violence to women's bodies; no to the sacrificial mass deaths. The stories of pain and violence and death and male desire ironically locate us in the same ideology of oppression as the Apocalypse" (ibid., 198).

only the surface level of the narrative. Because the *Apocalypse* simply mirrors hidden dimensions of gender patterns in the culture, those patterns continue to remain hidden in the *Apocalypse*."[53] Thus, in efforts to change this, Pippin brings the negative repercussions of such destructive texts to the fore.

In an honest reflection on a dialogue she had with some of her students, Pippin noted their insistence that the biblical text must—to paraphrase loosely—be left alone. According to these students, "a feminist reading that deconstructs and challenges a biblical text must reflect directly on the ['immoral'] lifestyle and ['unpatriotic'] politics of the author. . . . [Thus,] the authoritative borders of the biblical text must be protected against exegetical terrorists such as [Pippin], and the sacred plan of the canon must be allowed to proceed on course."[54] If the Bible is untouchable, then women—both fictional and real—have a problem. Pippin is right to suggest, then, that if these hierarchical gender patterns remain "hidden," dismissed, or ignored, it will continue to be a problem for "real" women, who, by the perpetuation of the negative stereotypes and the notion of patriarchal domination ever-present in this text, are constantly subjugated in present-day society. For Christian women who hope in the reversal of gendered stereotypes, Revelation is "limited in its destruction of the forces of oppression," and thus, is "untouched by the sword of God."[55]

For Pippin, metaphors matter. The same could be said about Schüssler Fiorenza as well. However, for Pippin, a gender-critical approach most clearly helps to reveal the implications of this text

---

52. Pippin, "The Heroine and the Whore," 131. Pippin notes that although the "*Apocalypse* focuses on the enemy in terms of class (Rome), [it] neglects the oppressed/oppressor categories of gender relations" (ibid., 143). "Apocalypse" is italicized throughout *From Every People and Nation*.

53. Ibid., 131–32.

54. Ibid., 141.

55. Ibid., 144.

for women—both real and fictional. Contemporary understandings of gender roles have been influenced by texts such as Revelation, and therefore, only help to perpetuate the oppression of real women. The inclusion of "good" and "bad" female stereotypes in this text presents contrasting models of what it means to be female. To be "good," a woman has to concede all of her power and autonomy ultimately to a masculine figure; however, to have independence and self-sufficiency apart from a male figure is to be "bad." Furthermore, a woman who has "stepped out of her place" is to be punished, and she is viewed as the cause of such punishment. Revelation is certainly not a liberating text for Pippin.[56]

Conclusion

The work of Schüssler Fiorenza and Pippin illustrates the dichotomy presented in the "Great Whore" debate that I seek to dismantle in this book. Specifically, it pertains to the interpretation of the figure of Babylon as either a city or a woman. Both scholars note the negative implications of this text on female readers; however, the difference in their interpretation is based on differences in methodological approach. As I stated above, I intentionally isolated their work from a much broader conversation in order to clearly explicate the contrasting perspectives—the two most directly related to my work.[57]

56. Pippin, *Apocalyptic Bodies*, 117.
57. This broader conversation also includes the work of scholars such as David L. Barr, who disagrees with both Pippin and Schüssler Fiorenza's approach to Revelation. In his 2009 essay, "Women in Myth and History: Deconstructing John's Characterizations" (in Levine and Robbins, *A Feminist Companion to the Apocalypse of John* 55–68), Barr argues that John's use of the female body as symbolic constructs, particularly, his depiction of them as either "good" or "bad," has led scholars to either "reject . . . and, if possible, discard" the book (like Pippin who focuses on the gender images), or "to read the Apocalypse against the grain" (such as Schüssler Fiorenza, who insists on reading it as "liberation from forces of domination") (ibid., 62–63). Discontented with both approaches, since the text and the gendered images therein are "too powerful to be ignored," Barr offers an alternative for women readers (albeit, not without first noting the "irony of his [own] male voice and eyes," ibid., 63–64). He

Should the figure Babylon be interpreted as a city? Or should *she* be interpreted as a woman? Pippin helps to set up my response to these questions. She writes, "Having studied the evils of Roman imperial policy in the colonies, I find the violent destruction of Babylon very cathartic."[58] Even as I reflect upon the harsh conditions and realities of my ancestors during the time of American slavery, I cannot help but applaud such a detailed and colorful reversal of colonial oppression. Yet, Pippin could not, and did not, end her analysis there: "But when I looked into the face of Babylon, I saw a woman."[59] Therein lies the tension between the depiction of the woman Babylon as an empress/imperial city and as a woman. Examining the gender-specific and rhetorical-political aspects of Revelation highlights the duality of her characterization. Although she represents the imperial center of Rome in all its excess, *she* is also a woman who is abused and horribly destroyed. Although Pippin ultimately topples the interpretive scale to understand the figure Babylon as a woman, and Schüssler Fiorenza's reference to Babylon as a city tips the scale in the other direction, I find myself doing a balancing act between the two.

As an African American woman who is both a victim and a participant in empire, I give both questions stated above a resounding yes. The fact that I find resonance with both of these aspects of the woman Babylon makes it difficult to choose between both readings, and thus, I embrace both. The figure of Babylon is a city because she reminds me of the imperial structures by which I and my ancestors have been victimized, and the very same structures from which I benefit. (I am torn.) The figure of Babylon is also a woman because I

suggests that one pays attention to the "gaps" between the historical and the mythical, because by focusing on these "gaps," one can see that although John employs mythic themes, he ultimately subverts their political intent (ibid., 66). See also an online version of his argument, David L. Barr, "Jezebel's Skinny Legs: (De)Constructing the Four Queens of the Apocalypse": http://www.wright.edu/~david.barr/jezebel.htm.
58. Pippin, *Death and Desire*, 80.
59. Ibid.

resonate with the violence that *she* experienced as a female. What she endures on the pages of John's text reminds me of what my female ancestors endured at the whim of their slavemasters. (I am incensed.) In short, her ambivalent subject position is a reflection of my own and incites within me all sorts of emotions.

It is quite evident, then, that "what we see depends on where we stand. Our social location or rhetorical context is decisive for how we see the world, construct reality, or interpret biblical texts."[60] This view is pertinent and appropriate because it highlights the fact that people of different racial and ethnic backgrounds, and those within similar identity groupings, have varied readings and approaches. In my reading of the woman Babylon I not only employ a reader-oriented approach, which takes into account my experiences as a concomitantly privileged and oppressed African American woman, but I also incorporate a gender-critical and rhetorical-political approach, as posited by Pippin and Schüssler Fiorenza, respectively, whose work we examined. My sociocultural context compels me to also consider the categories of race, ethnicity, and class when approaching the woman Babylon—a new perspective in the "Great Whore" debate—and leads me to argue that both aspects of the woman Babylon's characterization should be held in tension. Thus, instead of choosing sides in this debate, I set it on a different course. The combination of these approaches and sensitivities helps me to critically analyze the symbolic language of gender and sexuality as it pertains to the woman Babylon, and helps me to explain the occasion for this gendered metaphor without forfeiting the ability to contemplate its effects on me.

The experiences that are conjured up in my mind and the emotions that go along with it causes me to embrace the duality of the figure

60. Elisabeth Schüssler Fiorenza, *Wisdom Ways: Introducing Feminist Biblical Interpretation* (Maryknoll, NY: Orbis, 2001), 96. See also *Vision of a Just World*, 2.

of Babylon. She has already been ripped apart in the text; I intend to put her back together, interpretively speaking. My interpretation, which considers the implications of the figure Babylon's text for real women, has also led me to posit an interpretation that extends and complicates those previously posited by other African American scholars. Let us now turn to an examination of their scholarship in order to identify points of connection (ancestral historical experience), and points of departure (from Revelation as resistance to imperial and masculinist literature), between the works of those scholars and my own.

African American Interpretations of Revelation

In comparison to the above section on the "Great Whore" debate, a survey of African American interpretations of Revelation does not include readings specifically on Babylon or an analysis that includes a gender critique. Instead, these biblical scholars have engaged mainstream Revelation scholarship with questions about how the text has been, and may be, interpreted by African Americans, and its implications for this community. It is important that I engage this conversation not simply because as an African American biblical scholar, I too am interested and invested in how Revelation has been interpreted by blacks and the implications thereof, but also because my work adds a new perspective that takes the conversation in a different direction. The overall narrative of African American biblical interpretations of Revelation reads in unison; however, I am about to strike a different cord. Hopefully, with the addition of my work we can begin to harmonize.

The scholars in this section share an interest in how the text of Revelation, as one that presents a minority report, expresses the resistance and subversion of imperial powers by colonized peoples.

Despite this shared perspective, these scholars are differentiated by the various methods and approaches that they employ.[61] If my research is correct, there are only four trained African American New Testament scholars (three male and one female) who have published any works, whether monographs, articles, or essays, on the text of Revelation. Hopefully, there are others such as myself in the pipeline.[62] I will present their works in a rough chronological sequence.

Allen Dwight Callahan

Allen Dwight Callahan, in his article "The Language of Apocalypse," provides an overview of three traditional New Testament views regarding Revelation's unusual grammar and syntax, and suggests an alternative.[63] One view is that Revelation's original composition was of a Semitic language, either Hebrew or Aramaic, and that errors occurred during the translation process.[64] Another assessment is that the errors in the text's Greek grammar and syntax are the result of the author's carelessness and negligence.[65] The third viewpoint is that the author wrote in a "pidginized 'ghetto Greek' of a diasporan Jewish

---

61. For more on the shared emphasis of African American New Testament scholars regarding how cultural and social issues affect the African American community, all the while representing methodological diversity, see, e.g. Larry L. Enis, "Biblical Interpretation Among African-American New Testament Scholars," *Currents in Biblical Research* 4, no. 1 (2005): 57–82. The "hermeneutical approaches [of African American New Testament scholars], though diverse methodologically, [are] in some way fueled by African-American culture" (ibid., 78).

62. See, for example, Lynne St. Clair Darden, *Scripturalizing Revelation: An African American-Postcolonial Reading of Empire* (Atlanta: SBL Semeia Studies, forthcoming). Darden's work examines how John's signifying on the Roman Empire is a contradiction, since his anti-imperial rhetoric actually mimics aspects of imperial ideology. Her reading is also to be a caution to the African American community of the danger of being critically unaware of our tendency to embrace the dominant ethos.

63. Allen Dwight Callahan, "The Language of Apocalypse," *Harvard Theological Review* 88, no. 4 (1995): 453–70.

64. Ibid., 454.

65. Ibid.

community" whose strong Semitic accent was combined with an adapted form of the language.[66] These three negative views regarding the language of Revelation are problematic for Callahan because they deny a sort of credibility or writing expertise to the author. Countering these views, Callahan asserts that "the seer's language is due not to intellectual deficiency, but to an idiolectical peculiarity that is both intentional and insurgent."[67]

> The language of the seer is a subaltern language, the language of one who is disenfranchised from mainstream discourse, but must appropriate its articulations simply to be understood. He has chosen to write in the language of his own hegemonic moment, the language of the Roman empire. . . . [Being] aware that language as a system of discourse is necessarily a vector of power relations, . . . the seer, with strategy and premeditation, transgressed grammatical norms as an exercise of his own discursive power. . . . The language of the text—its discourse, the word of God—*is* the struggle. The terrain of contestation is the discourse itself.[68]

Callahan goes on to say that "the seer clearly knows how to follow the rules of the language game when he wants to . . . [because] most of the grammatical rules violated are flawlessly observed elsewhere in the work."[69]

Callahan asserts that these three traditional assessments of Revelation's diction not only offer "unsatisfactory explanations" for the text's language, but they also demonstrate the "inaccessibility of the language of the Apocalypse to the modern project of interpretation."[70] Instead of reading and analyzing the text in a "quest

---

66. Ibid. Callahan asserts, "The language of the Apocalypse presents not the dialect of a subaltern community that has only imperfectly internalized the dominant language, but an idiolect, the peculiar language of one author, unattested anywhere else in antiquity" (ibid., 458).
67. Ibid., 454. The term *idiolectical* refers to the author's specific use of a variant or form of a language.
68. Ibid., 464–65, emphasis original.
69. Ibid., 457.
70. Ibid., 459.

for meaning," one should focus on "*how* this text may have effected [*sic*] its hearers."[71] An idiolectical reading such as this, according to Callahan, is the "real critical task."[72] The author repeatedly emphasized reading the text aloud, which ultimately led to the transformation of the hearers.[73] "Reading the Apocalypse aloud, and hearing the Apocalypse read aloud, was effectual: through exhortations and exclamations, threats and thunder, the reading of the Apocalypse moved its hearers, effected [*sic*] them; the text *did* something to them."[74] In addition, in every instance that the text is read or heard, the author's deliberate and rebellious literary deviations are proclaimed, and "asserts anew the authenticity of its subaltern voices. . . . The bonds of linguistic convention are subverted; language for that moment ceases to be an imperialist prison. All those who read, recite, hear, and hold dear these words participate in the emancipation of discourse itself."[75]

Thomas B. Slater

In *Christ and Community: A Socio-Historical Study of the Christology of Revelation*, Thomas B. Slater combines historical criticism and sociology of knowledge to analyze three christological images of Revelation: "one like a son of man," the Lamb, and the Divine Warrior.[76] His goal is to understand the role of Christ within

71. Ibid., emphasis added.
72. Ibid.
73. See, for example, Rev. 1:3 ("Blessed is the one who *reads aloud* the words of the prophecy, and blessed are those who *hear* and who keep what is written in it," emphasis added). The repeated refrain in the letters to the seven churches states: "Let anyone who has an *ear listen* to what the Spirit is saying to the churches" (Rev. 2:7, 11, 17, 29; 3:6, 13, 22, emphasis added). See also 22:7b; 22:18a.
74. Ibid., 460, emphasis original.
75. Ibid., 466, 470.
76. Thomas B. Slater, *Christ and Community: A Socio-Historical Study of the Christology of Revelation* (Sheffield, UK: Sheffield Academic, 1999).

Revelation's symbolic universe, and the impact that these images may have had on the lives of the Christian communities experiencing suffering and persecution in first-century Asia Minor.[77] Slater argues that according to the text, the Christian communities experienced two types of tension. Chapters 2–3, the letters to the seven churches, reflect an *internal* conflict between the churches based on issues with "religious laxity," while chapters 4–22, the apocalyptic visions, speak to the *external* pressures and persecution experienced by the Christian community from the "greater society."[78]

With regard to the christological images and their social function in Revelation, Slater states that the "one like a son of man" (2–3; 14:14-16) is God's "eschatological divine agent who attains his *victory through suffering*, creating a new people of God composed of priest-kings."[79] This image encourages the suffering Christian community to remain faithful in order to attain the promise of becoming priestly coheirs and join God and Christ in the New Jerusalem.[80] The Lamb, "the major Christological image" in Revelation, positions Christ as the one who provides for the eschatological Christian community, protects it from Satan, and redeems it to God through his sacrificial death (5:9).[81] Reflecting a "victory-through-suffering motif," this Lamb imagery was used not only to help the Christian community recall Jesus' crucifixion, but also to convince them to remain faithful to God in the midst of persecution.[82] Lastly, the Divine Warrior (19:11-21) depicts Christ as one who vindicates the Christian community by judging the "worldly institutions" that had oppressed

77. Ibid., 63, 241. Slater notes that "there is no evidence that this [persecution of Christians] was an official Roman imperial policy. Rather, it appears that John placed a regional oppression on a worldwide plane" (ibid., 21).
78. Ibid., 208.
79. Ibid., 241, emphasis original.
80. Ibid, 242.
81. Ibid., 162, 200–1.
82. Ibid., 204, 245.

them.[83] This "negative form of legitimation wherein everything outside the system [the symbolic universe] is liquidated in some way" is referred to as "nihilation."[84] Slater concludes that all three images function as a symbol of Christ's unity with the Christian community.[85] During a time of "regional oppression of Christians in Asia," John wrote this text in order to persuade and challenge them to maintain their spiritual beliefs and "wait for divine deliverance."[86]

At this point in the survey, it is important to note a distinction between the scholarship of Callahan and Slater, on the one hand, and Brian K. Blount and Clarice J. Martin, on the other. Neither Callahan nor Slater ever explicitly relates the language or themes of Revelation to African American history or culture, even though each, in his own way, reads Revelation as minority discourse. A very different kind of "African American" reading of Revelation, however, is being performed by Blount and Martin, both of whom read Revelation explicitly out of their sociocultural locations as African Americans.

Brian K. Blount

Brian K. Blount, the only scholar in this section with multiple works on Revelation, including a commentary, numerous articles and essays, and a monograph, has an overarching focus on the language of witness and its function as a form of active resistance in Revelation.[87]

83. Ibid., 209, 244–45.
84. Ibid., 54. For further information on the term *nihilation*, see P. L. Berger and T. Luckmann, *The Social Construction of Reality: A Treatise in the Sociology of Knowledge* (Garden City, NY: Doubleday, 1966).
85. Slater, *Christ and Community*, 245.
86. Ibid.
87. Blount's *Revelation: A Commentary* and his essay "Revelation" in *True to Our Native Land: An African American New Testament Commentary*, ed. Brian K. Blount (Minneapolis: Fortress Press, 2007), 523–58, are excluded from this survey, not only because of their classification as commentary, but also because they are referenced numerous times throughout this book for their background information on, and exegesis of, Revelation.

For the purposes of this survey, I will explore Blount's arguments as thoroughly explicated in *Can I Get a Witness: Reading Revelation through African American Culture*.[88] He employs a cultural-studies approach in order to "ascertain how material written in and for that [original] community becomes meaningful for a particular twenty-first-century community."[89] In this case, it is the African American cultural experience that Blount uses to illumine the themes of witness and active resistance in the text of Revelation. It is a reading "from below."[90]

Blount argues that in the text of Revelation, the Greek word *martys* should not be defined as "martyr," but rather as "witness," an open and public expression of one's loyalty and commitment to Jesus Christ, which entails an active resistance to all persons and things that resist his sovereignty.[91] Dying for one's faith is not Revelation's

88. (Louisville: Westminster John Knox, 2005). I have chosen to focus solely on *Can I Get a Witness*, because his previous articles and essays—"Reading Revelation Today: Witness as Active Resistance," *Interpretation* 54, no. 4 (2000): 398–412; "Revelation: The Witness of Active Resistance," in *Then the Whisper Put on Flesh: New Testament Ethics in an African American Context* (Nashville: Abingdon, 2001), 158–84; and "The Witness of Active Resistance: The Ethics of *Revelation* in African American Perspective," in Rhoads, *From Every People and Nation*, 28–46—are all gathered up in this work, his most fleshed out to date.

89. Blount, *Can I Get a Witness*, 10. Through an exploration of cultural studies, Blount evaluates both historical and literary criticism, taking note of their limitations. Cultural studies indicates that the historical critics' aim of trying to determine what the text meant for its first-century audience is limiting not only because the original situations of these texts are inaccessible, but also because the critics themselves are bound and influenced by their own cultural contexts which affect their interpretation. It also shows that a literary critic's emphasis on the way in which the language of a text "abides by the textual and ideational constraints it imposes" only opens up the interpretive possibilities, as those very constraints are "filled with meaning potential that can be accessed in a multitude of appropriate ways" (ibid., 35).

90. Ibid., 17. Cultural studies "recognizes the intent of historical and literary critical methods to dismiss readings 'from below,' to appeal instead to 'objective' methodologies that valorize the dominant cultural ideology inscribed within them, while all the time arguing that no such ideology exists" (ibid.).

91. Blount states that to interpret *martys* as "martyr" is indicative of "contextual confusion"; it "has come to mean something quite different from what it meant for John and his hearers and readers. . . . When someone in John's turn-of-the-first-century environment said *witness*, she meant witness, not martyr" (ibid., 46, 47, emphasis original). Blount does not examine all the instances where the word *martys* appears, but rather where John combines "'witness' with word

appeal; instead, it is about bearing witness—expressing one's testimony and faithfulness to Christ through action—in which suffering is simply a byproduct.[92]

Similar to Revelation's plea for resisting accommodation to the Roman Empire, Blount recounts how African American slaves' "unauthorized [and 'unsupervised'] worship"[93] was an act of resistance, and how black churches in the civil rights movement served as meeting places to discuss plans for "social and political liberation."[94] Like the souls of Rev. 6:9-11, African Americans throughout history served as "defiant witnesses actively engaged in their own uplift through their preaching of the lordship of Christ."[95]

Blount concludes his work by analyzing the hymns of Revelation through the lens of African American music, such as "spiritual-blues" and rap music. By examining how music functioned as a "primary weapon" that blacks used to combat their negative experiences in the United States, Blount is then able to turn to the hymns of Revelation and assert that

the hymnic language in the Apocalypse . . . does more than "prepare

of God and then causally connects them both to some form of reactionary persecution. In 1:9, it was John's exile. In 6:9-11; 12:10-12; and 20:4-6, it will be his followers' deaths" (ibid., 50).

92. "The fact that punishment occurs as a result of witnessing implies that the witnessing is an active, public enterprise. Whether done in response to hostile inquiry by community leaders or voluntarily as a spontaneous act of faith declaration, witnessing appears very much to be a live action endeavor" (ibid.). In his chapter on the slain Lamb, Blount moves beyond the traditional association of Jesus' sacrifice with atonement, that is, Jesus' debt payment for human sinfulness. Instead, he situates it in the context of African American culture and experience, and examines sacrifice as it relates to a situation of injustice. As Rev. 6:9-11 indicates, "John appears to view unearned suffering as an evil" (ibid., 75). Suffering, in and of itself, does not bring about "liberation and transformation," but active resistance to wickedness does, the action that may *result* in suffering or death as expressed by Christ's dual representation as the slain Lamb and the Lion (Rev. 5:5-6) (ibid.). Blount states that "this lamb is no innocent; he *earns* the slaughter that comes his way. To be sure, this is an odd thing to say. And yet it is an accurate representation of both John's Apocalypse and some of the key transformative moments in the history of the Black Church tradition" (ibid., 83, emphasis original).

93. Ibid., 54.

94. Ibid., 43.

95. Ibid., 55.

and comment upon" plot movements. It also reinforces the plot thesis of resistance while it incites John's hearers and readers to initiate such resistance in their own lives. The hymns pump up the volume of worship to a frenzy of praise that describes God as the Lord of all creation who will crack *down* on Rome while raising *up* the Lamb. In doing this, the hymns first capture the combustible emotions of fear, loss, anger, deprivation, and hope, and then set those emotions cultically and politically ablaze in a way that only the poetry and melody of music can.[96]

Similarly to African American music, which draws attention to the ills of oppression and incites its audiences to action—to challenge, to resist, and to change—the hymns of Revelation exhort the Christian community to recall and rejoice over God's defeat of the enemy in order to continually resist the Roman Empire.[97] In Blount's reading of Revelation through the eyes of African American culture, he illustrates how a people can both maintain their faith and resist oppressive structures through public witness as a form of active resistance.

Clarice J. Martin

The last African American scholar in this survey, and the only woman in the group, is womanist biblical scholar Clarice J. Martin. In her essay, "Polishing the Unclouded Mirror: A Womanist Reading of *Revelation* 18:13," Martin examines how the phrase "slaves and human lives" in the cargo list in the above verse serves as a "mirror" or "looking glass" into African American history.[98] She also explores

---

96. Ibid., 93, emphasis original.
97. "The hymns in Revelation appear to pursue the same goal of resistance with the same strategy of remembrance" (ibid., 109).
98. Martin, "Polishing the Unclouded Mirror: A Womanist Reading of *Revelation* 18:13," in Rhoads, *From Every People and Nation*, 83. Martin is careful to note, however, that by this reflective lens, she does not "imply that the Seer's reference to 'slaves and human lives [human souls]' (18:13) mirrors *with exactitude* the American slave system of later centuries. The

how her reading may "shed new light on the rhetorical and ideological functions of *Revelation* 18:13 in its first-century socio-historical and rhetorical context."[99]

Martin states that when studying Rev. 18:13, she is reminded not only of the struggles of our ancestors during the "four-hundred-year-long history of slavery within the United States," but also of the sacrifices made by those during the Jim Crow era, the civil rights movement, and those of today who struggle against various forms of oppression such as racial inequality.[100] She notes, however, that the "gains and liberties" that African American people have struggled for are only "deposits whose yields are yet to be attained in full."[101] By privileging black women's experience, wisdom, and agency (to name a few), Martin's womanist lens helps her to "challenge the gender-exclusive hegemony of male-articulated understandings of the Christian faith."[102] What this means with regard to Revelation is a focus not only on themes of "resistance to oppression," but also of "activist moral agency."[103]

Martin asserts that Revelation, with its "social and world vision, . . . functioned as 'protest' literature," of which the primary goal was to stand in opposition to Roman imperialism.[104] With regard to the cargo list, Martin notes that John goes against the cultural view of his day that slaves were "defectively souled," by referring

---

reflection in the looking glass refracts historical parallels to the slave systems of Greece and Rome that are only *partially* commensurate with the American slave system. Nevertheless, the relative differences [such as a lack of 'ethnic' or 'racial' identifiers for slaves, and the fact that slaves usually worked 'side by side' with free persons] cannot diminish the often striking and conspicuous, albeit culturally differentiated, similarities [such as the violence used to 'maintain and perpetuate' slavery, and the notion of the slave as a 'dishonored,' and 'socially dead person']" (ibid., 87–89, emphasis added).

99. Ibid., 83, emphasis original.
100. Ibid., 83–84.
101. Ibid., 84.
102. Ibid., 85.
103. Ibid.
104. Ibid., 91.

to them as "*human* souls" (18:13).[105] This "inversion" is the author's way of "level[ing] a biting critique" against Roman enslavement.[106] Martin also states that John "signifies" on Rome, that is, he employs "language in indirect and covert ways to critique the larger hegemonic, imperial power arrangement of what he deems to be the 'evil empire.'"[107] As such, Revelation is resistance literature, reflecting a "minority report," which represents the views of marginalized and powerless persons via its "truculent rhetoric and oppositional ideological stance."[108] Similar to John's critique of the Roman Empire in 18:13, Martin asserts that black women have also "engaged in activist, prophetic critiques and resistance against . . . domination."[109]

Conclusion

All of the above African American scholars assert that Revelation, in one way or another, presents a minority report, one that gives voice to the voiceless and marginalized in an attempt to counter oppression. Callahan writes about the author's intentional misuse of Greek grammar and syntax, and suggests that it is a reflection of his attempt to emancipate discourse from the hands of imperialist society, and simultaneously give voice to the subaltern community of

105. Ibid., 89, emphasis added.
106. Ibid.
107. Ibid., 96. Martin asserts that this "signification" on Rome occurs in three ways. First, based on the placement of 18:13 within the larger literary context of God's judgment on Rome (17:1—18:24), John portrays Rome—in the figure of the woman Babylon—as "the condemned defendant in a criminal trial" (ibid.). Second, through "intertextual associations," he associates Rome with past evil empires, such as Babylon and Tyre (Ezekiel 27), who not only oppressed peoples, and boasted about their wealth, but who also were destroyed (ibid., 97–98). Finally, John signifies on Rome by rearranging the order of the cargo list. Compared to the list mentioned in Ezek. 27:12-25, John presents the "goods" in "descending order of value," placing slaves at the end (ibid., 99). Martin suggests that this "placement functions as a strategically crafted social critique of the widespread and 'taken for granted' practice of slave trade in the . . . Mediterranean world of John's day" (ibid.).
108. Ibid., 91.
109. Ibid., 105–6.

which he is a part. Slater, through an analysis of three christological figures of Revelation—"the one like a son of man," the Lamb, and the Divine Warrior—shows how these images function to encourage the suffering Christian community not only to endure both internal and external conflict and persecution, but also to remain faithful in the midst of it, in order to maintain the relationship between themselves and Christ in the New Jerusalem. Blount reads Revelation through the lens of African American culture, and argues that its witness language functions not as a call to self-sacrifice as a martyr, but as a form of active resistance to oppressive structures in which suffering may result. Lastly, Martin employs a womanist lens to analyze the phrase "slaves and human lives" in the cargo list of Rev. 18:13, and suggests not only that it functions as a "mirror" into African American history, but also that the rhetoric and ideological stance presented in that verse is reflective of resistance literature, which, in this case, is in opposition to Roman imperialism.

Although the above works reflect various types of readings and approaches that ultimately suggest that the author of Revelation writes in the interest of marginalized people against oppression, another perspective is warranted. As we shall see, John does not refrain from subscribing to the patriarchal and imperial rhetoric and ideologies of his day that both establish and perpetuate sexualized violence against women. In fact, he depicts the defeat of the Roman Empire by God's empire through the violent and vivid destruction of a woman'sbody. A postcolonial womanist approach to the woman Babylon that not only highlights John's reinscription of empire, but also seeks the well-being of all people, men *and* women, leads me to conclude that John does not present a minority report in the *full* sense, but rather a masculinist one.

3

The Book of Revelation

Texts and Contexts

The question that plagues most readers of Revelation is "What does it mean?" What does all the symbolism, gendered metaphors, riddles, visions of doom and destruction—including that of a woman—and the heightened sense of urgency reflect? What was happening, or what did the author sense was *about* to happen when he wrote this text? In an attempt to gain control of the vortex of questions that pulls interpreters into its winding and dizzying current, scholars have worked to determine the correlation between the situation behind the text and what is actually written on its pages. The range of foci one can explore for the purpose of contextualizing Revelation is quite broad. For this reason, the overview of scholarship included here is strictly functional, and thus, is dictated by direct relevance to themes explored in my exegetical analysis. I begin by briefly stating my working assumptions concerning the authorship and dating of Revelation. I then turn to a more thorough discussion regarding the social setting of the text, since an understanding of this context lends itself to an understanding of the occasion for its writing. A general overview of the scholarly positions pertaining to the "why" of Revelation, that is, the reason for its writing, will be presented, as it helps to illustrate how my work builds upon previous scholarship.

As we will see, the social context of the text leads to the rationale for the text's composition, which affects not only *what* the author writes, but also *how* he writes it. All of these components work together in order to help us determine what was happening in that point of history that prompted the writing of such a complex text. The task of "making sense" of this text, however, rests with the interpreter, and thus, the number of interpretations is multiple. This is the case not only because a simple variation in one's understanding of the social context leads to a different rationale for the text's composition, thus affecting how we read the text, but also because of the uniqueness of our very selves. The experiences, presuppositions, agendas, and questions that one brings to a text differ from one interpreter to the next. Context, therefore, matters—not only of the historical text, but also of the contemporary reader. Interpretation, or as we will see in my case, self-realization, occurs within this contextual encounter.

Authorship

Scholars have discussed various prospects for the authorship of this text; however, in this book, I will assume that the author was an itinerant prophet (as indicated by 1:3; 22:10, 18, 19) named "John,"[1]

---

1. The author of Revelation refers to himself as "John" in four instances (1:1, 4, 9; 22:8). "The consensus is that 'John' is . . . a personal self-reference to a real John" (G. K. Beale, *The Book of Revelation: A Commentary on the Greek Text*, The New International Greek Testament Commentary [Grand Rapids: Eerdmans, 1999], 34). The two most prominent candidates are: the Apostle John (the son of Zebedee) and John the presbyter. Justin Martyr (165 C.E.) assigns

who was not the apostle.[2] He was also a former Palestinian Jew, based upon his numerous references to the Hebrew Bible (particularly Ezekiel and Daniel), his familiarity with the apocalyptic genre associated with early Palestinian Judaism, and his knowledge of the Jewish temple and cult in Jerusalem (8:3-4; 11:1-2, 19).[3]

The social location of the author is another topic of interest, because it provides insight into the way that John writes, that is, the rhetorical moves he makes and the symbolism he employs. One of the ways this has been investigated is through a discussion of John's supposed banishment. Revelation 1:9 states, "I, John, your brother who share with you in Jesus the persecution and the kingdom and the patient endurance, was [egenomēn] on the island called Patmos because of [dia] the word of God and the testimony of Jesus." Scholars have debated the veracity of the tradition of John's banishment, which can be traced no further back than around 190 C.E. (see Clement of Alexandria, *Who Is the Rich Man That Shall Be Saved?* 42), arguing that it is either "reliable historical information or a legendary motif inspired by Rev. 1:9."[4] For example, by interpreting egenomēn as "I arrived," and *dia* in the purposive sense, Leonard L. Thompson asserts that John was on Patmos voluntarily, which underscores Thompson's argument against any type of persecution and banishment of John to Patmos.[5] David Arthur DeSilva argues that

authorship of Revelation to John the apostle in his *Dialogue with Trypho* (81.4 [ca. 155 C.E.]). Irenaeus, bishop of Lyons, later claims that the apostle John wrote both Revelation and the Gospel of John (*Against Heresies* 5.30). In the fourth century, citing Papias of Hierapolis, the historian Eusebius writes that the seer of Revelation was an elder or presbyter and not one of the apostles (*Hist. Eccl.* 3.39.5–7).

2. After taking into consideration the theological differences in the texts of the Johannine corpus, I find it hard to imagine, for example, the Gospel of John and Revelation coming from the same individual. Recall that the Gospel of John lacks a pronounced eschatology or apocalypticism.

3. Brian K. Blount adds that the author's use of "Semiticized Greek . . . suggests someone whose native language was not Greek but the Aramaic spoken by Palestinian Jews" (*Revelation: A Commentary* [Louisville: Westminster John Knox, 2009], 8).

4. Adela Yarbro Collins, *Crisis and Catharsis: The Power of the Apocalypse* (Philadelphia: Westminster, 1984), 55.

Thompson's assertion that John was on Patmos for "missionary intentions" is overreaching, stating that it "loses force on both a grammatical and judicial consideration."[6] Maintaining his critique, DeSilva states in a later work that Thompson's understanding of the preposition *dia* in the purposive sense "is not within the established range of meanings for [*dia*], which looks backward, never forward. Thus John was on Patmos 'on account of' prior activity connected with the Word of God and testimony of Jesus."[7] Adela Yarbro Collins holds a similar perspective, stating that the preposition *dia* should be interpreted as causative, connoting the "grounds, the *past* reason for something."[8] She continues, "If John was indeed banished, that fact tells us a great deal about the attitude of the Roman authorities toward him and his message and about his own probable attitude toward them."[9]

But what type of place was Patmos, and who went, or was sent, there? Aune argues that there is no historical evidence that Patmos was a Roman penal colony, but there is debate about the possibility of Romans using it as a place of exile.[10] If the exile interpretation of John's Patmos sojourn is maintained, it may be an indication of his relatively high social status. Aune notes that exile, which could be a voluntary or involuntary departure, was "permitted those of higher status who had been condemned to death, but they were usually subsequently deprived of both citizenship and property."[11]

5. Leonard L. Thompson, *The Book of Revelation: Apocalypse and Empire* (Oxford: Oxford University Press, 1990), 173.
6. DeSilva, "The Social Setting of the Revelation to John: Conflicts Within, Fears Without," *Westminster Theological Journal* 54, no. 2 (Fall 1992): 285.
7. DeSilva, *Seeing Things John's Way: The Rhetoric of the Book of Revelation* (Louisville: Westminster John Knox, 2009), 33.
8. Collins, *Crisis and Catharsis*, 55, emphasis original.
9. Ibid.
10. David Aune, *Revelation 1–5*, Word Biblical Commentary, vol. 52 (Dallas: Word, 1997), 78–79.
11. Ibid., 79.

John's high social standing—if that is truly implied by his presence on Patmos—which sits alongside his self-presentation as one who is persecuted, complicates the reconstruction of his identity. Despite being a member of the higher rung of the social system, John also sees himself as a victim—or such, at least, is the stance that he takes in the text. His complex identity could very well help to explain his construction of ambivalent characters such as the woman Babylon—a two-faced, mischievous image—and his tense relationship with power. One can surmise that perhaps John himself requires the use of a "veil"—a metaphorical covering that separates the duality of his bifurcated existence—as he constructs such a complex picture of God's empire overtaking the Roman Empire, in which the struggle between his identity as a persecuted individual and a privileged individual clearly emerges. If this admittedly speculative reconstruction of John's social location and consequent bifurcated identity is on or near the mark, it helps to explain why his text lends itself so well to a postcolonial womanist hermeneutics of ambi*veil*ence, one acutely attuned to class-driven identity conflicts of this kind.

Dating

There are two major schools of thought regarding the date of Revelation in its final form: (1) the late first century during the latter years of Emperor Domitian's reign, which ended in 96 C.E.; or (2) shortly following the death of Nero, whose reign ended in 68 C.E. Determining the date of Revelation is not an exact science, to put it mildly. Although the text uses numerical values to suggest names of persons (13:17-18; 17:9-11), this does not mean that the date of the Apocalypse is easily and definitely identifiable. I think that when one chooses a side on the debate (whether a Neronian or Domitianic date), it should be stated with a less than firm conviction.[12] Even scholars who argue for a particular date are not completely sure. For example, George H. van Kooten, who proposes a Neronian date, states that this period is one in which "Revelation can *most plausibly* be situated."[13] Similarly, Adela Yarbro Collins, who suggests a Domitianic date, states that "*it seems best*" to appeal to Irenaeus' remark about John witnessing his visions at the end of Domitian's reign.[14] Deciding on a certain time of writing is, however, important since the impetus for John's text varies in each case and can have an effect on how Revelation is interpreted.[15]

In this book, I maintain, with the majority of contemporary critical scholars, that the Domitianic date is the most plausible for Revelation's composition.[16] During this time, the persecution of

---

12. Aune argues that both dates are accurate in some respects. "The position taken in this commentary is that *both* views contain aspects of the correct solution, since it appears that while the final edition of Revelation was completed toward the end of the reign of Domitian . . . , the first edition of the book was composed as much as a generation earlier based on written and oral apocalyptic traditions that reach back into the decade of the ad 60s" (ibid., lviii, emphasis original). Aune's argument regarding the two sources of Revelation (before the final form), however, has been debated. See, for example, Ian Paul, "Ebbing and Flowing: Scholarly Developments in Study of the Book of Revelation," *The Expository Times* 119, no. 11 (2008): 525. Through a detailed study of word frequencies, he concludes that "words occurring with particular frequencies in the whole of Revelation are distributed across all sections of the text without any particular correlation to different section divisions" (525). G. K. Beale also sides with the consensus that Revelation was written by one author, "though he certainly alludes to many OT, Jewish, and Greco-Roman sources" (*The Book of Revelation*, 34).

13. George H. van Kooten, "The Year of the Four Emperors and the Revelation of John: The 'Pro-Neronian' Emperors Otho and Vitellius, and the Images and Colossus of Nero in Rome," *JSNT* 30 (2007): 241, emphasis added.

14. Collins, *Crisis and Catharsis*, 76, emphasis added.

15. Beale claims that "one can in fact affirm the early date or the late date without the main interpretative approach being affected. Under either dating position the book could be understood as a polemic against Rome and especially against compromise with ungodly Roman culture" (*The Book of Revelation*, 4). While Beale's statement certainly holds true, as John and his community (in either time) wrestle with negotiating the Roman Empire, a deeper, clearer understanding of the social situation during the writing of this text (which varies in each time period) can greatly affect the way the text is understood. Additionally, although Beale states that "there are no single arguments that point clearly to the early or the late date," he goes on to say that "the early date could be right, but the cumulative weight of evidence points to the late date" (ibid.).

Christians was local and sporadic. One would have to go to the empire-wide persecution of Decius of 250, or the Great Persecution by Diocletian in 303, to witness systemic, state-sponsored persecution.[17] I, therefore, embrace the idea that perhaps John was writing in between two persecutions, which would explain his message of endurance and judgment to communities of Christians. Now that the dating of Revelation has been established, let us explore the social setting in which John wrote in order to speculate the occasion for its writing.

Social Setting

During the time Revelation was written, there was no separation between the secular and the religious. S. R. F. Price argues in his *Rituals and Power: the Roman Imperial Cult in Asia Minor* that Roman imperial cults "confound our expectations about the relationship between religion, politics, and power."[18] Subjects of Rome had to make sense of the new reality that they inhabit; the emperor, who they had never seen and would never see, had absolute power. Thus,

16. For a comprehensive presentation of internal and external evidence used to support either an early or late date for Revelation, see, e.g. ibid., 4–27.
17. Loren L. Johns notes that in the text itself, there are only three mentions of a past or present *experience* of persecution (1:9; 2:13; and 6:9-11), and all the rest refer to persecution that is *anticipated* (cf. 2:10-11; 7:13-14; 11:7-9; 12:11; 16:6; 17:6; 18:24; 19:2; 20:4-6). A thorough examination of these passages, Johns argues, suggests that "evidence [of extensive persecution] is not as clear as one might think" (*The Lamb Christology of the Apocalypse of John: An Investigation into Its Origins and Rhetorical Force* [Tübingen: Mohr Siebeck, 2003], 122). For an examination of some of these passages, see also Collins, *Crisis and Catharsis*, 70–71.
18. Price, *Rituals and Power: The Roman Imperial Cult in Asia Minor* (New York: Cambridge University Press, 1986), 1. This texts provides an in-depth analysis of the inextricable ties between notions of the secular and religious as they pertain to the Roman imperial cults in Asia Minor, particularly in the first three centuries ce. Price's work has been described as "the dividing point in the history of research" on the Roman imperial cult in the field of classics (Michael Naylor, "The Roman Imperial Cult and Revelation," *Currents in Biblical Research* 8, no. 2 [2010]: 209). Prior to Price's aforementioned work, many scholars affirmed a stark distinction between the secular and the religious, and therefore, the Roman imperial cult was viewed as a strictly political phenomenon. See Naylor's article for a more detailed investigation of this topic.

they assimilated this new reality to the religious realities that were familiar to them by incorporating this external power of Rome "within the framework of traditional cults of the gods."[19]

A major polemical target in Revelation was the institution and observance of emperor worship, as evidenced by the prominence of the imperial cult in the text. John's contentious views about these imperial practices reflect the fact that the majority of the cities in Asia Minor were devoted to its advancement. However, countering emperor worship represents just one of the reasons why John may have written Revelation. The Apocalypse, by and large, is centrally about the relationship between Christianity and Rome in different facets, including Rome's economic exploitation, brutality, and politics of persuasion.

The imperial cult in the first century has frequently been viewed by the majority of scholars as the main reason the Apocalypse of John was written. However, it is important to realize that the imperial cult is synecdochal for the Roman Empire as a whole. Wes Howard-Brook and Anthony Gwyther argue,

> John's confrontation with the empire should not be reduced to a simple critique of the imperial cult. . . . In fact, the critique of Rome in Revelation is far broader than that of the imperial cult. While the imperial cult was a clear sign that the Roman Empire had transgressed the prerogatives of God, Revelation casts a critical eye on Rome's economic exploitation, its politics of seduction, its violence, and its imperial hubris or arrogance. To oppose the Roman Empire necessarily involved a rejection of the spirituality that helped the empire run like a well-oiled machine. Yet the rejection of that spirituality, manifest in the imperial cult, was part of a total rejection of the empire. This is a consequence of the inseparability of religion and politics in antiquity.[20]

---

19. Price, *Rituals and Power*, 1. Price thus argues that when these imperial cults are viewed simply as political observances, we are guilty of imposing modern conceptions of religion such as "Christianizing assumptions and categories" on an ancient phenomenon (ibid., 2).

20. Wes Howard-Brook and Anthony Gwyther, *Unveiling Empire: Reading Revelation Then and Now* (Maryknoll, NY: Orbis, 1999), 116.

John's attack on the imperial cult is thus representative of his attack on the Roman Empire as a whole. The imperial cult, "an indispensable element of the imperial order," was a major part of the "social glue" that bound the people together.[21] It not only refers to the worship of the emperor, but also reflects the relationship of the people with the emperor through "imperial statues, temples, inscriptions, coins, public festivals, and holidays."[22]

The imperial cult begins with Julius Caesar and progresses to Domitian and beyond.[23] Steven J. Friesen states that the imperial cult was extremely influential in the life of Roman Asia; however, it was not more influential under Nero or Domitian. He writes, "The two periods in which scholars have tried to locate the composition of Revelation [that of Nero and Domitian] have not yet produced much evidence to suggest any great increase in imperial cult activities in Asia."[24] John's multiple references to the imperial cult specifically,[25] were therefore, directed to the imperial way of life generally. One of the main issues that John addresses is the notion of eating meat sacrificed to idols, to which we shall now turn.

In chapter 2, John refers to the relationship between the figure of Jezebel[26] and the Nicolaitans (2:6, 15, 20) and their eating meat

---

21. Ibid., 102.
22. Ibid.
23. Julius Caesar was the first to be deified, albeit posthumously. He was declared *Divus Julius.*
24. Friesen, *Imperial Cults and the Apocalypse of John: Reading Revelation in the Ruins* (Oxford: Oxford University Press, 2001), 148. "The period of Nero seems to have been rather quiet with regard to imperial worship. . . . The evidence shows that imperial cult practices in Asia during this period were not unusual for their time. . . . The evidence for imperial cults in Asia from the Domitianic period also fit within the mainstream of imperial cult practice. There is no sign of exaggerated claims alleged for this period" (ibid., 148–50). Friesen concludes that "Revelation studies should focus less on alleged excesses in imperial cults under Nero and Domitian and more on the normative character of imperial cult activity" (ibid., 135).
25. For example, this is seen in the frequency with which the word *worship* is used in chapter 13(vv. 4, 8, 12, and 15).
26. The general assumption is that Jezebel, like Balaam in 2:14—a name that equals "false prophet" in the Jewish tradition of John's day—is a symbolic name. The author derived the name *Jezebel* from 1 Kgs. 16:31, which states the marriage of Ahab, king of Israel (860–850 B. C. E.), to

sacrificed to idols (*eidōlothyta*) and fornication (*porneusai*).[27] Scholars have argued that eating meat sacrificed to idols corresponds to a participation in the imperial cult. Brian K. Blount, for example, asserts that according to John, "persons who eat meat that has been sacrificed to foreign gods give credence to the reality and lordship of those gods; those persons have therefore prostituted themselves to a foreign faith."[28] Scholars debate the relationship between Revelation 2–3 and 1 Corinthians 8–10 regarding eating meat sacrificed to idols.[29] Paul argues for a situational ethic. It is acceptable for the strong in the faith to partake of such meat, because for them the gods of the idols do not really exist. However, it is not permissible if by eating meat you weaken the faith of others. It is commonly argued that Paul's stance on this issue would have been close to Jezebel's.[30] Nevertheless, John refuses to make exceptions based on spiritual maturity. His fundamental problem with this rival female Christian

Jezebel, daughter of King Ethbaal of the Sidonians. Jezebel is infamously known for influencing Ahab to worship Canaanite gods.

27. Further on the close connection between the Nicolaitans and Jezebel (and Balaam), see DeSilva, *Seeing Things John's Way*, 58–63; and "The Social Setting of the Revelation to John," 292–96. Fornication does not refer to sexual activity, but rather, from the Jewish Scriptures, is metaphoric of idolatry—unfaithfulness to one's god with whom one is supposed to be in covenant. Thus, fornication and eating food sacrificed to idols are just two names for the same thing. John uses these phrases to "indict prophetic circles and other members of the seven churches for participating in civic and imperial society" (Leonard L. Thompson, "Ordinary Lives: John and His First Readers," in *Reading the Book of Revelation: A Resource for Students*, ed. David L. Barr [Boston: Brill, 2003], 44). For further discussion on the symbolic use of fornication, see, e.g., Thompson, *The Book of Revelation*, 121–24; and Paul B. Duff, *Who Rides the Beast? Prophetic Rivalry and the Rhetoric of Crisis in the Churches of the Apocalypse* (Oxford: Oxford University Press, 2001), 51–59. Duff, for example, argues that John makes a strong connection between "Jezebel" and "Babylon," with regard to the eating of εἰδωλόθυτα [*eidōlothyta*] and the practicing of πορνεύω [*porneuō*], in order to "paint 'Jezebel' as an undisciplined woman, unfit to lead" (112).

28. Blount, *Revelation*, 10.

29. See, e.g., Aune, *Revelation 1–5*, 191–95. See also DeSilva, *Seeing Things John's Way*, 58–63, and "The Social Setting of the Revelation to John," 290–91.

30. "The 'strong' at Corinth—to some extent Paul himself, Jezebel, the Nicolaitans, and Christian Gnostics—thus shared in a similar attitude towards urban life, although they did not share the same philosophical and theological beliefs" (Thompson, *The Book of Revelation*, 123).

THE BOOK OF REVELATION

leader and the Nicolaitans is that they excessively accommodate themselves to the cultural norms of Roman society.

Thompson notes, however, that not all Asian Christians experienced or viewed the Roman Empire with the same stark perspective as John. Although it was a reality that

> anyone could be charged with being a Christian [and killed if found guilty] at any time, . . . those settled in the cities who made a living by "buying and selling," participating in the peace and prosperity of the empire and using their connections for spreading the Christian faith, would discount John's judgment that they carried the "mark of the beast," subject to evil Rome (Rev 13:17).[31]

DeSilva adds that those who accommodated to Roman society may have viewed it as a means of community survival by preventing complete marginalization that would lead to their demise, all the while "preserving the essential meaning [of their Christian beliefs] unharmed."[32] Alternatively, Schüssler Fiorenza highlights the fact that "whereas the vast majority of the population suffered from colonialist abuses of power, exploitation, slavery, and famine, some citizens in the senatorial province of Asia enjoyed the benefits of Roman commerce and peace as well as the comforts and splendor of urban life and Hellenistic culture."[33]

These insights aid in highlighting the possible perspectives of John's opponents; nevertheless, it is still John's revelation, and *his* side of the story. "The text reinterpreted the audience's experiences,

---

31. Thompson, "Ordinary Lives," 43.
32. DeSilva, "The Social Setting of the Revelation to John," 294; *Seeing Things John's Way*, 61.
33. Elisabeth Schüssler Fiorenza, *Revelation: Vision of a Just World*, Proclamation Commentaries (Minneapolis: Fortress Press, 1991), 127. She continues, "If Revelation stresses the economic exploitation and oppression perpetrated by Babylon/Rome's imperialist power, then it expresses an assessment of life in Asia Minor that was not necessarily shared by all Christians" (ibid.). Beale notes that the "economic factor was likely the reason that the teaching of Jezebel gained such a following" (*The Book of Revelation*, 261).

transforming their perspective and creating the potential for conflict."[34]

With the imperative to "Come out of her, my people" (Rev. 18:4; cf. Isa. 48:20; Jer. 50:8), John—a radical separatist—urges Christians to completely remove themselves from the Roman way of life, no matter the consequences. John is aware that this abandonment of Roman livelihood would not only be a difficult task for Christians because of the prevalence of the imperial cult in their society, but would also open them up to ostracism and persecution. In addition, "Christian abstention from emperor worship would have created difficulties regarding participation in other social organizations," such as trade guilds, and thus jeopardize the economic status and livelihood of successful Christians.[35] Nevertheless, John insists that Christians take a stand.

I agree with the majority of Revelation scholars that the persecution of Christians *before* John wrote was not virulent

---

34. Steven J. Friesen, "The Beast from the Land: Revelation 13:11–18 and Social Setting," in Barr, *Reading the Book of Revelation*, 64.

35. Naylor, "The Roman Imperial Cult and Revelation," 221. "Since there were many public festivals in each of the major cities of first century Asia Minor, we can envision the bind economically successful Christians often find themselves in" (Duff, *Who Rides the Beast?*, 53). For example, most of the meat sacrificed to idols was shared in communal meals, which "consisted of, among others, people who were in crafts and trades, who shared in civic responsibilities, and who were on the whole probably of the wealthier stratum of leadership in early Christian churches" (Thompson, *The Book of Revelation*, 123–24). As DeSilva notes, a "widely held view [is] that early Christianity was comprised largely of artisans and craftspersons" ("The Social Setting of the Revelation to John," 291). Additionally, cities had a lot of trade guilds that met regularly for communal meals, in which the emperor would be routinely honored. Food, including meat, would be distributed that might have been sacrificial meat. Beale notes that particularly in Thyatira, a city that was "the economic hub of a large number of prosperous trade guilds [all of which had patron deities] . . . Christian guild members would be expected to pay homage to pagan gods at official guild meetings, which were usually festive occasions often accompanied by immoral behavior. Nonparticipation would lead to economic ostracism" (*The Book of Revelation*, 261). Blount highlights that in Pergamum, "complicity in artisan, trade, and funeral associations allowed for upward social and economic mobility. They passed themselves off as Roman cultic devotees in order to avail themselves of Roman resources [unlike the Christians in Smyrna whose refusal to accommodate led to poverty and persecution]" (*Revelation*, 9).

persecution, in which worship of the emperor was being forced through very direct means. State-sponsored persecution under Domitian is not the context in which Revelation was produced; rather, during this time, as I asserted above, persecution was local and sporadic. Needless to say, scholars have attempted to ascertain what may have prompted John to write so urgently and uncompromisingly, and to foresee such imminent persecution. It is important at this juncture, therefore, to survey some of the major arguments that attempt to describe the situation behind Revelation. The following scholars wrestled with the relationship between the actual world and the narrative world of Revelation.

Occasion

Adela Yarbro Collins rejects the notion that Revelation was written as consolation for Christians undergoing "pressing external circumstances," such as pressure to engage in the imperial cult.[36] By highlighting John's rhetoric of crisis, she illustrates that John wrote this book "to point out a crisis that many of them [his fellow Christians] did not perceive."[37] It had nothing to do with past persecutions. Appealing to psychological, sociological, and anthropological studies, Collins states that with regard to intense crisis, "the crucial element is not so much whether one is actually oppressed as whether one *feels* oppressed."[38] Although there was no

---

36. Collins, *Crisis and Catharsis*, 77. Collins's view sharply opposes the "standard assumption" that Ian Paul states was held by many scholars for most of the twentieth century; namely, that Revelation "was written to Christians during a period of persecution or severe pressure and as an encouragement to them" (Paul, "Ebbing and Flowing," 523). This belief was based on the "sense of conflict and accusatory tone" in the language of the text itself, as well as the widespread belief that Christians were oppressed by Domitian in the late first century (ibid.). Certainly, others such as Leonard Thompson (to be discussed below) have gone in other directions as well.
37. Collins, *Crisis and Catharsis*, 77.
38. Ibid., 84, emphasis original.

intense persecution of Christians under Domitian, Collins notes that other factors, such as conflict of the Christian community with the Jews,[39] "mutual antipathy" toward the Gentiles, and unstable relations with Rome may have led to John's perceived crisis.[40] She states that John amplifies his perceived crisis by projecting it onto a "cosmic screen," which, in the end, provides catharsis for his readers by "clarify[ing] and objectify[ing] the conflict. Fearful feelings are vented by the very act of expressing them, especially in this larger-than-life and exaggerated way."[41] According to Collins, John employs apocalyptic rhetoric and the inclusion of catharsis in order to

39. Beale describes the tension between Jews and Christians after 70 C.E. "Jewish oppression of the churches of Smyrna (2:9) and possibly of Philadelphia (3:9)," for example, may be based on that fact that "the Jews made it clear to local government officials that Christians were not a legitimate sect within Judaism [which was allowed throughout the Empire] but a new religion, whose adherents had no legal right to practice their religion outside Palestine" (*The Book of Revelation*, 31). DeSilva also notes that "now that there was every indication that Roman confusion with regard to the distinction between Jew and Christian would be quickly resolved, it was the political cult, the cult with the power of life and death because administered by the local governor, which stood out as the place of a decisive standoff . . . [John was right to say that] these things would 'shortly come to pass,' [because] within fifteen years, confessing or cursing Christ, offering or not offering incense to the image of the emperor 'as to a god,' would become a life and death issue, a conscientious and rigorous trial, almost inquisition, for the Christian communities in Bithynia" ("The Social Setting of the Revelation to John," 290).

40. Collins, *Crisis and Catharsis*, 84–110. Eight years later, DeSilva acknowledges Collins's identification of the aforementioned factors, but states that they more accurately refer to an "assessment of the *larger* [social] situation" ("The Social Setting of the Revelation to John," 287). He then presents four factors that he believes are not only closer to *John's* analysis of the social situation, but also may "provide a closer key to the text itself": "(1) the hostility of the synagogue, (2) the external demand for conformity, (3) the internal threat of accommodation, and (4) the internal threat of distortion of the counter-definitions that define *communitas*" (ibid., emphasis original). DeSilva concludes that Revelation is a prophetic document in which John "perceives the shape of things to come, and seeks through the *medium* of apocalyptic to deliver a word of the Lord which will prepare the churches to meet the coming crisis effectively, that is, in such a way as to preserve *communitas* rather than to accommodate to the *societas*" ("The Social Setting of the Revelation to John," 302, emphasis added). "He thus enables the Christians in Asia Minor to reconsider how they will act in the world, freeing them from responding to the demands of a political and economic system as if these were the ultimate forces to be reckoned with and enabling them to respond instead to the invisible, but truly ultimate, God" (DeSilva, *Seeing Things John's Way*, 14).

41. Collins, *Crisis and Catharsis*, 153. Blount does not refer to a "cosmic screen" as Collins does, but he likens John to a "great sports coach who tries to rally his team before the most important game of their season. He wants to whip up a frenzy that will lift them to physical and emotional highs where confessing a subversive allegiance to Christ before hostile forces that promote the

create a tension between the Christian community and the imperial cult. He constructed this tension "for readers unaware of it, to heighten it for those who felt it already, and then to overcome it in an act of literary imagination," which is the Apocalypse.[42]

Leonard Thompson argues that the situation behind the book of Revelation does not pertain to any crisis, whether or not it was perceived. He opposes the views that Domitian was a tormenter of Christians, and that Christians were harassed by imperial and civic authorities. Instead, he posits that the basis of John's dissenting rhetoric against empire is rooted in ideological tensions between two parts of a single "dynamic cultural system"; namely, John's "literary religious vision" and "the world of actual, social relations."[43] Thompson writes, "In a nutshell, the conflict and crisis in the Book of Revelation between Christian commitment and the social order derive from John's perspective on Roman society rather than from significant hostilities in the social environment. . . . There is a crisis orientation in the Book of Revelation, but it is characteristic of the genre."[44] This genre, Thompson asserts, is more appropriately acknowledged as "revelatory literature," a "more basic element" of the apocalyptic genre.[45] This is not only because the writer "reveals" knowledge—namely, the point of view of the seer—that contrasts the knowledge of the Roman public order, but also because the apocalyptic genre entails "the formulation of 'crisis situations,'" which may or may not emerge from, or result in, social or political unrest, and therefore, "tells us nothing about the social and political

---

lordship of Rome becomes not only a possibility but also an imperative" (Blount, *Revelation*, 13).

42. Collins, *Crisis and Catharsis*, 141.
43. Thompson, *The Book of Revelation*, 8.
44. Ibid., 175.
45. Ibid., 192.

situation."[46] In other words, John "provokes crisis rather than reflects it" in his writing.[47]

Elisabeth Schüssler Fiorenza, in an earlier work, *The Book of Revelation: Justice and Judgment*, argues that persecution during the writing of Revelation was real, despite the lack of pressing evidence, the latter of which was due to the tainted and biased perspective of Roman history. Appealing to Roman sources that state that harassment and denunciation occurred not only in the later years of Domitian, but also even until Trajan's time, she asserts that John "has adopted the 'perspective from below' and expressed the experiences of those who were powerless, and in constant fear of denunciation."[48] Schüssler Fiorenza modifies her argument, albeit not significantly, in her later work, *Revelation: Vision of a Just World*, most probably due to recent scholarship, by stating that the issue of the existence of actual persecution is debated. "Whether Revelation's theological world of vision was engendered by a situation of persecution and conflict or is the outcome of psychological resentment and of wishful projection by the author remains a debated question."[49] She maintains, however, that although official persecution may not have been ordered by Domitian or Trajan, it does not make the Christian experience of persecution fictional or unfamiliar.[50] John's rhetoric resonates with what happened in the past—memories of persecution under Nero in 64 C.E.[51]—as well the "increase of harassments and difficulties" that may come in the near future.[52]

---

46. Ibid., 175, 192.
47. Paul, "Ebbing and Flowing," 528.
48. Elisabeth Schüssler Fiorenza, *The Book of Revelation: Justice and Judgment*, 2nd ed. (Minneapolis: Fortress Press, 1998), 9.
49. Schüssler Fiorenza, *Vision of a Just World*, 7.
50. Ibid., 127.
51. Ibid. Rev. 13:7, "Also it [the first beast] was allowed to make war on the saints and to conquer them," and John's introduction of the woman Babylon in 17:6, who is described as being drunk with the blood of the saints and witnesses to Jesus, are often viewed by scholars as a reference to Nero's persecution of Christians—the first and, for almost a century, most intense persecution.

Paul B. Duff posits yet another perspective, since, by the publication of his work, he states that "none has provided a fully adequate alternative explanation for the text's creation."[53] Focusing on the letters to the seven churches in chapters 2 and 3, Duff notes that there is no "crisis" per se, but rather "some kind of disturbance or conflict [that] functioned as the catalyst for the book."[54] Similarly to Robert M. Royalty Jr.'s *The Streets of Heaven: The Ideology of Wealth in the Apocalypse of John*, Duff argues that the discord in Revelation emerges from a social conflict within the churches.[55] According to Duff, the letters to the seven churches highlight internal issues that the churches were dealing with, despite the "blatant anti-Roman polemic of the visions sections," which often causes the former to be ignored.[56] The conflict between the churches is based on issues such as social position, economic mobility of *some* Christians within

---

52. Ibid., 54. John A. T. Robinson notes that John reflects on the Neronian persecution, "and then dispatch[es] his warning of what could lie ahead of them" (Robinson, *Redating the New Testament* [Philadelphia: Westminster, 1976], 252–53). Beale also gives a detailed analysis of various verses that may speak to both past and future persecution (*The Book of Revelation*, 28–29). For example, he cites 6:9-11 (the vision of the martyred saints), stating that it "could include reference to past outbreaks of persecution, but certainly refers clearly also to future oppression, which will lead up to the consummation (so 6:11)" (29). Robert H. Mounce also notes that "within the book itself are indications that the storm of persecution is about to break" (*The Book of Revelation*, rev. ed., New International Commentary on the New Testament [Grand Rapids: Eerdmans, 1998], 17). Blount concurs: "The problem [during John's time] lay with the imminent conflict he knew *would* erupt if his hearers and readers lived out the kind of nonaccommodating Christianity that he himself professed and refused to back away from the faith when Asia Minor officials demanded that they do so" (*Revelation*, 12, emphasis original).

53. Duff, *Who Rides the Beast?*, 14.

54. Ibid.

55. "The actual conflict that precipitated the 'crisis of the Apocalypse' was not conflict with the Romans or the Jews. Rather, it was conflict within the Christian churches over the authority of John and his circle of prophets against the authority of other Christian teachers, apostles, and prophets" (Robert M. Royalty Jr., *The Streets of Heaven: The Ideology of Wealth in the Apocalypse of John* [Macon, GA: Mercer University Press, 1998], 241). Royalty notes that by comparing the "high" social status and economic wealth one can receive with God and Jesus in the New Jerusalem with a low one that one can receive with Rome, John hoped to win Christians over to his worldview. Duff, however, discounts this portion of Royalty's arguments, stating that "John's audience . . . are themselves striving for the 'low status wealth' of merchants [of Rome]," especially those at "the bottom of the economic ladder" (*Who Rides the Beast?*, 13).

56. Duff, *Who Rides the Beast?*, 14.

Roman society, and theological difference with rival church leaders such as the Nicolaitans, those who follow the teachings of Balaam, and Jezebel.[57] John's rhetorical strategy, therefore, is to persuade his readers that the church was in a crisis due to the teachings of rival church leaders who are not only "threat[ening] the integrity of the church," but also his own authority.[58]

Conclusion

Fruitful scholarship builds upon itself. Certainly, the scholars I have discussed thus far have contributed to the advancement of scholarly analysis of the correlation between the history behind the text of Revelation and the story that Revelation actually tells. I think Duff was correct in saying that "a *fully* adequate alternative explanation for the text's creation" has not yet been provided; however, instead of positing another stand-alone interpretation, I believe that a *fuller*, and thus, more accurate understanding of this relationship is one that combines the arguments of several scholars—the works of whom I think are more complementary than contradictory.[59] For example, I agree with the majority of scholars that a state-wide Domitianic persecution did not occur at the time of writing; however, there was some type of crisis that John perceived or actually experienced, both from the Roman state via the imperial cult leading to Christian accommodation, and from competition within the churches themselves. While I do not agree with Thompson's view that negates the existence of any crisis, his analysis of the crisis-fixated nature of the apocalyptic genre itself proves helpful. I find Duff's assessment of

---

57. Ibid., 14–15. The "three terms—Nicolaitans, Balaam, and Jezebel—theologically label probably the same group of Christian prophets. . ." (Schüssler Fiorenza, *Vision of a Just World*, 56).

58. Duff, *Who Rides the Beast?*, 14–15.

59. Cf. ibid., 14.

Thompson most appropriate: Thompson "is forced to admit that the cognitive minority of Christians in Asia Minor might perceive a crisis between itself and the cognitive majority."[60] As Collins noted earlier, albeit in different terms, a "crisis" is still a crisis, whether it is abstract or concrete.[61]

Revelation is a text written with a sense of urgency, employing metaphors and grave images to heighten the awareness of the tension not only between John's community and the Roman Empire, but also among rival Christian communities, and including a demand for a call to resist. The attack on the imperial cult, which stands synecdochically for the Roman Empire as a whole, saturates certain of its central pages. Since there are no intense persecutions of Christians going on at this time, some of the Christians are beginning to get comfortable. As suggested by the treatment of the characters of Jezebel and the Nicolaitans, some are viewed as too accommodating of Roman culture and ideals, an attitude that generates competition among, and internal conflict within, the churches. John, therefore, pushes against hybridity in Revelation, and urges the Christians to separate themselves from Roman life, and endure. The latter part of his message, to endure, is included because John is well aware that a rejection of Rome elicits tension and danger. A major function of the book is to prepare the people for this; it is a preparation for martyrdom, which is why the word *witness* (*martys*) and its cognates frequently occur.[62] It is a word that signals "active engagement,

---

60. Ibid., 13.
61. Collins, *Crisis and Catharsis*, 84.
62. The word *martys* occurs five times (1:5; 2:13; 3:14; 11:3; and 17:6), and its feminine counterpart, *martyria*, appears nine times (1:2, 9; 6:9; 11:7; 12:11, 17; 19:10 [twice]; and 20:4). The verb *martyreō* occurs four times (1:2, 22:16, 18, 20). Richard Bauckham notes that John's "thoroughgoing prophetic critique of the system of Roman power," is due to the "evil of the Roman system," and includes unwavering Christian disassociation, which will most likely lead to their persecution. Despite the martyrdoms that have occurred (2:13; 6:9-10; 16:6; and 17:6), Bauckham understands persecution to be local and sporadic. Nevertheless, "John sees that the nature of Roman power is such that, if Christians are faithful witnesses to God, then they must

not sacrificial passivity."[63] Come what may, in the words of Blount, John's "prophetic charge" to the Christians is to "stand up and then opt out."[64]

suffer the inevitable clash between Rome's divine pretensions and their witness to the true God" (*The Theology of the Book of Revelation* [New York: Cambridge University Press, 1993], 38).

63. Blount, *Revelation*, 13. He goes on to say that "witness" in the first-century refers to one's "provocative testimony" and not necessarily the end of a "passive life" (13).
64. Ibid., 11.

4

The Woman Babylon and Marks of Empire

*Reading Revelation with a Postcolonial Womanist
Hermeneutics of Ambiveilance*

What I have been, I have had to be. I am a woman trying to make it in
a man's world.
Renita J. Weems[1]

The woman of Revelation 17 is no ordinary woman.[2] She appears

---

1. Renita J. Weems, *Just a Sister Away: A Womanist Vision of Women's Relationships in the Bible* (Philadelphia: Innisfree, 1988), 39, emphasis added.
2. Stephen D. Moore notes that a female symbol is used for imperial Rome because the "prototypical evil empire in Jewish tradition and the code name for Rome in Revelation, was already represented as female in that tradition" ("Metonymies of Empire: Sexual Humiliation and Gender Masquerade in the Book of Revelation," in *Postcolonial Interventions: Essays in Honor of R. S. Sugirtharajah*, ed. Tat-siong Benny Liew [Sheffield, UK: Sheffield Phoenix, 2009], 71). "As scholars have long surmised, Revelation renames Rome as 'Babylon', confers the name of another city upon it, because that city, also an empire, epitomizes in Jewish scripture and tradition human empire at its most destructive, but also at its most seductive. And that predatory and alluring empire (whose imagined antithesis is the Empire of God) comes already sexed and gendered, minimally at least, in the tradition that John of Revelation has inherited and internalized, Babylon being a feminine noun in both Hebrew (*Bābel*) and Greek (*Babylōn*)" (ibid., 71–72). See also John W. Marshall, "Gender and Empire: Sexualized Violence in John's

to live the good life. We find her exhibiting royalty: "The woman was clothed in purple and scarlet, and adorned with gold and jewels and pearls, holding in her a golden cup" (17:4).[3] Even John himself is captivated by her (17:6). Dressed by John, she represents Roman imperial power that will be destroyed and overtaken by God's empire.[4] However, this is not what makes her exceptional. She is marked on her forehead with an inscription that states, "Babylon

Anti-Imperial Apocalypse," in *A Feminist Companion to the Apocalypse of John*, ed. Amy-Jill Levine and Maria Mayo Robbins, Feminist Companion to the New Testament and Early Christian Writings, vol. 13 [New York: T & T Clark International, 2009], 27–28. Marshall adds, "John's depicting Rome/Roma as Babylon was also based on the long tradition of casting enemy capitals as whores. The choice of a female representation of Rome also reverses Roman statuary and coinage's traditional representation of Rome as male and conquered nations as female" (ibid.).

3. A common reading of the woman Babylon's dress is that it reflects that of a courtesan. "The description of the woman is drawn at least in part from the ancient courtesan *topos*. . . . Courtesans were used, particularly by moralist writers, as personifications of the vices, including incontinence, profligacy, covetousness, and flattery. . . . They had a recognizable way of dressing . . . and are often depicted as conspicuously well dressed" (David E. Aune, *Revelation 17–22* [Dallas: Thomas Nelson, 1998], 935). This familiar reading, as we will see, is challenged by Jennifer A. Glancy and Stephen D. Moore in their article, "How Typical a Roman Prostitute Is Revelation's 'Great Whore'?" (*Journal of Biblical Literature* 130, no. 3 [2011]: 551–69) based on a more accurate understanding of the word *pornē*. Moore asserts that in this verse (17:4), Babylon or "Roma [has been] stripped of her military attire and reclothed as a prostitute" ("Metonymies of Empire," 87). This is a "parody of the Roman imperial order"; John depicts the goddess Roma, known as having an "austere and noble personification," as "a tawdry whore" (ibid., 73). (I am aware that 17:4 continues with a description of what is *in* the cup, but will return to that below.)

4. Huber writes, "In Revelation, 'you are what you wear' and a significant part of John's description of the Whore focuses upon her attire, reflecting a traditional metaphorical connection between identity and appearance (IDENTITY IS APPEARANCE). . . . The reference to Babylon's purple garments is striking, as it was a color reserved for those at the top of the Roman social hierarchy and particularly for those associated with imperial powers. . . . The purple clothing suggests that this Great Whore not only dons imperial garb, she is an imperial woman" (Lynn R. Huber, *Thinking and Seeing with Women in Revelation* (New York: Bloomsbury/T & T Clark, 2013), 67–68, emphasis original).For a thorough analysis of not only John's reinscription of Roman imperial ideology, but also of his replacement of Rome's empire with God's empire, see chapter 5, "'The World Empire Has Become the Empire of Our Lord and His Messiah': Representing Empire in Revelation," in Moore's *Empire and Apocalypse: Postcolonialism and the New Testament*, Bible in the Modern World 12 (Sheffield, UK: Sheffield Phoenix, 2006), 97–121. Moore writes, "To construct God or Christ, together with their putatively salvific activities, from the raw materials of imperial ideology is not to shatter the cycle of empire but merely to transfer it to a transcendental plane, thereby reinscribing and reifying it" (ibid., 120).

the great, mother of whores [*pornōn*] and of earth's abominations" (17:5). Although markings on the body, such as tattoos and branding, were commonplace in antiquity, in the case of the woman Babylon, the mark of ownership on her forehead is linked to the profession of prostitution—details that, as we shall see, are consistent with her identification as a "brothel slave" [*pornē*].[5] This dual characterization of the woman Babylon, as an imperial figure (cf. 18:7: "I sit as a queen/empress (*basilissa*)," my translation) and as a slave, places her on both sides of the colonial relationship: she represents both the colonizer and the colonized.[6]

This twofold understanding of the woman Babylon, especially the identification of her as a slave, is not common in general Revelation scholarship. My reading of her in this regard is an essential connection that is made out of my own particular sociocultural location as a privileged African American woman.[7] When reading the Greek text of Revelation 17, and translating *pornē* as "brothel slave," there is a semiautomatic point, for me, where Revelation's characterization of the woman Babylon hooks into African American history.[8] Because of my particular cultural context, the description

---

5. Many classicists suggest that "throughout antiquity, the term *pornē* was, for all intents and purposes, a virtual synonym of *doulē* [female slave]" (ibid., 12).

6. I do not think that a slave and a colonized person are synonymous, as there are differences in their situations—potentially, the latter enjoys a degree of personal autonomy that the former does not. However, in this book, both terms will be used to describe the woman Babylon to denote her classification as *pornē* (a brothel slave), and to signify one side of her ambivalent characterization (the colonized).

7. Fernando F. Segovia, in talking about the move to cultural studies and the turn to the reader in biblical studies, writes, "Real readers lie behind all models of interpretation and all reading strategies, all recreations of meaning from texts and all reconstructions of history; further, all such models, strategies, recreations, and reconstructions are seen as constructs on the part of flesh-and-blood readers; and all such readers are themselves regarded as variously positioned and engaged in their own respective social locations" ("Cultural Studies and Contemporary Biblical Criticism: Ideological Criticism as Mode of Discourse," in *Reading from this Place*, Vol. 2: *Social Location and Biblical Interpretation in Global Perspective*, ed. Fernando F. Segovia and Mary Ann Tolbert [Minneapolis: Fortress Press, 2000], 7).

8. The use of ethnic language is found in several verses of Revelation. For example, David E. Aune writes, "Lists of three or (more frequently) four ethnic groups are found in six other passages in

of the woman Babylon (particularly, the punitive tattoo on her forehead) resonates racially with me. It is my historical and contemporary experience as an African American that compels me to maintain race as an analytical category along with the discussion of empire in my exegetical analysis—an important task, as discussed in chapter 1. It is important to note, however, that scholarship on slavery in antiquity does not commonly present ancient slavery as racialized, and with regard to Revelation, ethnic language is used to refer to peoplehood, rather than to those who share similar phenotypic characteristics.

Following the approach of Tina Pippin, whose work on the woman Babylon and particularly the depiction of her demise was the first of its kind, my reading strategy can be described as one of imaginative readerly engagement. Pippin writes,

> I realize that many biblical scholars want to revise and reconstruct the Apocalypse to relate it to modern sensibilities, but I want to take a postmodern turn: to read the Apocalypse as apocalypse (the designation the text gives itself), which involves entering into the fictional world as a participatory reader. I want to feel and see and hear and touch my way through the narrative. . . . This experience is cathartic, involving the emotional release of anger and grief and guilt and joy in the midst of

Revelation [in addition to 5:9], always in a polysyndetic list, but always in a different order. . . : (1) Rev 7:9, nations, tribes, peoples, tongues; (2) Rev 10:11, peoples, nations, tongues, kings; (3) Rev 11:9, peoples, tribes, tongues, nations; (4) Rev 13:7, tribe, people, language, nation; (5) Rev 14:6, nation, tribe, tongue, people; (6) Rev 17:15, peoples, crowds, nations, tongues" (*Revelation 1–5*; Word Biblical Commentary, vol. 52 [Dallas: Word, 1997], 362). (I also need to note the imperative in 18:4, "Come out of her, my people (*laos*)," where John urges his community to completely withdraw themselves from the Roman way of life, as this verse particularly relates to the woman Babylon.) "These lists," as Aune notes, "are meant to emphasize universality," since Christians "were drawn from many ethnic groups in the Roman empire," and therefore, did not "constitute an ethnic group themselves [leading] early Christian authors to refer to Christianity as a new people or a *tertium genus*, 'third race'" (ibid.). For deeper discussion of this type of Christian self-definition, see Denise Kimber Buell's, *Why This New Race: Ethnic Reasoning in Early Christianity* (New York: Columbia University Press, 2005). Buell focuses on the collective Christian identity, and its process of self-definition as a corporate body (over and against its Jewish counterparts and competing Christian communities), a process she calls "ethnic reasoning."

crisis. . . . Entering into the fictional world of the Apocalypse involves facing fear and a whole range of feelings.[9]

And this is exactly what happened to me as I engaged the woman Babylon's narrative. An unexpected rise of emotions—a whole range of them—welled up within me. I rejoiced with the completion of her demise. Representing empire with its domineering tactics, oppressive ideology, and inclination toward excess, I know who she is, what she has done, and of what she is capable; she deserves what she gets! I was sympathetic and sad. Denoting a female slave, violently abused and regarded as utterly dispensable, I also know her story, and I empathize with her plight. I was fearful. I know the negative connotations associated with her name, *Babylon*, and yet traces of all that she represents are recognizable in me. It is a revelation that still haunts me.

Nevertheless, it is important to explicitly state with the utmost clarity that my encounter with her text, and my interpretation thereof, is simply that—mine. Since "different real readers use different strategies and models in different ways, at different times, and with different results (different readings and interpretations) in light of their different and highly complex social locations," it is the case that my reading of the woman Babylon does not automatically reflect that of all African American women readers, although it may conjure up the collective memory of blacks in American slavery.[10]

As explicated in chapter 2, my interpretation of the woman Babylon engages and extends both feminist and African American trajectories of Revelation scholarship. It adds a fresh perspective in the "Great Whore" debate—the understanding of the figure Babylon as either a woman or a city, and the implications of such

---

9. Pippin, *Death and Desire: The Rhetoric of Gender in the Apocalypse of John*, Literary Currents in Biblical Interpretation (Louisville: Westminster John Knox, 1992), 16–17, 19.
10. Segovia, "Cultural Studies and Contemporary Biblical Criticism," 7.

classification—by bringing the categories of race, ethnicity, and class to bear on it. To recall, Tina Pippin employs a gender-critical approach to Revelation to critique the use and implications of gendered metaphors, which she asserts are dangerous to real women because the androcentric perspective underlying them helps to shape perceptions of reality.[11] Elisabeth Schüssler Fiorenza, while agreeing that Revelation posits a gender ideology that can be harmful for women, proposes that an examination of Revelation in both gender *and* political terms can help the reader to understand John's use of the conventionally coded feminine language for a city in his critique of empire.[12]

To describe the "Great Whore" debate as one between those who assert that metaphors matter and affect real women and those who oppose this view, as stated above, is inaccurate. The real question of the debate is how to respond and read for real women in one's analysis, both historically and theologically, and through which metaphors—woman or city?[13] My reading of the woman Babylon, which includes a consideration of the categories of race, ethnicity, and class, helps me to transcend this either/or dichotomy by highlighting the simultaneous duality of her characterization that should be held in tension; she is a brothel slavewoman *and* an empress/imperial city. Her participation in, and victimization by, imperial structures suggests that she is necessarily both/and, instead of either/or.

My reading of the woman Babylon also builds upon and complicates African American interpretations of Revelation. Instead of arguing that the text is essentially liberating, as expressed by

---

11. See Pippin, *Death and Desire*.
12. Schüssler Fiorenza, *The Power of the Word: Scripture and the Rhetoric of Empire* (Minneapolis: Fortress Press, 2007), 135–36.
13. I am indebted to New Testament scholar Melanie Johnson-DeBaufre for the insight she shared concerning the underlying issue of this debate.

scholars such as Brian K. Blount and Clarice J. Martin, I assert that a combined womanist (specifically, Martin's liberationist womanist approach) and postcolonial (drawing on extrabiblical postcolonial theory) approach illustrates that John does not present a *minority* report, but rather a *masculinist* minority report.[14] A postcolonial analysis highlights John's use of Roman imperial ideology displayed by his relegating and subjugating rhetoric. Certainly, John's reinscription of empire does not prevent him from being in solidarity with the oppressed; however, when this postcolonial lens is coupled with a womanist lens, this assertion changes. A womanist lens, which advocates for the well-being of *all* peoples, draws attention to, and seeks to counter the violent manner in which John deals with the woman Babylon. Although she represents a city, we cannot ignore the fact that John encases this city in feminine flesh.

John's detailed and vivid destruction of the *woman* Babylon (17:16), includes humiliation via the exposure of her naked body, the feasting on her flesh while she still has breath, and the burning up of whatever of her remains. John's carefully crafted description screams, "Look! Look at *her*!"[15] I find it really difficult to read this text and remain unaffected by the feminine-gendered devastation. It is hard for me to defer such imagery and remember that *she* is but a city. *She* has the same anatomical make-up as I do. *She* would have felt the contempt and disgust emanating from those who once were her loyal companions (17:2). *She*—with closed eyes or her head turned

14. See Blount, *Can I Get a Witness: Reading Revelation through African American Culture* (Louisville: Westminster John Knox, 2005), and Martin, "Polishing the Unclouded Mirror: A Womanist Reading of *Revelation* 18:13," in *From Every People and Nation: The Book of Revelation in Intercultural Perspective*, ed. David Rhoads (Minneapolis: Fortress Press, 2005), 82–109.
15. "The very first word of the book called Revelation, *apokalypsis* . . . implies the experience of seeing. . . . [John] coaxes his audience to look or envision with him. . . . Such vision-laden language in the text's opening verses primes the audience to think of the narrative as something to see and points to the importance of attending to the visual for understanding Revelation's interpretations" (Huber, *Thinking and Seeing with Women in Revelation*, 11–12).

away—would have felt the lingering gaze on her naked body, wondering how many are mentally raping her as they stare. *She* would have felt the agonizing pain as her flesh was being ripped from her body to be consumed as if she had a sign on her that said, "This is my body. Take. Eat all of it." (I wonder if they will remember her.) I can imagine that she would have felt these things because as a woman reading her text I did, and I abhor John for writing it. I can unequivocally say that this text has negative implications for real women. Therefore, contrary to the overall perspective of African American biblical interpretations of Revelation, I must assert that John does not, he simply cannot, write in *full* solidarity with the oppressed. Are not women included in this category?

I, therefore, propose a postcolonial womanist analysis that I call a hermeneutics of ambi*veil*ence. As discussed in chapter 1, this hermeneutics consists of two concepts, W. E. B. Du Bois's notion of the veil—a metaphorical covering that prevents African Americans from seeing themselves as they truly are—and Homi K. Bhabha's notion of ambivalence—a simultaneous attraction and repulsion experienced within a single individual, specifically under colonialism or its aftermath. This approach not only helps me to critically analyze the text of the woman Babylon by highlighting her duality—as simultaneously a brothel slavewoman and an empress/imperial city—but it also causes me to struggle with the tension that emerges from an engagement with such an ambivalent character. The woman Babylon functions as what Martin calls an "unclouded mirror" that reflects the conflicting characteristics within myself, and causes the veil that masks my own ambivalent characterization to be exposed.[16] As an African American woman, writing out of a very particular sociocultural context, and employing a hermeneutics of ambi*veil*ence,

---

16. Martin, "Polishing the Unclouded Mirror," 82.

I come face to face with an image of myself when I encounter the woman Babylon's text. I get glimpses of myself in her ambivalent identification as representing both imperial power as well as a victim of oppression. She is, therefore, more than just a metaphor, more than just a conventional code word for a city, because she reflects an image of me. So, what am I to do with her?[17]

Throughout this book, I employ ontological language when speaking about Babylon. I suggest that Babylon is a woman, an enslaved prostitute, and an empress/imperial city. Although these are metaphors, Babylon is also a literary character in a narrative, and therefore, as an implied reader I am led to imaginatively interact with, and relate to, *her*. This understanding frames the theoretical aspects of my interpretation.

My analysis shall proceed as follows: First, I discuss the larger context of Revelation around the issues of sealing and marking, and examine the practices of tattooing and branding in the Roman world as set forth by classicist C. P. Jones, in order to make sense of the inscription on the forehead of the woman Babylon. Second, I analyze the woman Babylon's marking, her association with prostitution, and the implications of the fact that she can be imaginatively identified as both a brothel slave and as an empress/imperial city. Finaly, I present a positional engagement with the text that shows how the dual characterization of the woman Babylon is one with which I, as a privileged African American woman, have an ambi*veil*ent relationship.

17. *Her* refers to both the woman Babylon and me as the reader.

Sealing and Marking in Revelation

"Marking" in the text of Revelation is described by different terms. Those who worship the beast and its image receive the mark (*charagma*) of the beast (13:16-17). The 144,000 in the company of the redeemed[18] are sealed (*sphragizō*) with the names of the Lamb and his Father (7:3-4; 14:1). Finally, Jesus has a name inscribed (*graphō*) on him when he returns in judgment (19:12, 16). Interestingly, the same word is used for the woman Babylon (17:5) and for Jesus; both of their names are *written* (*gegrammenon*) on them. The difference, however, lies in the locations of those names: Jesus is marked on his thigh (*mēros*), whereas, the woman Babylon is marked on her forehead (*metōpon*). These observations raise two questions: (1) What is the difference between the verbs "mark" (*charagma*), "seal" (*sphragizō*), and "write or inscribe" (*graphō*)?; (2) What is the significance of the location of the mark?

The word *charagma* appears in chapter 13, pertaining to the followers of the beast, and is a reference to a stamp or an imprinted mark.[19] Those who worship the beast and its image receive a mark either on their forehead (*metōpon*) or the right hand (13:16, 14:9). The term *sphragizō*, with reference to the 144,000, has three definitions, all of which are employed by John: (1) to mark with a seal for identification denoting ownership; (2) to seal for security; and, (3) since things sealed are concealed, it can also mean to hide or keep

---

18. For a comprehensive study about the identification of the 144,000, see, e.g., G. K. Beale, *The Book of Revelation: A Commentary on the Greek Text*, The New International Greek Testament Commentary (Grand Rapids: Eerdmans, 1999), 416–23. These identifications fall in two categories: those based on a literal interpretation ("a remnant of ethnic Israelites," "all ethnic Israel," or "a Christian remnant of ethnic Jews living in the first century"), and those based on a figurative one ("the complete number of God's people" or "the totality of the redeemed") (ibid).

19. The word *charagma* is found nine times in the New Testament, eight of which are found in Revelation: 13:16, 17; 14:9, 11; 15:2; 16:2; 19:20; and 20:4. The only other reference is made in Acts 17:29, and refers to something that is carved or sculpted, or a graven work such as an idol.

secret.[20] The 144,000 are sealed on their foreheads only (7:3; 9:4). Finally, the term *graphō* has the following connotations: to write, inscribe, or engrave.[21] The use of the word *graphō* associated with both the woman Babylon (17:5) and Jesus (19:16) leads me to draw yet another conclusion: the lexical meaning of the terms themselves is not as important as the location of the marking.

A comparative study of the three types of markings reveals a distinction between Jesus and the rest; Jesus is marked on his thigh

20. The word *sphragizō* is found fifteen times in the New Testament, eight occurrences of which are found in Revelation (7:3, 4 [twice], 5, 8; 10:4; 20:3; and 22:10). To mark with a seal for identification, and hence, indicating ownership occurs in Rev. 7:3, 4 (twice), 5, 8. See also Eph. 1:13, 4:30; 2 Cor. 1:22; John 6:27; and Tertullian, *The Prescription against Heretics* 40. To seal for security as a safety measure occurs in 20:3, when Satan is thrown into a pit that was sealed so that "he would deceive the nations no more." See also Matt. 27:66; *Gospel of Peter* 9:34; and *1 Clement* 43:3. To seal for the purposes of keeping secret occurs in Rev. 10:4, when John is told to "seal up what the seven thunders have said, and do not write it down," and in 22:10 when a seal is prohibited to block the prophecy of the book "for the time is near." Other interpretations of "seal," such as to certify the veracity of something and to seal for delivery (although not in Revelation) occurs in John 3:33 and Rom. 15:28, respectively.M. Eugene Boring associates sealing in antiquity with baptism: "'Sealing' . . . has particular overtones within the Pauline stream of tradition to which John and his churches belong. Incorporation into the body of Christ by baptism (1 Cor. 12:13) was sometimes pictured in Pauline churches as the seal which stamped the new Christian as belonging to God. . . . In the midst of the Roman threat baptism comes to have a new meaning: those who bear the mark of God are kept through (not from!) the coming great ordeal, whatever the beastly powers of evil may be able to do to them" (*Revelation*, Interpretation: A Bible Commentary for Teaching and Preaching [Louisville: Westminster John Knox, 1989], 129).Beale notes that "Ezekiel 9 is often correctly proposed as the best background for the divine sealing. There God commands an angel to put a mark on all genuine believers but instructs other angels to slay unfaithful Israelites. The mark on believers is to protect them from the coming wrath, which will be inflicted by the Babylonians and which unfaithful Israelites will suffer" (Beale, *The Book of Revelation*, 409). John's use of sealing, according to Beale, strays from the type of physical protection described in Ezekiel 9: "Uppermost in John's mind is . . . protection of the believers' *faith* and *salvation* from the various sufferings and persecutions that are inflicted on them, whether by Satan or by his demonic and earthly agents" (ibid, emphasis added). Exodus 12:7 and *Pss. Sol.* 15:6, 9 are also recalled due to the similarity of the function of the mark of the lambs' blood on the Hebrews' doors at Passover, and the mention of the seal of God on the righteous to protect them from the plagues, respectively (ibid., 409–10). Aune buttresses this notion of sealing as a means of divine protection of the 144,000 with a reference to Rev. 9:4, in which "only those people who do not have the seal of God on their foreheads" shall suffer from the plagues that comes forth after the blowing of the fifth trumpet.
21. The term *graphō* is a very common word in the New Testament, with twenty-nine references in Revelation alone.

(*mēros*) (19:16),[22] whereas all the other persons are marked on their right hand or, principally, their forehead (*metōpon*). Additionally, the writing on Jesus' thigh, "King of kings and Lord of lords" (19:16) is a reference to himself, and not anyone else, indicating independence from an external authority. This leads me to conclude that a mark on the forehead connotes a mark of ownership or loyalty in Revelation—to either Satan or to God.[23]

The 144,000 are the only ones explicitly labeled slaves (*douloi*) of God (7:3; 22:3, 6). They stand on Mount Zion with the Lamb (14:1), sing secret songs (14:3), and are redeemed from the earth (14:3). They are owned by, and faithful to, God and Christ. The other marked persons—those who worship the beast and its image, and the woman Babylon—are owned by, or loyal to, Satan, although they are not explicitly referred to as slaves (*douloi*). Additionally, other details connote ownership of these persons by the beast. The beast was given authority (*exousia*) by the dragon over "everyone whose name has not been written . . . in the book of life of the Lamb" (13:2, 7-8). To be aligned with the beast, such as the woman Babylon, also suggests that one is under the authority of the beast.[24] And those whom the

22. The word *mēron* appears only here in the entire New Testament. There is also no reference to *writing* on the thigh in the First Testament; however, the word *thigh* is used twenty-one times. Perhaps, based on the fact that majority of these references refer to a sign of honor and respect, the writing on Jesus's thigh should connote such a sign. (The name, "King of kings and Lord of lords" is also inscribed on Jesus' robe (19:16), a garb that further suggests honor.)

23. Beale writes, "In the Apocalypse names written on foreheads reveal the true character of people and their ultimate relationship, whether to God (7:3; 14:1; 22:4) or to Satan (13:16; 14:9; 20:4)" (*The Book of Revelation*, 857). He states that "σφραγίζειν [*sphragizein*] ('to seal') can . . . have the sense of 'to authenticate' and 'to designate ownership of,' which are included with the idea of 'protection.'" This understanding of *sphragizein* is "evident from the fact that John equates it with the name of Christ and God in 14:1 and 22:4" (ibid., 410–11). Beale also uses the association of the "mark" of the beast (that is, its name [13:17]) on the forehead of unbelievers to argue that the "seal" on the foreheads of the 144,000 is the divine name (ibid., 411).

24. "The 'name written on the forehead' of the whore reveals her seductive and idolatrous character, which further identifies her as on the side of the beast" (Beale, *The Book of Revelation*, 857–58).

beast was given authority over, worship [*proskyneō*] it, meaning they revere or pay homage to it to indicate respect or obeisance.[25]

A mark on the forehead also suggests that the bearers of this mark are protected. The 144,000 have "come out of the great ordeal," (7:14), and "will hunger no more, and thirst no more," (7:16) because "the Lamb at the center of the throne will be their shepherd" (7:17). Analogously, those who worship the beast and its image are economically protected. They are the ones permitted to buy and sell in the market places (13:17). Yet, what kind of protection does the woman Babylon receive? On the one hand, one may assume that she is granted the same financial advantage as the others who worship the beast because of her association with it, or because of her lavish attire. Caroline Vander Stichele writes,

> Albeit indirect, the only trace in the text that the whore is rewarded for her services is found in the description of her wealth [that is, her attire and accessories]. . . . [Although] the source of her luxury is never made explicit, the suggestion in the text seems to be that she is making profit from her lovers, one way or another. This connection may be fairly obvious as far as the wealth of Babylon as a colonial power is concerned, and it could even hold true for a whore.[26]

On the other hand, the woman Babylon is a brothel slave (*pornē*), and one must take into account the social reality of such sexual labor. Vander Stichele continues, "The cultural associations embedded in this discourse create a dynamic lens for characterizing the whore in purely negative terms, but the lens fails to engage the broader sociocultural contexts that engender prostitution in the ancient world and our own."[27] Although Babylon represents the imperial city of

---

25. Other references to the worship of the beast and its image are 13:4, 8, 12; 14:9, 11; 16:2; and 19:20.
26. Caroline Vander Stichele, "Re-membering the Whore: The Fate of Babylon according to Revelation 17.16," in Levine and Robbins, *A Feminist Companion to the Apocalypse of John*, 119.
27. Ibid.

Rome, *she* is also a sexually abused woman. "The two cannot be separated, and the dramatic consequences of such metaphorization are exposed in the violence done to [her]. The reader is supposed to rejoice in her death, but not every reader does—at least not the resistant reader."[28]

In his influential article on tattooing and branding in the ancient Mediterranean world, classicist C. P. Jones asserts that "the author [of Revelation] perhaps imagines the Woman not only as a whore, but as a whore of the most degraded kind, a tattooed slave."[29] His assertion is not only based on the fact that in the Roman world tattooing was commonly understood as a "sign of degradation," but also that it was usually inflicted as a form of punishment on the foreheads of slaves:[30]

> The penal tattooing of slaves seems to have been usual in the Hellenistic period. In the third century it is attested by a fragmentary legal code, one provision of which is that masters may not "sell slaves for export, nor tattoo (στίζειν) [*stizein*]" them. The ban seems only to have applied to good slaves, however, for another clause, referring to ones convicted of crimes, lays down that the injured party "shall give him not less

28. Ibid., 120.
29. C. P. Jones, "Tattooing and Branding in Graeco-Roman Antiquity" *The Journal of Roman Studies* 77 (1987): 151. See also Aune, *Revelation 17–22*, 936. Jones does not, however, attempt to tease out the implications of this statement.
30. Jones, "Tattooing and Branding," 146. Tattoos for "punitive purposes . . . came to the Greeks from the Persians, and was transmitted by the Greeks to the Romans" (ibid, 141). Aune writes that "slaves were tattooed on their foreheads, on the entire face, and sometimes on parts of the body such as the arm, hand, or leg. The tattoos could consist of texts, perhaps mentioning the crime committed; see Plato *Leges* 9.854D (LCL), 'Whosoever is caught robbing a temple, if he be a foreigner or a slave, his curse shall be branded on his forehead and on his hands'" (Aune, *Revelation 6–16* [Dallas: Word, 1998], 458). Jennifer A. Glancy (following Jones) mentions the jurist Ulpian, who "observed that some slaves were marked as chattel through fetters or branding, possibly a form of tattooing, often on the face. A slave who ran away would be placed in fetters or permanently tattooed to forestall future attempts to flee" (*Slavery in Early Christianity* [Minneapolis: Fortress Press, 2006], 13). Glancy notes Athenaeus's *Deipnosophists*, which includes descriptions of practices related to slavery along the Mediterranean trade routes: "Phyrgia supplied slaves, as did Pagasae. By noting that the slaves of Pagasae were often tattooed or branded . . . , the text implicitly draws attention to the many slaves who resisted enslavement and the practices of somatic marking, which enforced their corporal bondage" (ibid., 87). Pippin also notes that the name on the woman Babylon's forehead is "a sign of slavery" (*Death and Desire*, 65).

than a hundred lashes of the whip and tattoo his forehead (στιξάτω τὸ μέτωπον) [*stixatō to metōpon*]." In the same period there first appears a practice which may be as old as punitive tattooing itself, that of tattooing delinquent slaves with the name of their offence.[31]

The "profusion of evidence presented by Jones for tattooing in the ancient Mediterranean world, and the close associations with slavery and general degradation entailed in the practice," compel Jennifer A. Glancy and Stephen D. Moore to agree with Jones's statement regarding John's perception of the woman Babylon.[32] And I concur. The characterization of the woman Babylon as a brothel slave (*pornē*) intermingles issues of gender, ownership, profession, and the negative social implications in Roman culture. However, the other side of her characterization, namely, her association with, and participation in, empire is also firmly maintained. This is the paradox of the woman Babylon, and as the chapter proceeds, it is precisely this ambivalence that I see reflected in myself.

The Woman Babylon:
A Slavewoman *and* an Empress/Imperial City

Significantly, the woman Babylon is the only one marked on the forehead with a name: "Babylon the great, mother of whores (*pornōn*) and of the earth's abominations" (17:5).[33] This is the name that

31. Jones, "Tattooing and Branding," 148.
32. Glancy and Moore, "How Typical a Roman Prostitute," 559.
33. Beale states that "the first part of the name . . . 'Babylon the Great,' [was] already seen in 14:8 as an allusion to Daniel 4:27 MT (= 4:30 in LXX and English versions), where it reflects the extent of the king's power and glory" (*The Book of Revelation*, 858). In this text, King Nebuchadnezzar praises himself for building "magnificent Babylon . . . as a royal capital by [his own] mighty power and for [his own] glorious majesty," for which he is judged. Beale argues that "Babylon is called 'great' in Rev. 17:1, 5" not only because of "her power in any one age but also [because of] her influence and notoriety, which spans the ages" (ibid.). As "'mother' of idolaters" Babylon has "authoritative influence over and inspiration of the system of idolatry, which is an integral part of economic involvement" (ibid., 859).

associates her with prostitution, and aligns her with the beast.[34] Since the woman Babylon represents the imperial center of Rome, the label not only identifies her as a whore, but also associates her with idol worship. However, she is not just affiliated with this practice; the name, "mother [*mētēr*] of whores," suggests that she is the source—the creator of more just like her.[35] Blount states that the term *mother* suggests that "Rome has successfully co-opted other cities, that is, the 'children whores,' into her military-economic-political complex."[36] G. K. Beale adds that as "'mother' of idolaters" the woman Babylon has "authoritative influence over and inspiration of the system of idolatry, which is an integral part of economic involvement."[37] This understanding is reflective of the woman Babylon's lavish attire (17:4), and her ability to lure the ten kings (17:2, 12) and the inhabitants of the earth (17:2) into "an idolatrous, prostituting relationship with her pagan and imperial cults."[38]

Nevertheless, despite Babylon's association with Rome's practices of idolatry—in the metaphoric sense—a literal understanding of her identification as a "whore" must be maintained. David Aune's assertion that the word *mother* may be understood in the "superlative sense" heightens the impact of my analysis.[39] The location of the writing on herforehead and what that signified in the ancient Mediterranean world renders Babylon not simply a "whore," but one with an implied slave status. She is, therefore, not "the most

---

34. Glancy and Moore note, however, that "the very first mention of Babylon in Revelation, in which the city is already personified as female, declaims her spectacular promiscuity, even though the epithet πόρνη is not yet applied to her: 'Fallen, fallen is Babylon the great, she who made all the nations drink from the wine that induces lust for her prostitution/fornication' . . . (14:8)" ("How Typical a Roman Prostitute," 555).

35. Aune states that the term *mother* is "a figurative extension that means something like 'archetype,' . . . that indicates the source or origin of some activity or quality" (*Revelation 17–22*, 937).

36. Blount, *Revelation: A Commentary* (Louisville: Westminster John Knox, 2009), 316.

37. Beale, *The Book of Revelation*, 859.

38. Blount, *Revelation*, 315.

39. Aune, *Revelation 17–22*, 937.

depraved whore," as Aune asserts, but rather the most oppressed enslaved prostitute. [40] A better understanding of the word *pornē* further buttresses this point.

In an incisive article about the woman Babylon's identification as *pornē* and the perception of the term in the latter half of the first century c.e., Glancy and Moore argue that "although John terms Babylon a πόρνη [*pornē*], scholars have tended to treat her as a ἑταῖρα [*hetaera*, i.e. courtesan]." [41] They assert that once the main interpretive difference between courtesan (*hetaera*) and brothel slave (*pornē*) is properly understood, and the woman Babylon is correctly associated with the designation of the latter term without undue slippage into the former, it will add even more force to John's use of ancient Roman invective. [42] "The term '*pornē*' denoted a slave woman forced to have sex with whoever desired her and placed under the supervision of the *pornoboskos* (brothel keeper), while the

---

40. Ibid.

41. Glancy and Moore, "How Typical a Roman Prostitute," 551. They note, moreover, that "by the beginning of the Common Era . . . the ἑταῖρα [*hetaera*] was largely a literary construct" (ibid.). They suggest that "the scholarly approach to Babylon has been excessively 'bookish'. . . . By and large, the social realities of prostitution in the Roman world have not been adduced by such scholars [admittedly, due to the scant research on prostitution in the ancient Mediterranean world until recent years] to reconstruct the immediate connotations of the word πόρνη [*pornē*] for such audiences—connotations far from the scriptorium or the symposium, . . . and much closer to the πόρνειον [*porneion*] or brothel" (ibid., 552).

42. Glancy and Moore note that John's presentation of Babylon as *pornē* is a means of indicting the Roman Empire. "The servile associations of prostitution are crucial to Roman barbs indicting the imperial family for involvement in prostitution. . . . They are also crucial . . . for appreciating the full force of John's ironic portrayal of Babylon as a πόρνη [*pornē*] who services the kings of the earth" (ibid., 557).For a thorough treatment of how Christian "sex talk" is situated in the larger context of Greco-Roman invective, see Jennifer Wright Knust, *Abandoned to Lust: Sexual Slander and Ancient Christianity* (New York: Columbia University Press, 2006). Knust illustrates how sexual slander functioned as an instrument in the production and solidification of group boundaries (i.e., self-definition) by the earliest Christians and their contemporaries from the first through third centuries ce. She argues that "once the legitimacy of a position or a group has been linked to a particular definition of sexual virtue, accusations of sexual vice become a potent weapon for distinguishing insiders from outsiders, policing group boundaries, and eliminating rivals" (ibid., 3). Knust notes that sexual slander has also been used as a "resistance strategy designed to undermine the legitimacy of ruler and empire alike," certainly applicable to John's use of it in Revelation (ibid., 11).

hetaira more closely resembled a free-citizen wife in her ability to control her male partners' access to her body." [43] Additionally, the difference is inferred in the number of sexual relationships these types of women had. The courtesan (*hetaera*) had a strictly limited number of clients to whom she was expected to be loyal, whereas the brothel slave (*pornē*) "was distinguished by the anonymity and sheer number of her sexual partners."[44] The courtesan (*hetaera*) is "by definition an unmarriageable woman not under the control of a father, husband or *pimp*, who made a living by sexually attracting propertied men. Because of her social and economic *independence*, her affections had to be *won* by a prospective lover and could not be *permanently controlled.*"[45]

The woman Babylon, under the control of two pimps, does not have any type of independence, and her *pseudo*-affections are not won, but rather are coerced by the beast and by John, both of whose control the woman Babylon cannot escape.[46] The woman Babylon's two "johns" are the beast who pimps her, and the writer of Revelation who uses and abuses her body to symbolize the wickedness and later destruction of Rome.[47] I consider the beast as her first "john,"

43. Laura K. McClure, "Introduction," in *Prostitutes and Courtesans in the Ancient World*, ed. Christopher A. Faraone and Laura K. McClure (Madison, WI: University of Wisconsin Press, 2006), 11–12.
44. Glancy and Moore, "How Typical a Roman Prostitute," 555.
45. McClure, "Introduction," 16, emphasis added.
46. "In short, and in a fashion that is thoroughly circular, John constructs the sexual activity of Babylon in such a way that the epithet πόρνη [*pornē*] will be seen to stick to her. She is a πόρνη[*pornē*], in John's discourse of contempt, because she has had many sexual partners, and she has had many sexual partners because she is a πόρνη[*pornē*]" (Glancy and Moore, "How Typical a Roman Prostitute," 555). Glancy and Moore also reference part of the dialogue from Athenaeus's *Deipnosophistae*, which captures the horrid essence of the "πόρνη's [*pornē*] starkly commodified existence: 'The women stand naked that you be not deceived. Look at everything. . . . The door is open. One obol. Hop in. There is no coyness, no idle talk, nor does she snatch herself away. But straight away, as you wish, in whatever way you wish. You come out. Tell her to go to hell. She is a stranger to you' (569e–f)" (ibid., 554).
47. Tina Pippin refers to the text of Revelation as "Pornapocalypse" (*Apocalyptic Bodies: The Biblical End of the World in Text and Image* [New York: Routledge, 1999], 92). While I agree

because it has authority over the inhabitants of the earth (13:7-8), which include the kings of the earth with whom she fornicates (17:2). Presumably, the beast controls the sexual activities of all. In addition to being her pimp, the beast is also one of her clients; she "rides" him.[48] The woman Babylon is described as "sitting on a scarlet beast" (17:3). Since the beast possesses "seven heads and ten horns," one wonders if the woman Babylon endures unceasing penetration. The woman Babylon is also depicted as "seated on many waters" (17:1), which reflects "peoples and multitudes and nations and languages" (17:15). Although Eugene Boring states that the literal meaning of "seated on many waters" refers to Babylon's location on the Euphrates, "with many canals," as originally applied to the city of Babylon in Jer. 51:13,[49] another, more fitting, interpretation of the "waters" upon which the woman Babylon sits is that they refer to the places where men contacted prostitutes.[50]

John is the woman Babylon's other "john," because he uses and exploits the woman Babylon's body to speak metaphorically about Rome.[51] He provides much detail to describe the woman Babylon,

---

that some of the elements of pornography are present in Revelation, it is not a pervasive theme. This, however, does not negate the implications of such sexually infused violence. Moore argues that Revelation's "pornoprophecy, far from simply being siphoned, already fully fermented, from the pornoprophecy of the Hebrew prophets, is John's own distinctive concoction" ("Metonymies of Empire," 72).

48. Christopher Rowland states that "the ultimate inspiration for the immoral behavior lies with the beast supporting the woman" ("Revelation," in *Global Bible Commentary*, ed. Daniel Patte [Nashville: Abingdon, 2004], 566).

49. Boring, *Revelation*, 180.

50. Vander Stichele, "Re-membering the Whore," 119n68.

51. The identification of Babylon as either representing the entire Roman Empire or just the city of Rome has been debated. Susan R. Garrett states that "the details of John's description indicate that the beast symbolizes the Roman Empire as a whole, while the woman represents the city of Rome (17:18)" ("Revelation," in *Women's Bible Commentary*, ed. Carol A. Newsom and Sharon H. Ringe [Louisville: Westminster John Knox, 1998], 472). Alternatively, Blount notes that "the woman and the beast both seem to represent the same entity, the city of Rome. The fact that the woman rides the beast, however, suggests that they are different entities. Nevertheless, because of their parallel descriptions . . . John understands them to be one and the same entity, to which he gives the name 'Babylon'" (*Revelation*, 314). I assert that John of Revelation views the woman Babylon and the beast as interlocking yet separate figures. Following Tina Pippin,

which forces the reader to "see" her voyeuristically. Her beauty is emphasized as she is contrasted to the beast "that was full of blasphemous names" and had "seven heads and ten horns" (17:3). The woman Babylon, in contrast, is "clothed in purple and scarlet, and adorned with gold and jewels and pearls" (17:4).[52] Beale is right to suggest that "the woman is portrayed as draped with these products to identify her with a prosperous trading system. She is the symbol of [Roman] culture that maintains the prosperity of economic commerce."[53] He goes on to say that, "the expensive and attractive clothing reflects the outward attractiveness by which whores try to seduce others. . . . Babylon tries to seduce through her economic attractiveness."[54] She also "holds in her hand a golden cup" (17:4) that is full of the "wine of the wrath of her fornication" (14:8; 17:2).[55]

I also think that "the Whore of Babylon is *made* to symbolize *all the evil of the Roman Empire* and in particular, the city of Rome" ("The Heroine and the Whore: The Apocalypse of John in Feminist Perspective," in Rhoads, *From Every People and Nation*, 137, emphasis added). I also concur with Jean K. Kim's assertion that "by locating Revelation 17 in a (de)colonizing context, . . . the metaphor 'whore' is a double entendre, standing not only for the city of Rome (colonizing power) but also for a colonized woman, who is sexually exploited by two sets of men (foreign and native)" ("'Uncovering Her Wickedness': An Inter(con)textual Reading of Revelation 17 from a Postcolonial Feminist Perspective," *JSNT* 73 (1999): 64). This supports my assertion above that the woman Babylon has two masters: John and the beast.

52. The description of her garb is also mentioned in 18:16, in which she is referred to as "the great city," and elements of her attire are included in the cargo list (18:12-13). Beale notes that "behind the royal red colors of Babylon in 17:4 the perceptive person will be able to see her true blood-red color of persecution like that of the beast" (Beale, *The Book of Revelation*, 855). Both the dragon (12:3) and the beast (17:3) are described as being red in color, which "connote their persecuting nature" (ibid., 854). Additionally, the woman Babylon's dress is to be compared to that of the Lamb's bride, depicted as a city, which is described as being adorned with things such as "pure gold," "every jewel," and "pearls" (21:2, 9-21). In contrast to the deep, alluring colors of the woman Babylon, the bride "has the glory of God and a radiance like a very rare jewel, like jasper, *clear* as crystal" and the "pure gold" mentioned above is "*clear* as glass" (21:11, 18, emphasis added). Certainly, the purity of the bride is marked by her sheer and translucent appearance. She has nothing to hide.
53. Ibid., 854.
54. Ibid.
55. Beale writes that the metaphor of the nations' drunkenness "symbolizes Babylon's promise of a prosperous earthly welfare for its willing subjects, which intoxicates them. The intoxicating influence blinds them to Babylon's evil nature and her ultimate insecurity and deceives them about God as her future judge and as the only true foundation for true prosperity" (ibid., 855). This "intoxicating influence" also helps to deceive the people "so that they acquiesce

This is what Babylon serves to make the nations inebriated—so drunk that they cannot see Babylon's trickery—and therefore, participate in idol worship without protest. Despite its contents of "abominations and the impurities of her fornication" (17:4), the golden cup and the rest of the woman Babylon's dress signals her prestige, so much so that even John is amazed by her (17:6), his captivation quickly being corrected by the angel (17:7).[56] Blount writes, "John is awestruck

in idol worship" (ibid). Thus, he concludes that "the Babylonian whore is generally modeled after literal prostitutes, who offered sexual services for money, and particularly after whore-like Israel, who worshipped idols (= 'fornicated') for economic gain" (ibid., 856). Blount, however, suggests that the main use for the cup imagery is as a metaphor for divine judgment. "At both 14:10 and 16:19, he [John] narrates the cup of God's wrath. At the only other occurrence of the term, he declares that God gives to Babylon the very cup of desolation that she has mixed for others (18:6). Taken together, the images already suggest that while the call girl wields the cup in an effort to seduce and capture, God is preparing to make her elixir of abominations and impurities the means of her own punishing destruction" (*Revelation*, 315). An allusion to this "cup" is made in Jer. 51:7, "Babylon was a golden cup in the Lord's hand, making all the earth drunken; the nations drank of her wine, and so the nations went mad." Beale states that Jer. 51:7 "compares the exaltation of a precious golden cup to the exaltation of Babylon's sin" (*The Book of Revelation*, 855), while Blount points out that in both texts "the imagery of national seduction is the same" (*Revelation*, 315). Bauckham states that "God's wine [from the 'great winepress of the wrath of God,' 14:18] is the judgment on the nations (as can also be seen from the allusion to Isaiah 63:3, which is here combined with Joel 3:13)" (*The Theology of the Book of Revelation* [New York: Cambridge University Press, 1993], 95).Moore comments on the sexual nature of John's cup: "[John] recycles [the OT cup of wrath] . . . but he also sexualizes it. In John's sweaty hands the cup metaphor consistently becomes an allegory of Babylon/Rome's *porneia*: 'Fallen, fallen is Babylon the Great who caused all nations to drink of the wine of her lustful passion' (*tou thymou tēs porneias autēs*—14:8; the images of wine, drunkenness, and *porneia* recur in 17.2 and 18.3, and are implicit in condensed form in 19.2)" (Moore, "Metonymies of Empire," 72).Moore and Glancy refer to the cup as one of the aspects of Babylon (the other being her dress) that has made many a scholar associate her with the courtesan *topos*. "What could be more emblematic of the symposium, the drinking party, and hence, by extension, of the courtesan? But the courtesan *topos* called for the ἑταῖρα [*hetaera*] to be a model of decorum at table, at least as far as table manners, including *moderation*, were concerned. Babylon does not typify a courtesan in her relationship to the cup, however (even aside from the cup's singularly unappetizing contents), for that relationship is marked by *drunkenness*: 'And I saw the woman drunk [μεθύουσαν] . . . ' (17:6)" (Glancy and Moore, "How Typical a Roman Prostitute," 561, emphasis added).

56. "The Whore of Babylon is a siren calling to men, calling to the narrator John who stands amazed in the almost too near-distance" (Pippin, *Apocalyptic Bodies*, 92). Christopher A. Frilingos also notes, "Only those who can view the strange creatures of Revelation in the context of the 'great and amazing deeds' of God will be saved. Those unable to do so are enthralled by the prostitute and 'marvel' at the beast; these deceived spectators are 'the dwellers on the earth whose names have not been written in the book of life from the foundation of the world (Rev. 17:8). To be seduced by Babylon is to be amazed by the beast (Rev. 17:18)"

by what he sees. . . . <u>Even one who despises the idolatrous excess and despotic brutality of Rome must acknowledge her power and grandeur</u>."[57] John wants the reader to "buy" what he is, in fact, selling; that is, the grandiose picture of Rome that is doomed to destruction.[58]

The paradox of John's description of the woman Babylon, and the reason why many scholars understand her as a courtesan (*hetaera*) despite her identification as a brothel slave (*pornē*), relates to her attire. The woman Babylon is presented as a sumptuously well-dressed, promiscuous woman (who has fornicated with the kings of the earth, and has inebriated the inhabitants of the earth with her wine of fornication [17:2]), but she may still be considered lower class, and even of slave status. Glancy and Moore note that a "significant feature of Roman prostitution is that it was an activity almost universally associated with slaves or other persons on the bottommost rungs of the social ladder."[59] Additionally, although Babylon lacks the toga, "the garment that, rightly or wrongly, is often seen as the distinguishing dress not of the ἑταῖρα [*hetaera*], but of the common Roman brothel worker or streetwalker,"[60] classicist Kelly Olson states that Roman prostitutes were not uniform in attire: "Whores . . . appear in everything from expensive clothing down to little (or no) clothing at all."[61] Glancy and Moore state that "lavish female dress was not only compatible with slave status; such attire was among the

---

(*Spectacles of Empire: Monsters, Martyrs, and the Book of Revelation* [Philadelphia: University of Pennsylvania Press, 2004], 59). One wonders, then, how far John's amazement with the woman Babylon (and the beast) may have gone, without the angel's interception.

57. Blount, *Revelation*, 317.

58. "Revelation gleefully predicts the imminent destruction of Rome . . . which [John] mockingly renames 'Babylon'" (Stephen D. Moore, "The Revelation to John," in *A Postcolonial Commentary on the New Testament Writings*, ed. Fernando F. Segovia and R. S. Sugirtharajah [New York: T & T Clark, 2007], 441). However, as stated earlier, John's depiction of Rome as the *woman* Babylon is more than just a metaphor.

59. Glancy and Moore, "How Typical a Roman Prostitute," 557.

60. Ibid., 560.

61. Kelly Olson, "*Matrona* and Whore: Clothing and Definition in Roman Antiquity," in Faraone and McClure, *Prostitutes and Courtesans in the Ancient World*, 194.

tricks of the trade. . . . [Therefore,] Babylon's lavish dress does not cancel out the servile connotations of the term *pornê* or the (tattooed?) inscription on her forehead."[62]

Moreover, one might still be hesitant to attribute a "brothel slave" status to the woman Babylon based on her portrayal and supposedly professed assertion as an enthroned queen: "Since in her *heart* (*en tē kardia*) she says, 'I rule as a queen/empress [*basilissa*]; I am no widow, and I will never see grief'" (18:7, emphasis added and translation altered; cf. Isa. 47:8).[63] Blount comments on this scene,

> Self-glorification metastasizes into arrogance. In describing her own rule as a queen, she hijacks the language of royal seating (*kathēmai*) that John has used exclusively as a symbolic posture of divine rule: God's sitting in the heavenly throne (4:2-3, 10; 5:1, 7, 13; 6:16; 7:10, 15; 19:4; 20:11; 21:5). . . . But here for the first time she arrogantly defines such posturing as a ruling lordship that competes with God's.[64]

While I agree with Blount that a sure and blatant contrast is being established between the woman Babylon (representing the Roman Empire) and God's empire, I diverge from his assertion that these words and actions originate from the woman Babylon herself. I would argue that one must remember that she is enslaved. This is part of the function of her character; as a brothel slave, the woman Babylon does not have autonomy. Thus, similarly to John's dressing of the woman Babylon in royal attire to signify the excess of imperial

---

62. Glancy and Moore, "How Typical a Roman Prostitute," 561.
63. Glancy and Moore argue that 18:7 presents a discrepancy that causes them to assert that "in the final analysis, the figure of Babylon is not *simply* reducible to the lowest-status Roman sex worker, the tattooed brothel slave. . . . Not only does she sit, indeed, but she is enthroned. . . . Revelation 17–18 presents us, then, with the paradox of an enthroned πόρνη [*pornē*]. And it is precisely the combination of lowly and exalted elements in that paradoxical portrait that any adequate construal of it must ultimately hold in tension" (ibid., 561–62, emphasis added). They do argue, however, that the woman Babylon more closely resembles the "social type of the brothel slave" than the "literary *topos* of the courtesan" (ibid., 562). But neither of these types apply to the woman Babylon "pure and simple" (ibid.).
64. Blount, *Revelation*, 330.

Rome (17:4), and his inscribing on her forehead the words that forever plague and label her as a brothel slave (*pornē*) (17:5), he also mockingly imputes these thoughts to her, which, not surprisingly, is another way of abusing her and concomitantly enforcing her silence, since they are never spoken aloud (18:7). Thus, against those who suggest that this is the only time the woman Babylon speaks, I assert that in Revelation, she never utters a word of her own.[65] Although represented as a woman of means, with many "associates," and one who rides a beast, the woman Babylon is also an enslaved prostitute left to the whims of her two "johns."

The woman Babylon, when contextualized in this fashion, is a victim.[66] When her discursive construction is complete, John decides that she is expendable.[67] "For all the brilliance of her appearance, the prostitute's destiny is destruction rather than salvation."[68] She will be

65. Glancy and Moore state that "Babylon . . . is all but mute. John allows her only one line. . . . Ironically it is a line that declares her sovereignty—'I sit as a queen/empress . . . ' (18:7)—even as her otherwise voiceless role declares the stark limits of that sovereignty, at least within the world of the narrative. And yet John's characterization of her presupposes not just a voice, but an incomparably powerful voice. . . . 'And the woman whom you saw is the great city which has *imperium* [βασιλείαν] over the kings of the earth' (17:18). . . . However, Babylon's voice is banished to the interior spaces of Revelation's narrative world, so that we only hear its echos. To put it another way, John is careful to ensure that theβασίλισσα [*basilissa*] is subsumed in the πόρνη[*pornē*]" ("How Typical a Roman Prostitute," 567–68, emphasis original).The woman Babylon, in her inability to achieve authentic self-expression, exemplifies the discursive violence that contemporary postcolonial theorist Gayatri Chakravorty Spivak asserts is associated with marginal characters in dominant literature. See Spivak, "Three Women's Texts and a Critique of Imperialism," in *Postcolonial Criticism*, ed. Bart Moore-Gilbert, Gareth Stanton, and Willy Maley (New York: Longman, 1997), 145–65. This essay was originally published in *Critical Inquiry* 12 (1985): 243–61. See also her "Can the Subaltern Speak? Speculations on Widow Sacrifice," *Wedge* 7, no. 8 (1985): 120–30; reprinted in much expanded form, and without the subtitle, in *Marxism and the Interpretation of Culture*, ed. Cary Nelson and Lawrence Grossberg (Urbana: University of Illinois Press, 1988), 271–313.

66. Glancy and Moore assert that "the impact of John's representation of Babylon is contingent on the audience's recognition of the degradations to which enslaved brothel workers were subjected, including tattooed foreheads and perpetual vulnerability to violence" ("How Typical a Roman Prostitute," 569).

67. Although the text says that the woman Babylon's destruction is justified and purposed by God, ("For God has put it into their hearts to carry out his purpose by agreeing to give their kingdom to the beast, until the words of God will be fulfilled" [17:17]), one must not forget that this is John's literary construction.

hated (*miseō*), made desolate (*erēmoō*) and naked (*gymnos*) by the beast and the ten kings who have not yet received a kingdom (17:16). Similarly to slaveowners, John indicates his lordship over the woman Babylon as he dresses and undresses her at will. Blount writes,

> The slaveowner had a way of dressing slaves only in the essentials necessary to any given task. Slaves were only well dressed during those times when it suited the owner, say for example when they were placed on an auction block and paraded about like a cleaned up plantation tool. . . . By controlling appearance the owner demonstrated his symbolic control over the slave.[69]

Thus, John's robing and disrobing of the woman Babylon definitely corresponds to her identification as a brothel slavewoman.

Additionally, "The story of Babylon's demise is the story of a great many sex workers in every age, including our own. She is the victim of deadly violence on the part of her clients and . . . her pimp, the beast."[70] After taking one last look, they will eat (*esthiō*) her flesh and burn (*katakaiō*) her up with the fire (17:16). The very ones who were in relationship with the woman Babylon and who benefited from her "services" viciously turn on her. The woman Babylon "reveals the double jeopardy of the colonized wom[a]n, who [is] not only invaded by foreign men [John through his description and destruction of her] but also abandoned by their own men"—the beast and the ten kings who were affiliated with her.[71] Although the text later says that the kings of the earth ("who committed fornication

---

68. Robert W. Wall, *Revelation*, New International Biblical Commentary(Peabody, MA: Hendrickson Publishers, 1991), 206.

69. Blount, "Revelation," in *True to Our Native Land: An African American New Testament Commentary*, ed. Brian K. Blount (Minneapolis: Fortress Press, 2007), 530. Blount's assertion is found in his discussion of how clothing in the Black Church tradition is used as a form of identity formation. Although he is talking about African slaves in the United States, it can apply to the woman Babylon too.

70. Glancy and Moore, "How Typical a Roman Prostitute," 568.

71. Kim, "Uncovering Her Wickedness," 74.

and lived in luxury with her" [18:9]), the merchants (18:11), and all the shipmasters, seafarers, sailors, and all whose trade is on the sea (18:17) will mourn for her, their emotional outcry stems from selfish motives. Not only do these pseudolamenters "stand far off" while watching her burn (18:10, 15, 17), but they distance themselves "in fear of her torment" (18:10, 15). They are afraid of being associated with her, and thereby punished. I suggest that the kings of the earth are crying because they will no longer benefit from the woman Babylon's sexual pleasures, and the merchants and the remainder of the men stated above are losing money: "No one buys their cargo anymore" (18:11) and "In one hour all this wealth has been laid waste!" (18:17). When one considers the devastating and horrid manner in which the woman Babylon is rejected and ultimately destroyed, the masculinist logic that pervades John's supposed anti-imperial agenda becomes readily apparent.

Tina Pippin is the first scholar to thoroughly analyze verse 17:16 (which describes the woman Babylon's demise), and accurately and powerfully highlight the detriment that it causes for real women:

> The object of desire is made the object of death. The Whore/Goddess/Queen/Babylon is murdered (a sexual murder) and eaten and burned. This grotesquely exaggerated vision of death and desire accentuates the hatred of the imperial power—*and of women*. This story of death and desire is the most vividly misogynist passage in the New Testament. . . . In terms of an ideology of gender, *both women characters in the narrative and women readers are victimized.*[72]

Catherine Keller rightly inquires, "Why this trope to depict the defeat of the oppressor?"[73] Analyzing the use of gendered metaphors by the Hebrew prophets (yet undoubtedly later employed by John), Weems

72. Pippin, *Death and Desire*," 57–58, emphasis added.
73. Keller, *Apocalypse Now and Then: A Feminist Guide to the End of the World* (Boston: Beacon, 1996), 76.

asks, "What in the image of a naked, mangled female body grips the religious imagination?"[74] Indeed, the manner in which John depicts the destruction of Babylon, "the signifier *herself*," suggests that his "vision becomes voyeurism."[75] The *hear*ers of this text had to *see* the woman Babylon naked and mutilated. If John, like the Hebrew prophets, expected to "get through to [his] audience," then, using "rational, logical, coherent, reasonable, detached arguments" was not his modus operandi.[76] John employed graphic female sexual imagery in order to stir up within the hearers "strong, complicated emotions" that would hopefully convince them that the Roman Empire was conducting itself as an "impure, depraved wom[a]n" which was unacceptable, and punishable.[77] In Revelation, Babylon's gruesome, public death illustrates John's indictment of the Roman Empire. It has been argued that the purpose of this gendered metaphor ("Whore of Babylon") and her destruction is to "vilify . . . the enemy male, to feminize and abject, mock and reduce him (to ashes). But to claim that because the text does not intend misogyny it is innocent of its metaphoric subtext is to sweep *women's* ashes under the carpet." [78]

Describing the fate of Babylon, Rowland states that Babylon's "poverty will be seen for what it really is. Her wealth and 'false' clothes mask her need and destitution."[79] Although Rowland

---

74. Renita J. Weems, *Battered Love: Marriage, Sex, and Violence in the Hebrew Prophets* (Minneapolis, MN: Fortress Press, 1995), 1.

75. Keller, *Apocalypse Now and Then*, 75–76, emphasis original.

76. Weems, *Battered Love*, 66.

77. Ibid., 67. Weems takes note of the intended audiences of such gendered metaphors. "The first and most obvious feature of their imaginary audiences is that they were largely, if not exclusively, male. Only an audience that had never been raped or had never perceived rape or sexual abuse as a real threat could be expected to hear the kinds of ribald descriptions of abused women, sexual humiliation, assault, gang rape, violation, and torture . . . and not recoil in fear" (ibid., 41). The author of Revelation constructs his readers as male, as indicated by the sexually infused directive: "Come out of her" (18:4).

78. Keller, *Apocalypse Now and Then*, 77, emphasis original. Keller refers to this gendered metaphor, "The Whore of Babylon," as "a great 'queen' indeed: imperial patriarchy in drag" (ibid.).

79. Rowland, "Revelation," , 565.

understands Babylon to represent a city, his argument is transferrable to Babylon as a woman.[80] Once the object of amazement, the woman Babylon swiftly transitions into an object of hatred. Once naked by trade, she is now rendered naked in shame. Once a participant in fleshly relations, she is now just the flesh upon which her former clients feed. Nothing is left of her except ashes, as she is burned in the fire.[81] Indeed, when Babylon's "false clothes" of royalty are removed (both by John [17:16] and by the "kings of the earth" [17:2]), her "need" for cover, that is, for assistance, and her state of "destitution" are hard to miss. "Nakedness equals helplessness."[82]

The plight of the woman Babylon in this text is despicable. As I have mentioned, she has a forehead inscription that forever labels her as *pornē*, connoting her status as an enslaved prostitute, and she suffers under the command of two "johns"—the beast who she "rides," and the author of the text who abuses and destroys her in order to illustrate the destruction of the Roman Empire with his all-pervasive masculinist logic. However, being a victim of empire is only one part of her ambivalent characterization. As Rowland states, "Babylon is . . . *in part* a victim."[83] The other part of her depiction is evidenced by her extravagant attire and *excess*ories—her accessories (17:4) and her association with the excess of Rome—as well as her presentation as an imperial figure—that of an empress/queen (18:7). Her association with the Roman Empire is held in tension with her being a victim of the same imperial structure. It is the woman Babylon's paradoxical characterization that causes this African American woman to pause. A critical and thorough engagement with her text incites tension

---

80. Rowland admits that "reservations . . . about the negative image of woman . . . [in] 17:3" are warranted (ibid.). "Babylon as a woman has led the nations astray by virtue of her sexuality. We have to face squarely the male-centeredness of this text" (ibid.).
81. Pippin writes, "There is no 'proper' funeral for the Whore; her body is publicly burned" (*Death and Desire*, 61).
82. Ibid., 67.
83. Rowland, "Revelation," 566, emphasis added.

within me because her text reads like a mirror that reflects the seemingly conflicting characteristics within myself. It is to this encounter, this unexpected revelation, that I now turn.

Doubly Marked by Empire:
A Complex Identification

Writing out of a specific sociocultural context as an African American woman, my appropriation of the figure Babylon is for purposes that run counter to that of the author of Revelation. Similarly to Gayatri Chakravorty Spivak's category of catachresis[84]—a strategic reappropriation of imperial propaganda used to subvert its original meaning—I use John's feminine-gendered imperial metaphor of Babylon in order to highlight his own imperial, patriarchal, and misogynistic ways. Although I lean heavily into what John apparently intends to say—thus, taking with great seriousness his choice of words (such as brothel slave [pornē]and empress/imperial city [basilissa]) and unpack them, I also attempt to take this image of the woman Babylon away from the author altogether, "rescuing" her from his grasp.

I find the woman Babylon to be an ambivalent figure that calls to mind certain characteristics within myself that may appear conflicting. As stated above, her complexity is noted in the tension created by the amalgamation of external attributes. Her outward appearance simultaneously reflects the center of imperial power, and

---

84. "Catachresis is the process by which the colonized take and reinscribe something that exists traditionally as a feature of imperial culture." (Bill Ashcroft, Gareth Griffiths, and Helen Tiffin, *Post-Colonial Studies: The Key Concepts*, 2nd ed.[New York: Routledge, 2001], 34). Stephen D. Moore adds that it can be regarded as "a practice of resistance through an act of usurpation" (Stephen D Moore, *Empire and Apocalypse: Postcolonialism and the New Testament*, Bible in the Modern World 12 [Sheffield, UK: Sheffield Phoenix, 2006], 37). See, for example, Spivak, "Identity and Alterity: An Interview" (with Nikos Papastergiadis), *Arena* 97 (1991): 65–76 (70), in which she discusses the subaltern's catachretization of parliamentary democracy.

the physical markings of a colonized subject. The woman of Revelation 17 blurs the line between the colonizer and the colonized. It is her paradoxical nature that highlights the veil within me, namely, my simultaneous victimization by, and participation in, the capitalist structures of the United States. Let me explain these two sides of the veil based on my experience.

One Side of the Veil:
Victim of Empire

The woman Babylon, via her forehead inscription and labeling as a brothel slave (*pornē*), calls to mind the oppression from slavery that my ancestors endured, including my great-great-grandmother Indiana Grant, who was a former slave (1851–1956),[85] and the sexual violence that women continue to experience today. I share a similar understanding with Martin in her examination of the cargo list in Rev. 18:11-13: "With its reference to 'slaves and human lives,' [Rev. 18:11-13] functions for African American readers as a 'mirror' or 'looking glass' into their own history."[86] The difference between Martin and me, however, is that I find "unclouded" reflections of myself and my ancestors in the *woman* Babylon, which Martin refers to as a city.[87] Martin succinctly captures the traumatic experience of slavery:

---

85. My great-great-grandmother Indiana Grant was a slave in Texas. She obtained freedom, and moved to Sand Springs, Oklahoma in 1920. She was married in 1865 to W. C. Grant, who died in 1920. I am indebted to my paternal grandfather, Reverend Howard Bryant Sr., for sharing this ancestral history with me.
86. Martin, "Polishing the Unclouded Mirror," 83.
87. "Attacks on Rome are all achieved masterfully through the use of indirection, symbolism, allegory, irony, inter-textual allusions, and the strategic arrangement of narrative elements. The most obvious example of indirection is the author's address to the city of Rome as 'Babylon,' whereby he associates Rome not in terms of her own image of glory and honor but in terms of the tyranny and evil of a fallen empire of the past" (ibid., 96).

The four-hundred-year-long history of slavery within the United States
. . . is a history that began with the "indelicate" experience of the
overseas slave trade to the Americas, including the devastating genocide
of the Middle Passage and chattel enslavement in America, all of which
resulted in the tragic loss of what Pulitzer Prize-winning laureate
novelist Toni Morrison calls "The Sixty Million and More."[88]

Although slavery is said not to exist anymore, the crippling effects of
it remain.[89] Weems asserts that it may take double the amount of time
to move pass the anguish and pain that resulted from slavery.

Slavery was abolished in America a mere one hundred twenty-five years
ago; but evidently one hundred twenty-five years is not long enough
to abolish the memories and attitudes that slavery arouses in a nation.
Unless a miracle occurs, it is sad to say that it will probably take another
one hundred twenty-five years to erase the pain and antagonism bred
from two hundred fifty years of the cruelest brutality one race could
inflict upon another—especially in the name of God.[90]

African Americans are no longer *physically* marked as slaves; however,
the social, economic, and emotional residues of slavery live on.[91]

---

88. Ibid., 83–84.
89. Schüssler Fiorenza notes that "most of us are not conscious that millions of people in Europe,
    Africa, Asia and the Americas have been forced by traffickers into prostitution or debt bondage,
    because we believe that slavery was abolished in the nineteenth century. For most people
    'slavery' has become just a metaphor for undue hardship" ("Slave Wo/men and Freedom: Some
    Methodological Reflections," in Liew, *Postcolonial Interventions*, 123).
90. Weems, *Just a Sister Away*, 7.
91. "The movements of ancestors in every decade of every century advancing on freedom's
    tortuous path . . . is [*sic*]marked by treks through unholy vales of racial violence, Jim Crow
    segregation and politics, protest marches of men, women, and children amid menacing mobs,
    and the passionate rhetoric and legal forays of the Civil Rights Movement—all contested
    markers of hard-fought gains and liberties. These gains and liberties are deposits whose yields
    are yet to be attained in full" (Martin, "Polishing the Unclouded Mirror," 84, emphasis added).
    Womanist ethicist Katie G. Cannon, although writing over twenty years ago, expresses
    sentiments that still resonate with African Americans today: "I believe that it is important for us
    to trace the origin and expansion of these myths ['that served as the foundational underpinnings
    for slave ideology in relation to white Christian life': 1. African Americans were not human;
    2. Blacks were predestined by God to be subject to Whites; 3. Slavery is not against the
    law of God because it is not explicitly noted in the biblical text] because the same general
    schemes of oppression and patterns of enslavement *remain prevalent today* and because the

As stated earlier in chapter 1, Michelle Alexander's book, *The New Jim Crow: Mass Incarceration in the Age of Colorblindness*, explicates how racial discrimination experienced in the Jim Crow era still exists today, albeit in new ways; the criminal justice system's labeling of people of color as criminals has become a more implicit, and thus, more dangerous way to perpetuate the same form of racial injustice.[92]

Another example of the lasting effects of slavery pertains to the way African Americans read and approach biblical texts, especially since the Bible was used to justify the enslavement of Africans.[93] Vincent L. Wimbush writes, "Since every reading of important texts, especially mythic or religious texts, reflects a 'reading' or assessment of one's world, and since the Bible has from the founding of the nation served as an icon, a history of African Americans' historical readings of the Bible is likely to reflect their historical self-understandings—as Africans in America."[94] African slaves were forced to memorize the biblical text in the tainted manner in which it was taught by the colonizers. What the colonizers did not expect, however, was that the slaves would retool it to fit their needs. Blount contends that although slaves "possess[ed] an uncritical mind, [they] did not appropriate the biblical language uncritically but reoriented it. . . . Recogniz[ing]

biblical hermeneutics of oppressive praxis is *far from being dead* among contemporary exegetes" (Cannon, "Slave Ideology and Biblical Interpretation," *Semeia* 49 [1989]: 10, emphasis added).

92. Alexander, *The New Jim Crow: Mass Incarceration in the Age of Colorblindness* (New York: The New Press, 2012), 2.

93. Cannon provides a thorough treatment of how the Bible was used to support African slavery in the writings of slave apologists. She writes, "Slave apologists worked within an interpretative framework that represented the whole transcript of racial chattel slavery as ordained by God. They systematically blocked and refuted any discourse that presented contrary viewpoints. Using theo-ethical language, concepts and categories white superordinates pressed their claims of the supposedly inherent inferiority of Black people by appealing to the normative ethical system expressed by the dominant slaveholders. The political and economic context incorporated a structure of discourse wherein the Bible was authoritatively interpreted so as to support the existing patterns of exploitation of Black people" (Cannon, "Slave Ideology," 10).

94. Vincent L. Wimbush, "The Bible and African Americans: An Outline of an Interpretative History," in *Stony the Road We Trod: African American Biblical Interpretation*, ed. Cain Hope Felder (Minneapolis: Fortress Press, 1991), 82.

a difference in world situations, if not worldview, between biblical times and the nineteenth century, [slaves] adjusted [the] use of the conceptual imagery [of biblical texts] accordingly."[95]

Weems writes, "What the slavemasters did not foresee, however, was that the very material they forbade the slaves from touching and studying with their hands and eyes, the slaves learned to claim and study through the powers of listening and memory."[96] The learning of the Scriptures was very selective, and necessitated "'corrected' ideational interpretation."[97] Biblical stories that supported slavery ideology were ignored, and those that captured the essence of liberation and freedom from oppression were passed on, and "comprised the oral/aural Black biblical tradition," which would eventually become for the black community "a canon within the canon."[98] Wimbush describes the process by which the Bible was used to fit African slaves' needs:

A great many of the slaves did adopt—as part of the complex phenomenon of acquiring a number of new skills, symbols, and

95. Brian K. Blount, *Cultural Interpretation: Reorienting New Testament Criticism* (Minneapolis, MN: Fortress Press, 1995), 60. He continues, "Though not a demythologization, we might call what the slaves achieved an adaptive remythologization. They reoriented the biblical mythology by aligning it with a consciousness responsive to the nineteenth-century slave reality" (ibid.).

96. Renita J. Weems, "Reading *Her Way* through the Struggle: African American Women and the Bible," in Felder, *Stony the Road We Trod*, 61. Kelly Brown Douglas states that African slaves "were very cognizant of the power found in the Bible. . . . The enslaved Africans found a way to know this 'powerful' book for themselves. Rendered basically illiterate in terms of English by their slavery, they did this primarily through an oral/aural tradition of sermons, songs, and public readings" (Douglas, *Sexuality and the Black Church: A Womanist Perspective* [Maryknoll, NY: Orbis, 1999], 92).

97. Blount, *Cultural Interpretation*, 56.

98. Douglas, *Sexuality and the Black Church*, 92–93. "Stories from scripture that seemed to support enslavement and that were most used by the enslavers held little significance for the enslaved men and women and did not survive in the oral/aural tradition. The stories that did survive were those that were compatible with Black life and freedom" (ibid., 92). According to Wimbush, the "canon" that emerged for the black community included (among other texts) "narratives of the Hebrew Bible dealing with the adventures of the Hebrews in bondage and escaping from bondage, to the oracles of the eighth-century prophets and their denunciations of social injustice and visions of social justice, and to the New Testament texts concerning the compassion, passion, and resurrection of Jesus" ("The Bible and African Americans," 86).

languages for survival—the Bible as a "language" through which they negotiated both the strange new world that was called America and the slave existence. . . . In short, the Bible became a "world" into which African Americans could retreat, a "world" they could identify with, draw strength from, and in fact *manipulate* for self-affirmation.[99]

Wimbush refers to this phenomenon as "signifying on the Scriptures."[100] Henry Louis Gates Jr. states that "signifyin(g) presupposes an 'encoded' intention to say one thing but to mean quite another. . . . Signifyin(g), then, is a metaphor for textual revision."[101] Martin, elucidating Gates's work, writes,

> Signifying was a verbal means for marginalized, oppressed, and vulnerable people to expose the truth about oppressors and to subvert the arrogant assumptions of those in power over them. The signifying is usually done in verbally cryptic and clever ways in order to protect the oppressed signifier from the oppressor being signified upon—such that the insiders can discern the 'inside meaning of words,' while the outsiders, who are the oppressors, will encounter indirection, innuendo, and obfuscation.[102]

The interpretation of Scripture, therefore, was informed by social experience and not by the actual words of the text.[103] Blount adds that the "interpretative move . . . from experience to biblical image, [and] not the other way around," helps us to understand that "their key intent is not so much to understand the Bible as it is to understand their historical circumstance. The Bible becomes an interpretive means rather than an interpretative end."[104]

99. Ibid., 83, emphasis added.

100. Vincent L. Wimbush, "Signifying on Scriptures: An African Diaspora Proposal for Radical Readings," in *Feminist New Testament Studies: Global and Future Perspectives*, ed. Kathleen O'Brien Wicker, et al (New York: Palgrave Macmillan, 2005), 245–58.

101. Henry Louis Gates Jr., *The Signifying Monkey: A Theory of African-American Literary Criticism* (New York: Oxford University Press, 1988), 82, 88.

102. Martin, "Polishing the Unclouded Mirror," 93.

103. Wimbush, "The Bible and African Americans," 88.

104. Slaves did not "first read the Bible, or speak of its images, and then interpret those images through their experience. . . . They begin with the horrors of their experience and then

By identifying the lasting effects of the pain and trauma of slavery, African Americans were, and continue to be, able to embrace their whole self, and take it to the process of reading. According to Wimbush, African Americans' interaction with biblical interpretation, "should have to do not so much with [finding] the meaning *of* or *in* the Bible, but with the Bible *and* meaning."[105] Meaning-making of biblical texts involves the dual process of reading the Bible and a reading of the self, the latter of which involves "coming to terms with the pain and trauma of human existence as well as the psychosocial default response that involves either forgetting the past or . . . being haunted by it."[106] This process legitimates the voices of those on the margins because interpretation is intrinsically bound to their individual and collective experiences. "For African Americans to read Scriptures is to read darkness"; it "reflects and draws unto itself and engages and problematizes a certain complex order of existence associated with marginality, liminality, exile, pain, trauma." [107]

interpret those horrors through their understanding of biblical images" (Blount, *Cultural Interpretation*, 56).

105. Wimbush, "Signifying on Scriptures," 249. Wimbush's assertion indicates a change in his analysis of African Americans' engagement with the Bible. Michael Joseph Brown writes, "Drawing upon the history of readings . . . , which he calls the 'collective cultural wisdom' of African Americans, Wimbush argues for a shift in biblical investigation away from the texts *as* texts to human interactions *with* texts" (*Blackening of the Bible: The Aims of African American Biblical Scholarship* [Harrisburg, PA: Trinity Press International, 2004], 76, emphasis added). For an overview of these historical African American biblical reading strategies, from the start of the African experience in North America until the late twentieth century, see Wimbush, "The Bible and African Americans," 84–97. For a terse description and analysis of these historic reading strategies as well as a summary of some central themes that pervade Wimbush's work, see Brown, *Blackening of the Bible*, 72–74. Omitting the historic time periods, these reading strategies include suspicion and rejection, engagement of the Bible with the slave experience, an attempt to claim the Bible in its entirety, elitist and sectarian approaches, and fundamentalism. Wimbush notes, however, that in no way are these strategies "strictly chronologically successive," but rather "overlap . . . in different historical periods" ("The Bible and African Americans," 84).

106. Wimbush, "Signifying on Scriptures," 256.

107. Vincent L. Wimbush, "Reading Darkness, Reading Scriptures," in *African Americans and the Bible: Sacred Texts and Social Textures*, ed. Vincent L. Wimbush (New York: Continuum, 2001), 17.

This experience of "marginality, liminality, exile, pain, and trauma" continues most markedly for African American women. Weems analyzes the ways black women have approached and negotiated the Bible despite its use to maintain both racial and gender inequality. For African American women, the Bible has been used to "restrict and censure the[ir] behavior"; thus, they have had to learn to "resist those things within the culture and the Bible" that offend them or threaten their dignity.[108] Although the Bible is viewed as an authoritative text in the Christian community, the negative ways in which it has been used by the dominant society to oppress rather than liberate African American women has caused the latter to approach the text with a hermeneutics of suspicion. Approaching the Bible in this way is a widely accepted practice, since the process of reading has been understood in the African American community as an interaction between the text and the reader.[109] Unfortunately, the power of the dominant group to privilege some readings over others, and in that way, determine how to treat certain groups, is still an unresolved issue. For example, one of the tenets of womanist theology is to begin with the experience of black women; however, the dominant reading process suggests that in order to attain "the true meaning of a text," one must "abandon oneself completely to the world of that literary work"—in this case, the Bible.[110]

This marginalization of African American women's experience unfortunately is also experienced in the company of African American men in the black church. Clarice J. Martin, in a truth-telling essay entitled "The *Haustafeln* (Household Codes) in African American Biblical Interpretation: 'Free Slaves' and 'Subordinate Women,'" argues for consistent hermeneutics in the Black Church—a

This helps me to understand it better

108. Weems, "Reading *Her Way*," 63.
109. Ibid., 64.
110. Ibid., 65.

160

call, I believe, that is not strictly for black congregations, but for any community where gender biases are present. With regard to the perpetuation of the "paradoxical hermeneutical tensionsin traditional African American approaches to the slave regulation and the regulation regarding women in the *Haustafeln*," Martin asserts that it is unacceptable for black male preachers and theologians to employ a "liberated hermeneutic while preaching and theologizing about slavery," and a "literalist hermeneutic with reference to women."[111] "The patriarchal model of male control and supremacy that typifies the Eurocentric, Western, Protestant tradition in general," she asserts, is not normative, despite the number of African Americans who believe that it is.[112] If the household codes are "provisional" and are not to be "absolutized, universalized, or eternalized," then "African American believing communities need to assume a new and more profoundly integrative praxis that moves women 'from the margins' of the church and ecclesial structures 'to the center.'"[113]This is especially true if African American biblical interpretation is supposed to be aimed at focusing on paradigms in biblical texts that explicitly highlight and uphold the liberating acts of God. African American faith communities, therefore, must work together not only to fight against perpetuating models of slavery, but also against the subjugation and marginalization of black women. If this does not occur, then not only will the enslavement of black women, that is, their relegation and confinement to roles determined by males persist, but the goals of African American biblical hermeneutics will justifiably be called into question.

Although it was more than twenty years ago, Weems was correct to suggest that reading for African Americans continues to be viewed

111. Clarice J. Martin, "The *Haustafeln* (Household Codes) in African American Biblical Interpretation: 'Free Slaves' and 'Subordinate Women,'" in Felder, *Stony the Road We Trod*, 226.
112. Ibid., 227.
113. Ibid., 228.

as "an act clouded with mystery, power, and danger."[114] As if passing through the blood of the slaves to their living descendants, the strained, forbidden disposition toward the act of reading persists. Orally taught the Bible, along with the oppressive ideological perspectives of the colonizers, the slaves were to absorb the Scriptures and live them out accordingly. Even though slaves reinterpreted the Scriptures for their own benefit, it is possible that passages pertaining to the relegation of women may not have been seen as needing much reworking, as evident by the perpetuation of the subjugation of black women by black men and even some black women today. Despite the contextual shift—it is no longer "us slaves" versus "them colonizers" (to an extent, at least)—some black men and women blinded by "freedom" continue to assume Westernized patriarchal gender roles, and have placed black men in a superior position to (black) women. Enslaved even in thought.

Weems says that a person's "experience of reality" becomes the measure by which she or he evaluates Bible passages.[115] Our experiences influence not only the questions we bring to the task of interpretation, but also how we read biblical texts. When I embrace my experience of reality and allow it to inform the way I read the woman Babylon's text, glimpses of myself begin to be reflected back to me in what Martin calls an "unclouded mirror."[116] Although she looks the part of an imperial queen, her heart beats uneasily like a slave's. Representing both sides of the colonial divide, she exhibits confusion: she is linked to Jesus as the object of the verb *graphō* (to write), and yet differentiated in the location of the writing; she is associated with the 144,000 in the location of the mark, and yet they are distinguished by different owners; she is comparable to

---

114. Weems, "Reading *Her Way*," 60.
115. Ibid., 62.
116. Martin, "Polishing the Unclouded Mirror," 83

the ones who worship the beast and its image, and yet set apart by her profession; she is labeled a prostitute, and yet classifiable as a slave. Ultimately, with regard to this side of the veil, that is, her characterization as a victim, the woman Babylon is constantly displaced. This notion of displacement is not foreign to African Americans. Our ancestors were forcibly displaced to North America—royalty relegated to slave status—and had to find ways to adjust to their new environment.[117]

Although referred to in this book as a woman, Babylon's body has also become "text" via the inscription on her forehead, and the graphic visual image of her ravaged and burned body which (is) forever "remains." Her labeling and experience as a brothel slave recalls the sexual abuse to which my female ancestors were, and women today are, subjected. The fact that both the woman Babylon and African slave women's bodies were at the disposal of their imperial pimps and masters and then destroyed at their whim is not easy to ignore. The scarlet beast that the woman Babylon had to "ride" (17:3) reminds me of the slaveowners or white colonizers who forced black women to pleasure them in whatever way they desired, only to be hated (17:16), ridiculed, and punished afterward. The woman Babylon pales in comparison to the Woman Clothed with the Sun or the Bride of Christ, similar to the female slave when juxtaposed with the female slave owner.[118] Although not verbally

---

117. "African slaves brought to the plantations of North America were radically dislocated from their own worlds. In their new environments, they had to construct an understanding of their social context that brought meaning to their experiences and helped them survive their ordeals" (Brown, *Blackening of the Bible*, 70). As mentioned earlier in the chapter on womanist biblical interpretation, some African American women decided to create a discursive space to call their own (black feminism), instead of denying parts of themselves—either their race in the company of white feminists, or their gender when among black theologians—in order to fit into an interpretive community.

118. Marshall writes, "The contrast between . . . Babylon on the one hand and on the other hand the Queen of Heaven [the Woman Clothed in the Sun] and the Lamb/Bride is the contrast between active woman and passive woman, between impure and pure, between the woman condemned by God to suffer sexual violence and the woman protected therefrom by divine

castigated by these two exemplary female figures in Revelation, one can imagine the evil gaze that may be directed to the woman Babylon just for being who she is and for what she does to their imperial men.[119] As Vander Stichele notes, "She is quite *literally caught in the middle* between the positive images of the woman giving birth in ch. 12 and the new Jerusalem in ch. 21 [the Bride]."[120]

and male power, between the woman engaged in human political and cultural contest and the woman on whose behalf a man acts, the contrast between the whore and the virginal bride/ idealized mother" ("Gender and Empire," 31). Although Marshall states that these distinctions "are basic to John's vision of an ideal future and his critique of an imperial present," he also admits that they are "problematic . . . in their restriction of options for women to the extremities of virtue or depravity" (ibid., 31–32).Although the woman Babylon is closely identified with the accommodating Jezebel (2:18-28) in contrast to the Woman Clothed with the Sun and the Bride, a thorough treatment of such similarities and distinctions is beyond the scope of this book. In brief, the negative characteristics and stereotypes associated with the woman Babylon are also attributed to Jezebel. For example, they both entice others to practice fornication (17:4; 18:3; cf. 2:20), and share the fate of the devouring of their flesh (17:16; cf. 2 Kgs. 9:36-37). A distinction can be made, however, regarding their punishment. Jezebel's death is not described; however, she will be thrown "on a bed" (2:22, implying sexual violence [cf. 17:16]) and "her children" will be killed (2:23). The woman Babylon's death, as I have discussed, is much more explicit and gruesome. Interestingly, in both cases, those who commit adultery or fornicate with these women are given a way out, either through the opportunity to repent (2:22), or by divine intervention (17:17). Nevertheless, John's intention is to establish a connection between the woman Babylon and Jezebel. "The underlying story about Jezebel evoked in Revelation 2 and further used in chs 17–18 merges both pictures and thus facilitates the identification of the woman called 'Jezebel' with the whore called Babylon. The terms 'whore' and 'woman' used for Babylon in Revelation 17 are then used not just as metaphors, but are also meant to establish a link with a real person mentioned earlier in the book" (Vander Stichele, "Re-membering the Whore," 113). These women, in contrast to the pureness, passiveness, and sacredness of the Woman Clothed with the Sun and the Bride, are not to be trusted, envied, or modeled. Such characters of binary opposition may put "real" women in the position of having to choose with which female stereotype they will identify.

119. Pippin notes that although a "new social order is created in the utopian vision, . . . as God's law unfolds in the narrative, the desire for the Whore remains strong. The tension this creates is never fully resolved in the Apocalypse. The symbols of the pregnant woman [the Woman Clothed with the Sun] and the Bride as the city of God only accentuate that tension" (*Death and Desire*, 64).

120. Caroline Vander Stichele, "Apocalypse, Art and Abjection: Images of the Great Whore," in *Culture, Entertainment and the Bible*, ed. George Aichele, Journal for the Study of the Old Testament Supplement Series, vol. 309 (Sheffield, UK: Sheffield Academic, 2000), 134, emphasis added. In this essay, Vander Stichele gives an overview of some of the visual presentations of the woman Babylon. She also analyzes the "cultural codes [such as food, taboo, and sin] operating in both the text and its representations" (ibid., 124, 135, 137).

It is this same predicament that my mother-ancestors found themselves in with regard to slave owners and their wives, except physical abuse was also inflicted by colonial women, either directly or by an appointed person, most often another slave.[121] "The [slave] owner's wives stigmatized slave women for the sexual misconduct their husbands, the slave owners, directed toward female slaves. They referred to these slave women as concubines, which suggested that slave women had a choice in the matter."[122] Weems, who compares the relationship between Sarai and Hagar (the Egyptian slavewoman) to the experiences of African American slavewomen with their female masters, fittingly writes,

> The story of the Egyptian slave and her Hebrew mistress is hauntingly reminiscent of the disturbing accounts of black slavewomen and white mistresses during slavery. Over and over again we have heard tales about the wanton and brutal rape of black women by their white slavemasters, compounded by punitive beatings by resentful white wives who penalized the raped slavewomen for their husbands' lust and savagery.[123]

We cannot forget the forehead inscription that eternally labels the woman Babylon a whore. Black slaves, although perhaps branded for punitive purposes, did not require such explicit identification. Their skin color alone was enough to identify them as that which has no value. Even today, the beautiful hues of the black skin are viewed as ugly and perceived as a license to discriminate, to hate, and in

121. "Slaveholders relied on slaves as surrogate bodies to do their dirty work when they wanted to keep their own hands clean" (Glancy, *Slavery in Early Christianity*, 16).

122. Delores S. Williams, "African-American Women in Three Contexts of Domestic Violence," in *Violence against Women*, ed. Elisabeth Schüssler Fiorenza and M. Shawn Copeland, Concilium Series, vol. 1 (Maryknoll, NY: Orbis, 1994), 37. Weems notes that some slavewomen "willingly conceded to their slavemasters' sexual advances: first, as a way of protecting their husbands, children, and loved ones from being beaten; second, as a way to keep themselves and those close to them from being sold away; or, third, as the only way of elevating their social rank in order to protect themselves from vicious overseers and mistresses" (*Just a Sister Away*, 7).

123. Ibid., 7.

other cases to kill. In recent years, this has become quite evident, since wearing a hoodie and playing loud music has become reason enough to kill and prevent the future production of black life.[124]

The American slave system, a particularly pernicious form of colonization, has had tremendous disheartening and long-lasting effects on African American people, despite how many generations removed we may be from those who were the primary recipients of such cruelty and dehumanization. The pain of our ancestors and the horrid stench of the colonizers' disgust for African slaves are thrust to the forefront of our minds with each incident that stems from racism and discrimination. The effects of systemic racism continue to plague, cripple, and arrest the advancement of some African American people today, and can no longer be ignored.

Reading the woman Babylon's text includes a reading of myself and the pain and trauma associated with my existence, and I sympathize with her. The manner in which she is horridly used, abused, and killed captures and reflects the historical black experience of American slavery. The negative connotations associated with her name that continue to survive reminds me of the racist underpinnings of imperial ideology that remain in effect today. However, the woman Babylon's characterization as a victim of empire is only half of her ambivalent nature. As a *privileged* African American woman, I also resonate with what lies on the other side of the woman Babylon's veil: her association with, and participation in, empire. It is, therefore, difficult to employ the interpretive process of my ancestors, that

---

124. Trayvon Martin was shot and killed at age seventeen by George Zimmerman, a neighborhood watch volunteer, on February 26, 2012 in Sanford, Florida. This tragic occurrence, which led to his demise, began because according to Zimmerman, Martin, wearing a hoodie, looked suspicious. Jordan Davis, seventeen, was shot and killed on November 23, 2012 (nine months after Martin) in Jacksonville, Florida by Michael Dunn because of a confrontation over loud music playing from his car. Still, there are others such as Darrin Manning, sixteen, who was stopped by police on January 7, 2014 in Philadelphia, Pennsylvania while en route to a basketball game and suffered a ruptured testicle at the hands of a female officer during a pat-down. Although he was not killed, his chances of producing children of his own may be.

is, to ignore the texts that further perpetuate slave ideology and embrace—albeit with adaptation—the texts that give me hope, when it comes to the "text" of the woman Babylon. I cannot tear her apart like the beast and the kings (17:16), and pick and choose which aspects of her I will embrace, nor do I want to. The woman Babylon—in all her suffering and involvement in empire—functions as a mirror and I behold an image of myself. Let me now explicate my likeness with the woman Babylon's association with empire; certainly, a topic much more difficult to engage.

The Other Side of the Veil:
Participant in Empire

The woman Babylon's association with imperial power, as suggested by her regal attire and accessories (17:4), and her characterization as an empress (18:7), calls to mind my participation in "the city," that is, the socioeconomic metropolis that is America. We are both highly *emplaced*. As a privileged black woman, not only do I have individual educational privilege, but I also benefit from other structural privileges such as home ownership, safety, healthcare, wealth accumulation, private transportation, and access to luxury goods and services (to name a few).

I am loosely bound to the woman Babylon because of my access to higher education. Certainly, in my position as a professor—a profession marked by prestige, privilege, and power—I too dress the part. The only difference between me and the woman Babylon, on this matter, is that I can choose to disrobe myself of my "professional" attire—without fear of impending punishment and dismemberment (17:16)—before entering contexts where my scholastic affiliation need not be advertised. She is not so lucky.

Such academic privilege and access to scholastic platforms cause me to be a bit hesitant to claim a minority status when in the company of, or in dialogue with, other minority women, including my two-thirds-world sister scholars, who do not share the same benefits. As mentioned earlier in chapter 1 on womanist biblical interpretation, Renita J. Weems admits that she herself struggles with a similar conflict. The tensions of our horrible collective memory of being slaves in America, and the privilege we experience as recipients of the benefits of simply being American, causes Weems to suggest that privileged African American women must, therefore, intentionally engage in scholarly dialogue with sister-scholars who hail from third-world countries, taking seriously what they consider to be "scripture" and other pressing matters in their context. Weems aptly asserts that she is a "First World woman with Third World commitments."[125] Potentially many more African American women, who experience the academy as a space of ambivalence, share the same sentiment.

With regard to access to luxury goods and services, however, I am an individual in a much larger narrative of global capitalism. The woman Babylon's *excess*ories—her embellishments including fine linen, jewelry, a golden cup, etc. (17:4), as well as the cargo list (18:11-13)—reflect the abundance and overindulgence of the economically privileged class:

> And the merchants of the earth weep and mourn for her, since no one buys their cargo anymore, cargo of gold, silver, jewels and pearls, fine linen, purple, silk and scarlet, all kinds of scented wood, all articles of ivory, all articles of costly wood, bronze, iron, and marble, cinnamon, spice, incense, myrrh, frankincense, wine, olive oil, choice flour and wheat, cattle and sheep, horses and chariots, slaves—and human lives. (Rev. 18:11-13)

125. Renita J. Weems, "1–2 Chronicles," in *The Africana Bible: Reading Israel's Scriptures from Africa and the African Diaspora*, ed. Hugh R. Page Jr. et al (Minneapolis: Fortress Press, 2010), 286.

Scholarly studies of Revelation's economic critique of Rome relate this text to the present situation of the global economy. They highlight the callous manner in which the prosperity of empire is attained and maintained by any means necessary, including the harsh treatment of minority populations around the globe—even children. For example, Néstor Míguez, who makes connections between Revelation's economic critique and contemporary global capitalism in his essay, "Apocalyptic and the Economy: A Reading of Revelation 18 from the Experience of Economic Exclusion," writes,

> Behind the mask of luxury and progress lies the true visage of human destruction. The repulsive spirits of violence, racial hatred, mutilation, and exploitation roam the streets of our Babylons in Latin America (and the globe); their presence is clear once one looks beyond the glimmering lights of the neon signs. It is the accumulation of goods as such that gives birth to these spirits.[126]

Those of us with access to, and an accumulation of, luxury goods—things we may *want* but not *need*—should not allow the sheer pleasure and enjoyment of these items to eclipse or render invisible the suffering of people who labor—as de facto slaves—to produce them. As Míguez states, "The basic needs of all human beings yield to the luxury markets of great merchants and traders,"[127] but especially those of the underprivileged who, at times, have no choice but to labor in sweatshops and other inhumane workplaces.

Even as I approach the cargo list as a privileged *African American* woman, I cannot readily dismiss the mention of the "slaves and human lives" (18:13) simply because I do not personally possess any. Instead, this phrase, which, according to Martin, functions as a mirror for the horrible experience of African Americans in American

---

126. Néstor Míguez, "Apocalyptic and the Economy: A Reading of Revelation 18 from the Experience of Economic Exclusion," in Segovia and Tolbert, *Reading from this Place*, 260.
127. Ibid., 261.

slavery,[128] should compel me to consider the struggles of these laborers, the severe conditions in which they work, and find ways to improve their situation—or at the least, join the discussions or movements of activist groups who are already attempting to do so.

The economic *excess*ibility of the woman Babylon highlights my association with empire, and I am distressed about it. Thinking about John's message in Revelation, that is, his directive to withdraw from empire and align oneself with God's empire, I wonder if I have crossed over to the "dark side." It is confusing and unsettling to wonder if my participation in empire, that is, my access to, and utilization of, all that American has to offer, is perceived as accommodating to imperial culture or simply an indication that I worked my tail off, and am now reaping the benefits of my hard labor, and of those who came before me. Have I "'baptized' dominant viewpoints, political positions, or economic systems so that [I] can benefit from the prevailing views of the world around [me?]. . . . [Have I] tame[d] the demands of the Kingdom so that [I] can have one foot in the Kingdom of God and one in the realm where success is measured in terms of financial success[?]"[129] John would say yes, but I disagree. As I will explicate below, having access to the benefits of empire presents us with an opportunity to effect change for the betterment of others. This, I would say, is a "demand of the kingdom of God."

This side of the veil, which reflects my participation in the American economy, is much more difficult to discuss than the other side of the veil that is marked by my victimization in the same structure. Indeed, it is much easier to posit a positive image of the self (in terms of being free from blame or guilt), than to present oneself

128. Martin, "Polishing the Unclouded Mirror," 83.
129. Jerry L. Sumney, "The Dragon Has Been Defeated—Revelation 12," *Review & Expositor* 98, no. 1 (2001):112.

as one who is aligned with, and who benefits from, a potentially oppressive system. And yet, both sides of the veil make up the reality of who I am.

Approaching the text of the woman Babylon with a hermeneutics of ambi*veil*ence not only highlights her ambivalent characterization, but also my own. Her paradoxical description as simultaneously a brothel slavewoman *and* an empress/imperial city has underscored my oppression by, and participation in, capitalistic America. A critical and thorough examination of her text has taken me through various emotions, inciting tension within me by drawing attention to my own conflicting realities. Although the woman Babylon is John's "poster child" for ambivalence, I find my ambivalence on display in her.

Rending the Veil

The veil that separates these two seemingly conflicting realities, following Du Bois's thinking, must be rent.[130] I suggest that privileged African American women such as myself rend the veil that separates both our victimization by, and association with, the American empire. I understand that this might be difficult to do, especially when the veil may be self-imposed. As stated earlier, Toni Morrison, who expands Du Bois's notion of the veil, explains how autobiographers of their own slave narratives masked their complex experience as if with a veil, tempering the harsh and violent experience with slavery so that their texts may be better received

---

130. As stated earlier, having argued that blacks in America suffer from a double consciousness that results from their experience with racial discrimination and othering, Du Bois asserts that this veil be rent in order for blacks to see themselves for who they truly are, and not from the perspective of white America. In so doing, the "strivings of black folks" will be revealed and make an enriching ethnic, that is, cultural, contribution to the world. See Du Bois, *The Souls of Black Folk* (New York: Library of America, 1969).

by white literary critics.[131] This self-muting, hiding, or softening of oneself and one's experience transcends time. When among the dominant culture, I have found it necessary to hide behind a veil, concealing my body in nonfitted suits and downplaying my ambition in order to prevent me from being labeled aggressive, instead of assertive, or as an "angry black woman." At times, in a negotiation with my environment, I have consciously masked my true self, keeping my inner thoughts, goals, and dreams unspoken, in order to remain in solidarity with the oppressed, and to thwart any possibility of being labeled as an "uppity" black woman, one who does not truly understand "the struggle." Certainly, I am not alone. Maintaining a veil, in some respects, is a means of survival. Unfortunately, if I can bring myself to admit it, there was a time when this veiling was done in efforts to remain *seemingly* ignorant of the discrimination and oppression of others in order to protect my place at the American elitist table from which I am "f.e.d." (finding enjoyment [by] default—de fault of either being the token minority, or by de fault of all those who struggled to make my place of privilege possible).[132] I am disgusted and embarrassed by this recollection; however, I am grateful for enlightenment. I have changed.

The. Veil. Must. Be. Rent. Despite the tension that emerges from the coexistence of my dual(ing) relationship with the American capitalist system, I have to be true to myself. By rending the veil, I can simultaneously embrace both aspects of myself, and come into a fuller consciousness and love of myself. This coming into a full realization of myself does not have to be daunting, but rather can

---

131. Toni Morrison, "The Site of Memory," in *Inventing the Truth: The Art and Craft of Memoir*, ed. William Zinsser (Boston: Houghton Mifflin, 1987), 110.

132. This play on the word *default* is adapted from Ann DuCille, *Skin Trade* (Cambridge, MA: Harvard University Press, 1996), 128. In speaking about the difference between Afrocentricity and postcoloniality, she states that "whereas the [former] is 'unembarrassingly black,' . . . the other is black only by default—de fault of being nonwhite" (ibid).

be empowering. An understanding of how it feels to be oppressed helps me to frame the right questions and determine the appropriate and pertinent conversations that I then take with me when I go to get f.e.d. at any American elitist soirée. My duality, if I welcome it wholeheartedly, can help to achieve a greater standing for the oppressed. In my profession as a New Testament professor and as an ordained minister, I help to prepare leaders for ministry in today's multifaith world; my students are within my reach, but the many lives I will touch through them are far-reaching. Thus, I remain dedicated to enhancing the status of women both in the profession and in local communities, mentoring students by helping them recognize, embrace, and capitalize on their potential to evoke change, publish works such as this that will not only further New Testament scholarship but also incite within others the need for self-reflection, love of the self, and a desire to act on the behalf of others, especially, those who are suffering. Rending the veil is personal but its effects are communal.

Approaching the text of the woman Babylon has initiated this process of self-realization. To my surprise, what began as a comprehensive examination of *her* duality resulted in the disclosure of mine. A revelation, indeed. Despite my initial hesitance to admit my simultaneous victimization by, and participation in, capitalistic structures, when approaching the woman Babylon the veil was difficult to maintain. It is not easy to sustain a "poker face" when confronting aspects of the woman Babylon that so closely resemble myself. Her traumatic experience forces the negative, almost-forgotten memories buried in the deep recesses of my mind—and often buried so that I can effectively function—to come to the fore. (*I shudder at the notion of similarity.*) The way she is scripted and (mis)represented by John parallels the ways in which I have been ill-spoken *for*, or spoken *to*, without any opportunity of voicing my own thoughts. (*The likeness cannot be possible.*) The manner in which she is used by her two pimps, hated, and turned against by her former associates, runs too close to the times when I was manipulated and "stabbed in the back" by those whom I thought were my allies. (*I contemplate risking self-exposure.*) The fashion in which she is made desolate, stripped naked, ravished, and burned alive—the text never says she dies before then—compels me to remember, recall, recount, recollect, restore, and revisit any and all types of oppression, subjugation, violence, and crime (past and present) against black women. (*The parallels are profoundly perplexing.*) The ways in which she also participates in, and benefits from, imperial structures, resembles my position as a privileged black woman in America. (*I slowly reach for the veil.*) The luxury goods that she has at her disposal, and in excess, correspond to the abundance and surplus of my possessions, most of which is indicative of my access to what I *want* rather than what I *need*. (*I grip the veil.*) Although I do not benefit from the consumption of blood as the woman Babylon does of her victims (17:6), I am reminded that I benefit from the "blood, sweat, and tears" that were shed, and continue to be shed, by the many women and men who work to make my imperial life comfortable. (*The veil is ripped off.*)

And I am filled with emotions: from dejection and rage about all that I as a black woman have had to deal with, to contentment and gratitude regarding the benefits and privileges I receive from the capitalist system of America, to disbelief and confusion that I have so much in common with such a negatively regarded figure—the woman Babylon. I have come face to face in what Martin calls "an unclouded mirror," seeing an almost the same, but not quite, reflection of myself. And I love her.

Conclusion

It's more than just interpretive business; it's personal. What started out as an innovative reading of the woman Babylon, based on a theoretical comparison of the interpretations of my predecessors, quickly morphed into something for which I was not prepared. I expected to read the woman Babylon's text, not to be *read by it*.[1] However, I had no choice but to succumb to this mutual engagement, since the more I read about her, the closer I came to discovering more about myself.[2] And oh, how I longed to know her.

But I struggled. How can a text—a biblical text—and one that depicts the destruction of a woman be so enticingly familiar? There has to be something wrong here. And yet, this is the paradoxical relationship between the Bible and black women about which Renita J. Weems speaks. She attests that though the Bible has been used to subordinate, violate, and silence African American people, especially women, it remains an authoritative text to which we turn for spiritual guidance and comfort. She therefore rightly advises black women to

---

1. Located after a broad "rhetorical-ethical turn" in biblical studies, this book is indicative of the shift of the scholar's focus to the interaction between the flesh-and-blood reader and the text. Cf. Elisabeth Schüssler Fiorenza, *Rhetoric and Ethic: The Politics of Biblical Studies* (Minneapolis: Fortress Press, 1999), 32.
2. This mutual interaction is certainly not experienced by all black women, and I have studiously avoided attempting to speak for all black women in this book.

read with caution and resistance, being careful not to internalize that which offends or jeopardizes their self-worth.[3] But as I have shown, my mutual interaction with the text has problematized this type of protective reading. My ability to cast aside that which is offensive is frustrated because the woman Babylon, functioning in Martin's terms as an "unclouded mirror," reflects back to me an image of myself. How can I not internalize her? I am her, at least in the ways I have—at the risk of exposing myself—so honestly described. And since the interpretive task has been infused with the emotive, I cannot deny the fact that it has definitely gotten personal.

A postcolonial womanist analysis of the woman Babylon not only fills a scholarly gap, but also recognizes a trend. It both builds upon and complicates previous scholarship on the book of Revelation as presented by feminists and African American scholars. Transcending the dichotomous divide of the "Great Whore" debate, which has often seemed to presuppose that the woman Babylon refers to either a "whore" or a "city," I have argued for a new alternative. By bringing the categories of race, ethnicity, and class to bear on the debate, I have been led to propose that she necessarily be understood as *simultaneously* a brothel slavewoman *and* an empress/imperial city. Her participation in, and victimization by, imperial structures suggests that she is both/and, instead of either/or.

Correspondingly, instead of adhering to the general African American scholarly notion that John, in his critique of the Roman Empire, presents a *minority* report, I have made the case—by appealing to postcolonial *and* womanist hermeneutical inquiry—that

---

3. "The experience of oppression has forced the marginalized reader to retain the right, as much as possible, to resist those things within the culture and the Bible that one finds obnoxious or antagonistic to one's innate sense of identity and to one's basic instincts for survival" (Weems, "Reading *Her Way* through the Struggle: African American Women and the Bible," in *Stony the Road We Trod: African American Biblical Interpretation*, ed. Cain Hope Felder [Minneapolis: Fortress Press, 1991], 63).

he puts forth a *masculinist* minority report. Postcolonial analysis helped to highlight John's reinscription of Roman imperial ideology, which was displayed not only by his relegating and subjugating rhetoric, but also by the violent manner in which he deals with the woman Babylon. A womanist analysis foregrounded the experiences of African American women, and maintained the notion of advocating for the well-being of *all* people. A thorough examination of John's treatment of the woman Babylon in Revelation undermines the notion that John simply writes as one in solidarity with the oppressed. Certainly, women are included in this category.

Babylon in Revelation is a metaphor, a code word for a city, but Babylon is also a literary character, a female character in a narrative. As such, she invites not just decoding but imaginative readerly engagement. I have attempted to make myself John's implied reader/ hearer in that regard, but I have also felt it necessary, as a woman and an African American, to read John's narrative resistantly. For these reasons, I have not only paid very close attention to what the author of Revelation apparently intends to say by thoroughly examining his choice of words, but have also appropriated the figure of Babylon for ends that run counter to his.

A postcolonial womanist analysis revealed that the woman Babylon of Revelation 17 is not the wanton, lustful, over-the-top, and unrestrained prostitute that John matter-of-factly presents. She is more complex than that. The careful interpretive gaze of this African American woman has identified her as representing both imperial power *and* servitude. The royal attire in which John clothes her, and the unspoken words ascribed to her, reflect her participation in, and benefit from, empire. Contrastingly, the word *whore* that he stamps on her forehead—the location of choice by colonizers for runaway or insurrectionist slaves—and the violence he unleashes on her at his whim, reflects her perpetual castigation and domination. She is doubly marked by empire.

A postcolonial womanist hermeneutics of ambi*veil*ence makes the duality of the woman Babylon's characterization readily identifiable. This combined lens, analyzing not only issues of empire but also those pertaining to race from my experience as a black woman, makes for a worthwhile interdisciplinary venture. My hermeneutics is a combination of Du Bois's notion of the veil—the metaphorical covering that prevents African Americans from seeing themselves as they truly are because they view themselves from the perspective of white America—and Bhabha's notion of ambivalence—the simultaneous attraction to and repulsion from an object or person experienced within a single individual, particularly under colonialism or its long, complex aftermath. It helps to more accurately capture the experience of one's engagement with texts such as that of the woman Babylon. It causes the interpreter to wrestle with the tension that emerges from an encounter with an ambivalent text or character, because the latter has functioned as a mirror, and exposed the conflicting characteristics within the interpreter about which she was either unaware or, until then, chose to ignore.

I have shown that the dual characterization of the woman Babylon generated distressing thoughts about African American experience with slavery and simultaneously produced anxieties about my privilege in capitalistic America. The woman Babylon's identification as a brothel slave stirred up memories of the African American woman's experience of being repeatedly raped and subjected to other forms of violence under slavery. Regarded as property, black women's bodies were the receivers of whatever sexual acts or expressions of lust their masters threw at them. They were also beaten and mutilated at the command of their masters and mistresses—the latter often blaming them for their husbands' sexual advances and misconduct. A brothel slave, the woman Babylon is also victimized by her two "johns," the author John and the beast, establishing a powerful connection with African American identity. However, this is only one side of the veil.

The other side of the veil, illustrated by the woman Babylon's association with, and benefit from, imperialism, reflects my participation in empire. As Weems noted, being both educated and employed is suggestive of one's privileged status. It is the case that higher education and a steady paycheck are not offered or accessible to everyone. Additionally, women with these intellectual and economic riches occasionally have the opportunity to exploit other women.[4] As I reflected on certain structural privileges from which I benefit—such as access to higher education and luxury goods and services—my association with empire became more apparent. Like Weems, I became "painfully aware" that I am doubly implicated in empire, due to my acceptance of the capitalist *handouts* from which I benefit, as well as due to my *hand in* perpetuating systems of domination by either ignoring or refusing to concern myself with the needs of the less privileged.[5] I am thus forced to consider: How much different am I from the woman Babylon?

One of the greatest tensions in this book was making sure that my identity-related approach remained balanced and authentic. I could not allow my connection with the woman Babylon's slave status to overpower or prevent me from seeing my participation in other imperial communities. Additionally, I had to be mindful not to efface any difference that exists among African Americans themselves, or ignore any similarities that may exist between me and my white sister-scholars. A hermeneutics of ambi*veil*ence compels the

---

4. Renita J. Weems, *Just a Sister Away: A Womanist Vision of Women's Relationships in the Bible* (Philadelphia: Innisfree, 1988), 11.
5. Ibid.

interpreter to look intently at the image that the text reflects back to her, and consider truthfully how much of herself she discovers.

I have argued that the veil that separates the twoness of the woman Babylon's characterization revealed the veil that separates the twoness of my privileged African American female identity. Ambivalence is experienced because these two seemingly conflicting characteristics—participant in, and victim of, empire—reside together within me, appearing in varying degrees depending on the circumstance. This ambivalence is veiled because the last thing that anyone, not just me, wants to reveal about themselves is an apparent contradiction. However, this is what a hermeneutics of ambi*veil*ence calls us to do. By exposing the veil in our lives and forcing us to confront it, we are now in a position to make a decision. Hopefully, the decision made is to rend the veil in order to attain true self-consciousness, which, according to Du Bois, is the full awareness and acceptance of oneself for which blacks are always striving. This, in turn, will hopefully incite the will to act—to act on behalf of those who do not have access to the "finer" things in imperial life like higher education, employment, private transportation, healthcare, and so on—those, who according to Weems, are the "potential victims" of our privileged ways.[6] A womanist-based hermeneutics "does not simply *postulate* theoretical formulations, but it also seeks to assist African American women in *living out* the gospel message and *addresses* issues that affect them."[7] Words must be put into action. The ultimate goal of this hermeneutics, of this book, is to stir up within individuals not only the desire to help achieve a greater standing of the oppressed, but also to help them break free from whatever has them bound.

6. Ibid.
7. Raquel A. St. Clair, *Call and Consequences: A Womanist Reading of Mark* (Minneapolis: Fortress Press, 2008), 83, emphases added.

I further suggest that a postcolonial womanist hermeneutics of ambi*veil*ence ultimately has potential relevance for the future of biblical interpretation. By removing the veil, African American women can each attain a better sense of self, and thus become better equipped and positioned for critical dialogue. Following Weems, African American scholars are to be able to have third-world commitments, while admitting their first-world privilege.[8] Kwok Pui-Lan writes, "Women can benefit from reading together with others in community in order to challenge our own biases and investment in a particular interpretive method. We have the challenge to turn the postcolonial 'contact zones' into places of mutual learning, and places for trying out new ideas and strategies for the emancipation of all."[9]

A hermeneutics of ambi*veil*ence is not limited to the text of Revelation, but is designed to be used in one's analysis of any biblical text. What it necessitates is not only a critical investigation of a text, but also, and more importantly, a willingness to be read and exposed by the text. Certainly, every text will not resonate with our experiences, but when it does, it is up to us to allow this awakening to occur. We are to own up to the characteristics, especially the flaws, that we see reflected back to us in the text. We are to embrace those qualities, change what needs to be changed, and tear the veil that seeks to prevent us from coming into our full selves. We are to, as Toni Morrison states, "rip [the] veil drawn over 'proceedings too terrible to relate.'"[10] Although Morrison refers to what is omitted or tempered in African American discourse, particularly, in slave

8. Weems, "1–2 Chronicles," in *The Africana Bible: Reading Israel's Scriptures from Africa and the African Diaspora*, ed. Hugh R. Page Jr. et al (Minneapolis: Fortress Press, 2010), 286.
9. Kwok, "Making the Connections: Postcolonial Studies and Feminist Biblical Interpretation" in *The Postcolonial Biblical Reader*, ed. R. S. Sugirtharajah (Malden, MA: Blackwell Publishing, 2006), 60. She defines a "contact zone" as "the space of colonial encounters where people of different geographical and historical backgrounds are brought into contact with each other, usually shaped by inequality and conflictual relations" (ibid., 48).

narratives, her assertion is appropriate. We cannot hide behind the veil that separates the "terrible proceedings" of our experiences as both victims of oppression and as participants in empire; it must be rent. It is a process of coming into the full(aware)ness of ourselves, where no part of ourselves has to be denied (unless deemed appropriate), and where everything about ourselves can be embraced.

Additionally, and of equal importance, a hermeneutics of ambi*vei*lence, although informed by certain tenets of womanist thought, need not be employed solely by African American women, who self-identify in that respect. What I have resolved to do in this book is identify from the womanist conversation what I think is important for my intellectual, ethical, and political work with regard to biblical interpretation. These tenets are, however, readily transferrable across gender, racial, and class lines. To begin with, it is important to foreground one's experiences (cultural, religious, political, etc.) in the task of interpretation, since they directly affect how we approach the text, and inform the questions we take to the text. One should be relentless in bringing attention to the sufferings of marginalized peoples, seeking to counter any form of oppression or domination, whether expressed in the biblical text or found in any aspect of life. At the same time, one must also acknowledge one's privilege and participation in dominating systems. This power, no matter the degree, should be used to foster solidarity with the oppressed, by being open to dialogue with marginalized voices, taking seriously their interpretations of their life situations and of the biblical text, even if the interpreter is considered to be nonacademic. One way to achieve this is to read and interrogate the text within a community of other, including minority, voices to ensure one's accountability to the text, oneself, and others. Finally, it is important

---

10. Toni Morrison, "The Site of Memory," in *Inventing the Truth: The Art and Craft of Memoir*, ed. William Zinsser (Boston: Houghton Mifflin, 1987), 110.

to keep the task of biblical inquiry relevant and applicable to the church and the community. Abstract theories and concepts that are not readily transferrable to real life, or as Cone states, cannot help people "live out their faith in the world" are not useful for effecting change and promoting survival.[11]

It is my goal, then, that everyone can benefit from a hermeneutics of ambi*veil*ence because it is an approach that not only critically analyzes biblical texts, but also seeks to help readers attain a better sense of themselves through some tough, but much-needed self-realization, reflection, and transformation. As Weems writes,

> It will not be easy. In fact, it will be very difficult. It will require a deliberate effort on our part to listen [to the text and to our inner voice] when it is easier to dismiss. At times, it will mean that we must be as willing to confront and confess the evil in us, as a community of women [and men], as we are to point to the evil in the world. It will require a resolve to work [at bettering ourselves and the situations of others] . . . both in spite of and because of the pain. . . . The future of our world depends upon our resolve to walk headlong into that which makes us different as diverse tribes of a vast world and to march straight into that which binds us as people of God. If we don't, who will?[12]

As difficult as it may be to confront the reality of our true selves, it is a task that must be performed. The future of biblical studies depends on it, because the interaction between the text and a fully self-cognizant flesh-and-blood reader makes for a more well-informed and honest interpretation. The future of our world depends on it, because the biblical text, and the interpretations thereof, are more often than not what are used to either oppose or justify systems of oppression.

---

11. James Cone, "Black Theology, Black Churches, and Black Women," in *Out of the Revolution: The Development of Africana Studies*, eds. Delores P. Aldridge and Carlene Young (Lanham, MD: Lexington, 2000), 417.

12. Weems, *Just a Sister Away*, 17–18. Although Weems was speaking about the work that is needed to build the broken relationships between black and white women both in terms of race and economic stratification, her sentiments are relevant here.

Hence, it really *is* more than just interpretive business; it is personal and interpersonal. Womanists seek the well-being of all people; a hermeneutics of ambi*veil*ence is just one way to get there.

Bibliography

Adell, Sandra. *Double-Consciousness/Double Bind: Theoretical Issues in Twentieth Century Black Literature*. Urbana, IL: University of Illinois Press, 1994.

Agnani, Sunil, et. al. "Editor's Column: The End of Postcolonial Theory? A Roundtable with Sunil Agnani, Fernando Coronil, Gaurav Desai, Mamadou Diouf, Simon Gikandi, Susie Tharu, and Jennifer Wenzel." *PMLA: Publications of the Modern Language Association of America* 122 (2007): 633–51.

Aland, Kurt, et al. *The Greek New Testament*. 3rd ed. West Germany: Biblia-Druck GmbH Stuttgart, 1983.

Ashcroft, Bill, Gareth Griffiths, and Helen Tiffin. *Post-Colonial Studies: The Key Concepts*. 2nd ed. New York: Routledge, 2001.

———, eds. *The Post-Colonial Studies Reader*. 2nd ed. New York: Routledge, 2006.

Attridge, Harold, ed. *The HarperCollins Study Bible: New Revised Standard Version, including the Apocryphal Deuterocanonical Books*. Student ed. San Francisco: HarperCollins Publishers, 2006.

Aune, David E. *Revelation 1–5*. Word Biblical Commentary, vol. 52. Dallas: Word, 1997.

———. *Revelation 6–16*. Word Biblical Commentary, vol. 52b. Dallas: Thomas Nelson, 1998.

————. *Revelation 17–22*. Word Biblical Commentary, vol. 52c. Dallas: Thomas Nelson, 1998.

Austen, Jane. *Mansfield Park*. Edited by John Wiltshire. New York: Cambridge University Press, 2005. (Orig. pub. 1814.)

Baker-Fletcher, Karen. "Anna Julia Cooper and Sojourner Truth: Two Nineteenth-Century Black Feminist Interpreters of Scripture." In *Searching the Scriptures*, vol. 1: *A Feminist Introduction*, edited by Elisabeth Schüssler Fiorenza, 41–51. New York: Crossroad, 1993.

————. *A Singing Something: Womanist Reflections on Anna Julia Cooper*. New York: Crossroad, 1994.

————. "A Womanist Journey." In Floyd-Thomas, *Deeper Shades of Purple*, 158–175.

Barr, David L. "Doing Violence: Moral Issues in Reading John's Apocalypse." In Barr, *Reading the Book of Revelation*, 97–108.

————. "The Lamb Who Looks Like a Dragon? Characterizing Jesus in John's Apocalypse."In *The Reality of Apocalypse: Rhetoric and Politics in the Book of Revelation*, edited by David L. Barr, 205–20. Symposium Series, no. 39. Atlanta: Society of Biblical Literature, 2006.

————, ed. *Reading the Book of Revelation: A Resource for Students*. Atlanta: Society of Biblical Literature, 2003.

————. *Tales of the End: A Narrative Commentary on the Book of Revelation*. Santa Rosa, CA: Polebridge, 1998.

————. "Towards an Ethical Reading of The Apocalypse: Reflections on John's Use of Power, Violence, and Misogyny." In *Society of Biblical Literature 1997 Seminar Papers*, 358–373. Society of Biblical Literature Seminar Papers Series, no. 36. Atlanta: Scholars Press, 1997.

————. "Women in Myth and History: Deconstructing John's Characterizations." In Levine and Robbins, *A Feminist Companion to the Apocalypse of John*, 55–68.

Barrett, Lindon. Review of *Double-Consciousness/Double Bind: Theoretical Issues in Twentieth Century Black Literature*, by Sandra Adell. *American Literature* 68, no. 2 (1996): 476–77.

Bauckham, Richard. *The Climax of Prophecy: Studies on the Book of Revelation*. Edinburgh: T & T Clark, 1993.

———. *The Theology of the Book of Revelation*. New Testament Theology Series. New York: Cambridge University Press, 1993.

Beale, G. K. *The Book of Revelation: A Commentary on the Greek Text*. The New International Greek Testament Commentary. Grand Rapids: Eerdmans, 1999.

Berger, P. L., and T. Luckmann. *The Social Construction of Reality: A Treatise in the Sociology of Knowledge*. Garden City, NY: Doubleday, 1966.

Bhabha, Homi. *The Location of Culture*. New York: Routledge, 1994.

Blount, Brian K. *Can I Get a Witness: Reading Revelation through African American Culture*. Louisville: Westminster John Knox, 2005.

———. "Reading Revelation Today: Witness as Active Resistance." *Interpretation* 54, no. 4 (2000): 398–412.

———. "Revelation." In Blount, *True to Our Native Land*, 523–58.

———. *Revelation: A Commentary*. Louisville: Westminster John Knox, 2009.

———. *Then the Whisper Put on Flesh: New Testament Ethics in an African American Context*. Nashville: Abingdon, 2001.

———, ed. *True to our Native Land: An African American New Testament Commentary*. Minneapolis: Fortress Press, 2007.

———. "The Witness of Active Resistance: The Ethics of *Revelation* in African American Perspective." In Rhoads, *From Every People and Nation*, 28–46.

Boesak, Allan. *Comfort and Protest: The Apocalypse from a South African Perspective*. Philadelphia: Westminster John Knox, 1987.

Boring, M. Eugene. *Revelation*. Interpretation: A Bible Commentary for Teaching and Preaching. Louisville: Westminster John Knox, 1989.

Brontë, Charlotte. *Jane Eyre*. Edited by Jane Jack and Margaret Smith. Oxford: Clarendon, 1975, 1969.

Brown, Michael Joseph. *Blackening of the Bible: The Aims of African American Biblical Scholarship*. New York: Trinity, 2004.

Buell, Denise Kimber. *Why This New Race: Ethnic Reasoning in Early Christianity*. New York: Columbia University Press, 2005.

Butler, Judith. *Gender Trouble: Feminism and the Subversion of Identity*. New York: Routledge, 1990.

Byron, Gay L. "The Challenge of 'Blackness' for Rearticulating the Meaning of Global Feminist New Testament Interpretation." In Wicker, Miller, and Dube, *Feminist New Testament Studies*, 85–101.

———. *Symbolic Blackness and Ethnic Difference in Early Christian Literature*. New York: Routledge, 2002.

Callahan, Allen Dwight. "The Language of Apocalypse." *Harvard Theological Review* 88, no. 4 (1995): 453–70.

Cannon, Katie Geneva. "The Emergence of Black Feminist Consciousness." In *Feminist Interpretation of the Bible*, edited by Letty M. Russell, 30–40. Philadelphia: Westminster John Knox, 1985.

———. *Katie's Canon: Womanism and the Soul of the Black Community*. New York: Continuum, 1995.

———. "Slave Ideology and Biblical Interpretation." *Semeia* 49 (1989): 9–23.

Carter, Warren. *John and Empire: Initial Explorations*. Maiden Lane, NY: T & T Clark, 2008.

———. *Matthew and Empire: Initial Explorations*. Harrisburg, PA: Trinity, 2001.

Coleman, Monica. "Roundtable Discussion: Must I Be a Womanist?" *JFSR* 22 (2006): 85–134.

Collins, Adela Yarbro. *Crisis and Catharsis: The Power of the Apocalypse*. Philadelphia: Westminster, 1984.

———. "Feminine Symbolism in the Book of Revelation." *Biblical Interpretation* 1, no.1 (Fall 1993): 20–33.

———. "Feminine Symbolism in the Book of Revelation." In Levine and Robbins, *A Feminist Companion to the Apocalypse of John*, 121–30.

———. "Women's History and the Book of Revelation." In *Society of Biblical Literature 1987 Seminar Papers*, edited by Kent Harold Richards, 80–91. Society of Biblical Literature Seminar Papers Series, no. 26. Atlanta: Scholars Press, 1987.

Cone, James. "Black Theology, Black Churches, and Black Women." In *Out of the Revolution: The Development of Africana Studies*, edited by Delores P. Aldridge and Carlene Young, 407– 25. Lanham, MD: Lexington Books, 2000. An earlier version was published in *For My People: Black Theology and the Black Church*, edited by James Cone. Maryknoll, NY: Orbis, 1984.

Cone, James H., and Gayraud S. Wilmore, eds. *Black Theology: A Documentary History*. Vol. 2: *1980–1992*. Maryknoll, NY: Orbis, 1993.

Cooper, Anna Julia. "Womanhood a Vital Element in the Regeneration and Progress of a Race." In *A Voice from the South*, edited by Mary Helen Washington, 9–47. New York: Oxford University Press, 1988.

Copeland, M. Shawn. "A Thinking Margin: The Womanist Movement as Critical Cognitive Praxis." In Floyd-Thomas, *Deeper Shades of Purple*, 226–35.

———. "'Wading through Many Sorrows': Toward a Theology of Suffering in Womanist Perspective." In *A Troubling in My Soul: Womanist Perspectives on Evil and Suffering*, edited by Emilie M. Townes, 109–29. Maryknoll, NY: Orbis, 1993.

Cummings, Lorine. "A Womanist Response to the Afrocentric Idea: Jarena Lee, Womanist Preacher." In Sanders, *Living the Intersection*, 57–64.

Darden, Lynne St. Clair, *Scripturalizing Revelation: An African American-Postcolonial Reading of Empire*. Atlanta: SBL Semeia Studies, forthcoming.

DeSilva, David Arthur. *Seeing Things John's Way: The Rhetoric of the Book of Revelation*. Louisville: Westminster John Knox, 2009.

———. "The Social Setting of the Revelation to John: Conflicts Within, Fears Without." *Westminster Theological Journal* 54, no. 2 (Fall 1992): 273–302.

Douglas, Kelly Brown. "Marginalized People, Liberating Perspectives: A Womanist Approach to Biblical Interpretation." *Anglican Theological Review* 83, no 1 (2001): 41–48.

———. *Sexuality and the Black Church: A Womanist Perspective*. Maryknoll, NY: Orbis, 1999.

———. "Twenty Years a Womanist: An Affirming Challenge." In Floyd-Thomas, *Deeper Shades of Purple*, 145–57.

———. "Womanist Theology: What Is Its Relationship to Black Theology." In Cone and Wilmore, *Black Theology*, 290–299.

Douglas, Kelly Brown, and Cheryl J. Sanders. "Introduction." In Sanders, *Living the Intersection*, 9–17.

Dube, Musa W. *Postcolonial Feminist Interpretation of the Bible*. St. Louis: Chalice, 2000.

———. "Rahab is Hanging Out a Red Ribbon: One African Woman's Perspective on the Future of Feminist New Testament Scholarship." In Wicker, Miller, and Dube, *Feminist New Testament Studies*, 177–202.

Du Bois, W. E. B. *Dusk of Dawn: An Essay Toward an Autobiography of A Race Concept*. New York: Harcourt, Brace & Co., 1940.

———. *The Souls of Black Folk*. New York: Library of America, 1986. (Orig. pub. 1903.)

DuCille, Ann. *Skin Trade*. Cambridge, MA: Harvard University Press, 1996.

Duff, Paul B. *Who Rides the Beast? Prophetic Rivalry and the Rhetoric of Crisis in the Churches of the Apocalypse*. Oxford: Oxford University Press, 2001.

Elliott, Neil. *Liberating Paul: The Justice of God and the Politics of the Apostle*. Sheffield, UK: Sheffield Academic, 1994.

Enis, Larry L. "Biblical Interpretation Among African-American New Testament Scholars." *Currents in Biblical Research* 4, no. 1 (2005): 57–82.

Exum, J. Cheryl. *Plotted, Shot, and Painted: Cultural Representations of Biblical Women*. Sheffield, UK: Sheffield Academic, 1996.

Fanon, Franz. *Black Skins, White Masks*. Trans. Charles Lam Markmann. New York: Grove, 1991. (French orig. pub. 1952.)

———. *The Wretched of the Earth*. Trans. Constance Farrington. New York: Grove, 1963. (French orig. pub. 1961.)

Faraone, Christopher A., and Laura K. McClure, eds. *Prostitutes and Courtesans in the Ancient World*. Madison, WI: University of Wisconsin Press, 2006.

Felder, Cain Hope, ed. *Stony the Road We Trod: African American Biblical Interpretation*. Minneapolis: Fortress Press, 1991.

Floyd-Thomas, Stacey M. "'I am Black and Beautiful, O Ye Daughters of Jerusalem . . . ': African American Virtue Ethics and a Womanist Hermeneutics of Redemption." In *African American Religious Life and the Story of Nimrod*, edited by Anthony B. Pinn and Allen Dwight Callahan, 35–51. New York: Palgrave Macmillan, 2008.

———, ed. *Deeper Shades of Purple: Womanism in Religion and Society*. New York: New York University Press, 2006.

———, ed. "Introduction: Writing for Our Lives—Womanism as an Epistemological Revolution." In Floyd-Thomas, *Deeper Shades of Purple*, 1–16.

Foucault, Michel. "The Discourse on Language." In *The Archaeology of Knowledge*, trans. A. M. Sheridan Smith, 215–37. New York: Pantheon, 1972. (French orig. pub. 1969.)

Fuller, Margaret. *Woman in the Nineteenth Century*. New York: Greeley & McElrath, 1845.

Friesen, Steven J. "The Beast from the Land: Revelation 13:11-18 and Social Setting." In Barr, *Reading the Book of Revelation*, 49–64.

————. *Imperial Cults and the Apocalypse of John: Reading Revelation in the Ruins*. Oxford: Oxford University Press, 2001.

Frilingos, Christopher A. *Spectacles of Empire: Monsters, Martyrs, and the Book of Revelation*. Philadelphia: University of Pennsylvania Press, 2004.

Gafney, Wilda. "A Black Feminist Approach to Biblical Studies." *Encounter* 67 (2006): 391–403.

Gallagher, Susan VanZanten, ed. *Postcolonial Literature and the Biblical Call for Justice*. Jackson, MS: University Press of Mississippi, 1994.

Garrett, Susan R. "Revelation." In *Women's Bible Commentary*, edited by Carol A. Newsom and Sharon H. Ringe, 469–74. Louisville: Westminster John Knox, 1998.

Gates Jr., Henry Louis. "Critical Fanonism." *Critical Inquiry* 17, no. 3 (1991): 457–70.

Gilbert, Sandra M., and Susan Gubar. *The Madwoman in the Attic: The Woman Writer and the Nineteenth-Century Literary Imagination*. 2nd ed. New Haven, CT: Yale University Press, 2000.

Glancy, Jennifer A. *Slavery in Early Christianity*. New York: Oxford University Press, 2002.

Glancy, Jennifer A., and Stephen D. Moore, "How Typical a Roman Prostitute Is Revelation's 'Great Whore'?" *Journal of Biblical Literature* 130, no. 3 (2011): 551–69.

Grant, Jacquelyn. *White Women's Christ and Black Women's Jesus: Feminist Christology and Womanist Response*. Atlanta: Scholars, 1989.

————. "Womanist Theology: Black Women's Experience as a Source for Doing Theology, with Special Reference to Christology." In *African-American Religious Studies: An Interdisciplinary Anthology*, edited by Gayraud S. Wilmore, 208–27. Durham: Duke University Press, 1989.

Hawley, John C., ed. *Encyclopedia of Postcolonial Studies*. Westport, CT: Greenwood, 2001.

Hegel, Georg Wilhelm Friedrich. *Phenomenology of Spirit*. Trans. A. V. Miller. Oxford: Oxford University Press, 1952.

hooks, bell. *Ain't I a Woman: Black Women and Feminism*. Boston: South End, 1981.

Horsley, Richard A. *Hearing the Whole Story: The Politics of Plot in Mark's Gospel*. Louisville: Westminster John Knox, 2001.

———, ed. *In the Shadow of Empire: Reclaiming the Bible as a History of Faithful Resistance*. Louisville: Westminster John Knox, 2008.

———, ed. *Paul and Empire: Religion and Power in Roman Imperial Society*. Harrisburg, PA: Trinity, 1997.

———, ed. *Paul and Politics: Ekklesia, Israel, Imperium, Interpretation: Essays in Honor of Krister Stendahl*. Harrisburg, PA: Trinity, 2000.

Howard-Brook, Wes, and Anthony Gwyther. *Unveiling Empire: Reading Revelation Then and Now*. Maryknoll, NY: Orbis, 1999.

Huber, Lynn R. *Like a Bride Adorned: Reading Metaphor in John's Apocalypse*. Emory Studies in Early Christianity; New York: T & T Clark, 2007.

———. "Sexually Explicit? Re-Reading Revelation's 144,000 Virgins as a Response to Roman Discourses." *Journal of Men, Masculinities and Spirituality* 2, no. 1 (2008): 3–28.

———. *Thinking and Seeing with Women in Revelation*. New York: Bloomsbury/T & T Clark, 2013.

———. "Unveiling the Bride: Revelation 19.1-8 and Roman Social Discourse." In Levine and Robbins, *A Feminist Companion to the Apocalypse of John*, 159–79.

Ipsen, Avaren. "Sex Worker Standpoint and Sacred Text." PhD diss., University of California at Berkeley, 2006.

———. *Sex Working and the Bible*. Bible World Series. London: Equinox, 2009.

Jones, C. P. "Tattooing and Branding in Graeco-Roman Antiquity." *The Journal of Roman Studies* 77 (1987): 139–55.

Jones-Warsaw, Koala. "Toward a Womanist Hermeneutic: A Reading of Judges 19–21." *Journal of the Interdenominational Theological Center* 22 (1994): 18–35.

Joyce, Joyce A. "The Black Canon: Reconstructing Black American Literary Criticism." *New Literary History* 18 (1987): 335–44.

Keller, Catherine. *Apocalypse Now and Then: A Feminist Guide to the End of the World.* Boston: Beacon, 1996.

———. *God and Power: Counter-Apocalyptic Journeys.* Minneapolis: Fortress Press, 2005.

———. "Ms.Calculating the Endtimes: Additions and Conversation." In Levine and Robbins, *A Feminist Companion to the Apocalypse of John,* 205–27.

Kim, Jean K. "'Uncovering Her Wickedness': An Inter(con)textual Reading of Revelation 17 from a Postcolonial Feminist Perspective." *JSNT* 73 (1999): 61–81.

Kwok Pui-Lan. "Making the Connections: Postcolonial Studies and Feminist Biblical Interpretation." In Sugirtharajah, *The Postcolonial Biblical Reader,* 45–63.

———. *Postcolonial Imagination and Feminist Theology.* Louisville: Westminster John Knox, 2005.

Leclair, Thomas. "'The Language Must Not Sweat': A Conversation with Toni." In *Toni Morrison: Critical Perspectives Past and Present,* edited by Henry Louis Gates Jr. and K. A. Appiah, 369–77. Amistad Literary Series. New York: Amistad, 1993.

Lee, Jarena. *The Life and Religious Experience of Jarena Lee: A Colored Lady Giving an Account of Her Call to Preach the Gospel.* In *Early Negro Writing 1760–1837,* edited by Dorothy Porter, 49–514. Boston: Beacon, 1971. (Orig. pub. 1836).

Levine, Amy-Jill, and Maria Mayo Robbins, eds. *A Feminist Companion to the Apocalypse of John.* New York: T & T Clark International, 2009.

Lewis, Reina, and Sara Mills, eds. *Feminist Postcolonial Theory: A Reader.* Edinburgh: Edinburgh University Press, 2003.

Loewenberg, James, and Ruth Bogin, eds. *Black Women in Nineteenth-Century American Life.* University Park: Pennsylvania State University Press, 1976.

Marshall, John W. "Gender and Empire: Sexualized Violence in John's Anti-Imperial Apocalypse." In Levine and Robbins, *A Feminist Companion to the Apocalypse of John,* 17–32.

Martin, Clarice J. "The *Haustafeln* (Household Codes) in African American Biblical Interpretation: 'Free Slaves' and 'Subordinate Women.'" In Felder, *Stony the Road We Trod,* 206–31.

———. "Polishing the Unclouded Mirror: A Womanist Reading of *Revelation* 18:13." In Rhoads, *From Every People and Nation,* 82–109.

———. "Womanist Interpretations of the New Testament: The Quest for Holistic and Inclusive Translation and Interpretation." *JFSR* 6 (1990): 41–61.

McClure, Laura K. "Introduction." In Faraone and McClure, *Prostitutes and Courtesans in the Ancient World,* 3–18.

"Medieval Sourcebook: Pliny on the Christians." *The Internet Medieval Source Book,* Fordham University Center for Medieval Studies.http://www.fordham.edu/halsall/source/pliny1.asp.

Míguez, Néstor. "Apocalyptic and the Economy: A Reading of Revelation 18 from the Experience of Economic Exclusion." In Segovia and Tolbert, *Reading from This Place,* vol. 2, 250–62.

Moore, Stephen D. *Empire and Apocalypse: Postcolonialism and the New Testament.* Sheffield, UK: Sheffield Phoenix, 2006.

———. *God's Beauty Parlor: And Other Queer Spaces in and around the Bible.* Stanford: Stanford University Press, 2001.

———. *God's Gym: Divine Male Bodies of the Bible.* New York: Routledge, 1996.

———. "Hypermasculinity and Divinity." In Levine and Robbins, *A Feminist Companion to the Apocalypse of John*, 180–204.

———. "Metonymies of Empire: Sexual Humiliation and Gender Masquerade in the Book of Revelation." In *Postcolonial Interventions: Essays in Honor of R. S. Sugirtharajah*, edited by Tat-siong Benny Liew, 71–97. Sheffield, UK: Sheffield Phoenix, 2009.

———. *Poststructuralism and the New Testament: Derrida and Foucault at the Foot of the* Cross. Minneapolis: Fortress Press, 1994.

———. "The Revelation to John." In Segovia and Sugirtharajah, *A Postcolonial Commentary*, 436–54.

———. "Situating Spivak." In *Planetary Loves: Spivak, Postcoloniality, and Theology*, edited by Stephen D. Moore and Mayra Rivera, 15–30. Transdisciplinary Theological Colloquia. New York: Fordham University Press, 2011.

Moore, Stephen D., and Fernando F. Segovia, eds. *Postcolonial Biblical Criticism: Interdisciplinary Intersections*. New York: T & T Clark International, 2005.

Moore-Gilbert, Bart. *Postcolonial Theory: Contexts, Practices, Politics*. London: Verso, 1997.

———. "Spivak and Bhabha." In *A Companion to Postcolonial Studies*, edited by Henry Schwartz and Sangeeta Ray, 451–66. Malden, MA: Blackwell, 2000.

Moore-Gilbert, Bart, Gareth Stanton, and Willy Maley, eds. *Postcolonial Criticism*. New York: Longman, 1997.

Morrison, Toni. "The Site of Memory." In *Inventing the Truth: The Art and Craft of Memoir*, edited by William Zinsser, 101–24. Boston: Houghton Mifflin, 1987.

Mostern, Kenneth. "Postcolonialism after W. E. B. Du Bois." In *Postcolonial Theory and the United States: Race, Ethnicity, and Literature*, edited by

Amritjit Singh and Peter Schmidt, 258–76. Jackson, MS: University Press of Mississippi, 2000.

———. Review of *Double-Consciousness/Double Bind: Theoretical Issues in Twentieth Century Black Literature*, by Sandra Adell. *MELUS* 22, no. 4 (1997): 193–97.

Mounce, Robert H. *The Book of Revelation.* Rev. ed. New International Commentary on the New Testament. Grand Rapids: Eerdmans, 1998.

Naylor, Michael. "The Roman Imperial Cult and Revelation." *Currents in Biblical Research* 8 (2010): 207–39.

Nkrumah, Kwame. *Neo-Colonialism: The Last Stage of Imperialism.* London: Nelson, 1965.

Økland, Jorunn. "Why Can't the Heavenly Miss Jerusalem Just Shut Up?" In Levine and Robbins, *A Feminist Companion to the Apocalypse of John*, 88–105.

Olson, Kelly. "*Matrona* and Whore: Clothing and Definition in Roman Antiquity." In Faraone and McClure, *Prostitutes and Courtesans in the Ancient World*, 186–204.

Paul, Ian. "Ebbing and Flowing: Scholarly Developments in Study of the Book of Revelation." *The Expository Times* 119, no. 11 (2008): 523–31.

Pauli, Hertha. *Her Name Was Sojourner Truth.* New York: Camelot/Avon, 1962.

Pippin, Tina. "'And I Will Strike Her Children Dead': Death and the Deconstruction of Social Location." In Segovia and Tolbert, *Reading from This Place*, vol. 1 191–98.

———. *Apocalyptic Bodies: The Biblical End of the World in Text and Image.* New York: Routledge, 1999.

———. *Death and Desire: The Rhetoric of Gender in the Apocalypse of John.* Louisville: Westminster John Knox, 1992.

———. "Eros and the End: Reading for Gender in the Apocalypse of John." *Semeia* 59 (1992): 193–210.

————. "The Heroine and the Whore: The Apocalypse of John in Feminist Perspective." In Rhoads, *From Every People and Nation*, 127–45.

————. "The Revelation to John." In *Searching The Scriptures*, vol. 2: *A Feminist Commentary*, edited by Elisabeth Schüssler Fiorenza, 109–30. New York: Crossroad, 1994.

Pippin, Tina, and J. Michael Clark. "Revelation/Apocalypse." In *The Queer Bible Commentary*, edited by Deryn Guest, Robert E. Goss, Mona West, and Thomas Bohache, 753–68. London: SCM, 2006.

Price, S. R. F. *Rituals and Power: The Roman Imperial Cult in Asia Minor.* New York: Cambridge University Press, 1986.

Prior, Michael. *The Bible and Colonialism: A Moral Critique.* Sheffield, UK: Sheffield Academic, 1997.

Rhoads, David, ed. *From Every People and Nation: The Book of Revelation in Intercultural Perspective.* Minneapolis: Fortress Press, 2005.

Robinson, John A. T. *Redating the New Testament.* Philadelphia: Westminster, 1976.

Rolfe, J. C., ed. and trans. *Suetonius: The Lives of the Caesars and the Lives of Illustrious Men.* 2 vols. The Loeb Classical Library. Cambridge, MA: Harvard University Press, 1913–14.

Rossing, Barbara R. *The Choice between Two Cities: Whore, Bride, and Empire in the Apocalypse.* Harrisburg, PA: Trinity Press International, 1999.

————. "For the Healing of the World: Reading *Revelation* Ecologically." In Rhoads, *From Every People and Nation*, 165–82.

————. "Prophecy, End-Times, and American Apocalypse: Reclaiming Hope for Our World." *Anglican Theological Review* 89, no. 4 (Fall 2007): 549–63.

Rowland, Christopher. "Revelation." In *Global Bible Commentary*, edited by Daniel Patte, 559–70. Nashville: Abingdon, 2004.

Royalty Jr., Robert M. *The Streets of Heaven: The Ideology of Wealth in the Apocalypse of John.* Macon, GA: Mercer University Press, 1998.

Ruiz, Jean-Pierre. "Taking a Stand on the Sand of the Seashore: A Postcolonial Exploration of Revelation 13." In Barr, *Reading the Book of Revelation*, 119–35.

Said, Edward W. *Culture and Imperialism*. New York: Knopf, 1994.

———. *Orientalism*. New York: Vintage, 2003. (Orig. pub. 1978.)

Sanders, Cheryl J., ed. *Living the Intersection: Womanism and Afrocentrism in Theology*. Minneapolis: Fortress Press, 1995.

———. "Roundtable Discussion: Christian Ethics and Theology in Womanist Perspective" in *Journal of Feminist Studies in Religion* 5, no 2 (1989): 83–112.

Schueller, Malini Johar. *Locating Race: Global Sites of Post-Colonial Citizenship*. Albany, NY: SUNY, 2009.

Schüssler Fiorenza, Elisabeth. "Babylon the Great: A Rhetorical-Political Reading of Revelation 17–18." In *The Reality of Apocalypse: Rhetoric and Politics in the Book of Revelation*, edited by David L. Barr, 243–69; Symposium Series, no. 39. Atlanta: Society of Biblical Literature, 2006.

———. *The Book of Revelation: Justice and Judgment*. 2nd ed. Minneapolis: Fortress Press, 1998.

———. *But She Said: Feminist Practices of Biblical Interpretation*. Boston: Beacon, 1992.

———. *Invitation to the Book of Revelation: A Commentary on the Apocalypse with Complete Text from the Jerusalem Bible*. Garden City, NY: Image Books, 1981.

———. *The Power of the Word: Scripture and the Rhetoric of Empire*. Minneapolis: Fortress Press, 2007.

———. *Revelation: Vision of a Just World*. Proclamation Commentaries. Minneapolis: Fortress Press, 1991.

———, ed. *Searching the Scriptures: A Feminist Introduction*. New York: Crossroad, 1997.

———. *Wisdom Ways: Introducing Feminist Biblical Interpretation.* Maryknoll, NY: Orbis, 2001.

Schüssler Fiorenza, Elisabeth, and M. Shawn Copeland, ed. *Violence against Women.* Concilium Series, vol. 1 Maryknoll, NY: Orbis, 1994.

Schwartz, Henry, and Sangeeta Ray, eds. *A Companion to Postcolonial Studies.* Malden, MA: Blackwell, 2000.

Scott, James C. *Domination and the Arts of Resistance: Hidden Transcripts.* New Haven, CT: Yale University Press, 1990.

Segovia, Fernando F. "Biblical Criticism and Postcolonial Studies: Toward a Postcolonial Optic." In Sugirtharajah, *The Postcolonial Biblical Reader,* 33–44.

———. "Cultural Studies and Contemporary Biblical Criticism: Ideological Criticism as Mode of Discourse." In Segovia and Tolbert, *Reading from This Place,* vol. 2 1–17.

———. "Mapping the Postcolonial Optic in Biblical Criticism: Meaning and Scope." In Moore and Segovia, *Postcolonial Biblical Criticism,* 23–78.

Segovia, Fernando F., and R. S. Sugirtharajah, eds. *A Postcolonial Commentary on the New Testament Writings.* New York: T & T Clark, 2007.

Segovia, Fernando F., and Mary Ann Tolbert, eds. *Reading from This Place.* Vol. 1: *Social Location and Biblical Interpretation in the United States.* Minneapolis: Fortress Press, 1995.

Segovia, Fernando F., and Mary Ann Tolbert, eds. *Reading from This Place.* Vol. 2: *Social Location and Biblical Interpretation in Global Perspective.* Minneapolis: Fortress Press, 2000.

Slater, Thomas B. *Christ and Community: A Socio-Historical Study of the Christology of Revelation.* Sheffield, UK: Sheffield Academic, 1999.

Smith, Brian C. *Understanding Third World Politics: Theories of Political Change and Development.* Bloomington: Indiana University Press, 1996.

Smith, Shanell T. "A Perspective on Revelation." In *Global Perspectives on the Bible*, ed.Mark Roncace and Joe Weaver. Upper Saddle River, NJ: Pearson Prentice Hall, forthcoming.

Spivak, Gayatri Chakravorty. "Can the Subaltern Speak?" In *Marxism and the Interpretation of Culture*, edited by Cary Nelson and Lawrence Grossberg, 271–313. Urbana: University of Illinois Press, 1988.

———. "Can the Subaltern Speak? Speculations on Widow Sacrifice," *Wedge* 7, no. 8 (1985): 120–30.

St. Clair, Raquel. *Call and Consequences: A Womanist Reading of Mark*. Minneapolis: Fortress Press, 2008.

———. "Womanist Biblical Interpretation." In Blount, *True to Our Native Land*, 54–62.

Stanton, Elizabeth Cady. *The Woman's Bible*. New York: European, 1895–98.

Stenström, Hanna. "'They Have Not Defiled Themselves with Women . . .': Christian Identity according to the Book of Revelation." In Levine and Robbins, *A Feminist Companion to the Apocalypse of John*, 33–54.

Sugirtharajah, R. S. *Asian Biblical Hermeneutics and Postcolonialism: Contesting the Interpretations*. Sheffield, UK: Sheffield Academic, 1999.

———. *The Bible and the Third World: Precolonial, Colonial, and Postcolonial Encounters*. New York: Cambridge University Press, 2001.

———, ed. *The Postcolonial Biblical Reader*. Malden, MA: Blackwell, 2006.

———. *Postcolonial Criticism and Biblical Interpretation*. New York: Oxford University Press, 2001.

———. "A Postcolonial Exploration of Collusion and Construction in Biblical Interpretation." In *The Postcolonial Bible*, edited by R. S. Sugirtharajah, 91–116. The Bible and Postcolonialism, 1. Sheffield, UK: Sheffield Academic, 1998.

———, ed. *Voices from the Margin: Interpreting the Bible in the Third World*. Maryknoll, NY: Orbis, 1991.

Sumney, Jerry L. "The Dragon Has Been Defeated—Revelation 12." *Review & Expositor* 98, no. 1 (2001): 103–15.

Thompson, Leonard L. *The Book of Revelation: Apocalypse and Empire.* Oxford: Oxford University Press, 1990.

———. "Ordinary Lives: John and His First Readers." In Barr, *Reading the Book of Revelation*, 25–47.

Townes, Emilie M. "The Womanist Dancing Mind: Speaking to the Expansiveness of Womanist Discourse." In Floyd-Thomas, *Deeper Shades of Purple*, 236–50.

Trible, Phyllis. *Texts of Terror: Literary-Feminist Readings of Biblical Narratives.* Philadelphia: Fortress Press, 1984.

Vander Stichele, Caroline. "Apocalypse, Art and Abjection: Images of the Great Whore." In *Culture, Entertainment and the Bible*, edited by George Aichele, 124–38. Journal for the Study of the Old Testament Supplement Series, vol. 309. Sheffield, UK: Sheffield Academic Press, 2000.

———. "Just a Whore: The Annihilation of Babylon According to Revelation 17:16." *Lectio Difficilior* 1 (2000): 1–14.

———. "Re-membering the Whore: The Fate of Babylon According to Revelation 17.16." In Levine and Robbins, *A Feminist Companion to the Apocalypse of John*, 106–20.

Van Kooten, George H. "The Year of the Four Emperors and the Revelation of John: The 'Pro-Neronian' Emperors Otho and Vitellius, and the Images and Colossus of Nero in Rome." *Journal for the Study of the New Testament* 30 (2007): 205–48.

Walker, Alice. "Coming Apart." In *Take Back the Night: Women on Pornography*, edited by Laura Lederer, 95–104. New York: William Morrow and Company, 1980.

———. *In Search of Our Mothers' Gardens: Womanist Prose.* Orlando: Harcourt, 1983.

———. Review of *Gifts of Power: The Writings of Rebecca Jackson (1795–1871), Black Visionary, Shaker Eldress*, by Rebecca Jackson. *Black Scholar* 12 (1981): 64–67.

Wall, Robert W. *Revelation.* New International Biblical Commentary. Peabody, MA: Hendrickson Publishers, 1991.

Weems, Renita J. "1–2 Chronicles." In *The Africana Bible: Reading Israel's Scriptures from Africa and the African Diaspora*, edited by Hugh R. Page Jr., et al., 286–90. Minneapolis: Fortress Press, 2010.

———. *Battered Love: Marriage, Sex, and Violence in the Hebrew Prophets.* Minneapolis: Fortress Press, 1995.

———. *Just a Sister Away: A Womanist Vision of Women's Relationships in the Bible.* Philadelphia: Innisfree, 1988.

———. "Reading *Her Way* through the Struggle: African American Women and the Bible." In Felder, *Stony the Road We Trod*, 57–77.

———. "Womanist Reflections on Biblical Hermeneutics." In Cone and Wilmore, *Black Theology*, 216–24.

West, Traci C. "Is a Womanist a Black Feminist? Marking the Distinctions and Defying Them: A Black Feminist Response." In Floyd-Thomas, *Deeper Shades of Purple*, 291–95.

Westhelle, Vítor. "Revelation 13: Between the Colonial and the Postcolonial, a Reading from Brazil." In Rhoads, *From Every People and Nation*, 183–99.

Whitaker, Richard E., and John R. Kohlenberger III. *The Analytical Concordance to the New Revised Standard Version of the New Testament.* New York: Oxford University Press, 2000.

Wicker, Kathleen O'Brien, Althea Spencer Miller, and Musa W. Dube, eds. *Feminist New Testament Studies: Global and Future Perspectives.* New York: Palgrave Macmillan, 2005.

Williams, Delores S. "African-American Women in Three Contexts of Domestic Violence." In Schüssler Fiorenza and Copeland, *Violence against Women*, 34–43.

———. *Sisters in the Wilderness: The Challenge of Womanist God-Talk.* Maryknoll, NY: Orbis, 1993.

———. "Womanist/Feminist Dialogue: Problems and Possibilities." *JFSR* 9 (1993): 67–73.

Wimbush, Vincent L. "The Bible and African Americans: An Outline of an Interpretative History." In Felder, *Stony the Road We Trod*, 81–97.

———. "Introduction: Reading Darkness, Reading Scriptures." In *African Americans and the Bible: Sacred Texts and Social Textures*, edited by Vincent Wimbush, 1–43. New York: Continuum, 2001.

———. "Reading Texts as Reading Ourselves: A Chapter in the History of African-American Biblical Interpretation." In Segovia and Tolbert, *Reading from This Place*, vol. 1, 95–108.

———. "Signifying on Scriptures: An African Diaspora Proposal for Radical Readings." In Wicker, Miller, and Dube, *Feminist New Testament Studies*, 245–258.

———. "'We Will Make Our Own Future Text': An Alternate Orientation to Interpretation." In Blount, *True to Our Native Land*, 43–53.

Winbush, Raymond A. *The Warrior Method: A Parents' Guide to Rearing Healthy Black Boys.* New York: Amistad, 2001.

Wisker, Gina. *Post-Colonial and African American Women's Writing: A Critical Introduction.* New York: Palgrave Macmillan, 2000.

Young, Robert J. C. *Postcolonialism: An Historical Introduction.* Oxford: Blackwell, 2001.

———. *Postcolonialism: A Very Short Introduction.* Oxford: Oxford University Press, 2003.

Zamir, Shamoon. *Dark Voices: W. E. B. Du Bois and American Thought, 1888–1903.* Chicago: University of Chicago Press, 1995.

Index

Barr, David L., 79n13, 90n57

Basilissa, 3n4, 127, 148n65. *See also* Babylon, Empress/imperial city

Bauckham, Richard, 123

Beale, G.K., 140, 144

Beast, The, 136–137, 142–143

Bhabha, Homi K., 18, 62, 63–64, 178. *See also* ambivalence.

Bible: African American interpretations, 156–162; Colonial symbol, 65; Racist interpretations, 155n91, 156n93; Subversive readings, 45, 65, 65n162; Womanist interpretations, 19, 32, 35–37. *See also* Women, African American: Relationship to Bible

Black Church, 7, 8

Blount, Brian K., 7, 98–101, 114, 118n41, 147, 149

Boring, M. Eugene, 143

Branding, 127, 165

Branding, Relation to skin color, 165–166

Bride, The, 77, 86, 88, 144n52. *See also* Revelation: Feminine symbolism

Callahan, Allen Dwight, 94–95

Cannon, Katie Geneva: 20, 27–28

Cargo list. *See* Martin, Clarice J., Cargo list.

Catachresis, 153

Charagma, 134

Christology: Feminist, 29; Womanist, 33

Collins, Adela Yarbro, 78, 84, 108, 110, 117–119

Cone, James, 21

Copeland, M. Shawn, 67

Darden, Lynne St. Clair, 94n62

Davis, Angela, 24

Davis, Jordan, 166n124

Decian persecution, 111

DeSilva, David Arthur, 107–108, 115, 118n40

Diocletian persecution, 111

Domitian, 109, 113, 119, 120

Double consciousness, 57–58, 59n141, 60, 171. *See also* Du Bois, W.E.B.; veil

Double jeopardy: 21, 149

Douglas, Kelly Brown, 21, 32, 33n60

Doulos, 30, 136

Du Bois, W.E.B.,18, 19, 54, 53n128, 54; *Souls of Black Folk,* 57, 60n147, 178

Dube, Musa W., 48n113, 56n134

Participatory reading strategy, 128–129

Pornē, 3, 126n3, 137, 139, 141–142, 141n42. *See also* Babylon, Brothel slavewoman

Postcolonial biblical criticism, 45–46

Postcolonial criticism: 9–10, 39–40, 43, 46, 46n110, 50; Definition, 37–38; Genealogy, 41, *see also* hermeneutics, contextual; biblical criticism, historical

Price, S.R.F., 111, 111n18

Privilege: Analytic category, 167–170; Connection to empire, 168–170; Economic, 168–170, *see also* Babylon, Attire and goods; Educational, 167–168

Proskyneo, 137

Prostitution, Roman, 146–147

Protowomanists: Baker-Fletcher, Karen, 22–23, 24; Cooper, Anna Julia, 22–23; Lee, Jarena, 23, 35; Truth, Sojourner, 22, 35; Tubman, Harriet, 23, 24; Wells-Barnett, Ida B., 23, 24

Psychoanalytic theory, 64

Race: Analytic category, 50, 51, 51n119; Systemic, 166

Revelation: African American interpretations, 93–102; Apocalyptic genre, 119; Minority discourse, 94–98, 103. *See also* John, Author of Revelation, Masculinist Minority Discourse; Authorship of, 106–108; Christological images, 96–98. *See also* Slater, Thomas B.; Cultural-studies approach, 99. *See also* Blount, Brian K.; Dating, 109–111; Economic critique of, 169; Feminine symbolism, 77, 77n8, 78, 82, 86–89. *See also* Babylon, Jezebel, Woman Clothed with the Sun, and Bride, The; Gender-critical approach, 80, 84, 89–90, *see also* Pippin, Tina; Hymns of, 100–101; Idiolectal strategy, 95. *See also* Callahan, Allen Dwight; Internal conflict, 121–122; Occasion, 117–121; Persecution, 111n17, 116–117, 120, 121n52; Rhetoric of crisis, 117–119, *see also* Collins, Adela Yarbro; Sexual violence,

85–87, 150–151; Social setting,
111–117
Rome, feminine symbolism,
125n2
Rossing, Barbara R., 77n8
Rowland, Christopher, 143, 151,
152
Royalty Jr., Robert M., 121

Said, Edward, 62–63, 62n150, 63
Sanders, Cheryl J., 26
Sarai, 165
Schueller, Malini Johar, 52–53
Schüssler Elizabeth Fiorenza, 5,
76–84; Babylon as city, 5–6,
82–83; Critique of postcolonial
studies, 47–48; Feminist
rhetorical perspective, 78,
78n10, 80–81; Persecution in
Roman Empire, 120
Sealing, see graphizō
Segovia, Fernando, 40–41, 42,
127n7
Slater, Thomas B., 96
Slavery: African American, 7,
154–155, 163n117, 166;
Ancient, 128
Sphragizō, 132, 134, 135n20,
136n23
Spivak, Gayatri Chakavorty,
62n148, 148n65, 153

St. Clair, Raquel A., 32, 71
Stichele, Caroline Vander, 85, 137,
164
Sugirtharajah, R.S., 42, 43, 47, 49

Tattoos, 127, 138n30, 138–139
Thompson, Leonard L., 107, 119,
122–123
Trible, Phyllis, 31

Van Kooten, George H. 110
Veil, 11, 18, 57–58, 172–173;
Protection, 60n147, 61;
Rending, 61, 171–173

Walker, Alice, 24, 26
Weems, Renita J., 1–2, 12, 27n34,
28, 155, 157, 160, 161, 165,
168, 183; Bible and African
American women, 30–31;
Gendered metaphors, 150–151
Williams, Delores S.: 21, 36–37
Wimbush, Vincent L., 58, 156,
157, 158, 159, 159n105
Witness, 123. See also Martys,
witness
Woman Clothed with the Sun, 86,
88, 163–164, 164n118. See also
Revelation: Feminine
symbolism

Womanist: Biblical interpretation,
27-37; Criticism, 9; Definition
of, 1–2, 20n4, 24–27;
Hermeneutical approaches, 35;
History of, 20–24. *See also*
Protowomanists; Theology
and Critique, 27–35

Women, African American:
Experience, 18, 56, 91, 102,
160–161; Relationship to
slaveowners, 163, 165;
Relationship to Bible, 1, 30,
160, 175–176; Slavery, 36, 100

Zimmerman, George, 166n124

CPSIA information can be obtained at www.ICGtesting.com
Printed in the USA
LVOW04s0929230814

400579LV00004B/7/P